The Complete Probate Kit

Jens C. Appel, III

F. Bruce Gentry

JOHN WILEY & SONS, INC.

New York · Chichester · Brisbane · Toronto · Singapore

Library of Congress Cataloging-in-Publication Data:

Appel, Jens C., 1948–
  The complete probate kit / by Jens C. Appel, III and F. Bruce Gentry.
    p.   cm.
  Includes index.
  ISBN 0-471-53579-6. —ISBN 0-471-53492-7 (pbk.)
    1. Probate law and practice—United States—Popular works.
2. Probate law and practice—United States—States—Popular works
I. Gentry, F. Bruce, 1946–   II. Title.
KF765. Z9A66   1991
346.7305′2—dc20
[347.30652]   90-23444

Printed in the United States of America

10 9 8 7 6

This book is dedicated to our families:

Amelia Hough Gentry

Amelia Elizabeth Gentry
Morgen Adrienne Gentry

and

Linda Diane Riddle Appel

Fawn Autumn Sky Rememberance Appel
Joy Charmain Appel
Jade Christa Appel

Preface

Sooner or later, almost all of us will take part in settling the estate of a family member or close friend. Preparation, and a fundamental understanding of the probate system, can help prevent costly errors when that time comes. Knowledge of the probate process can also be useful in preparing your own estate plan. Since probate is not often the subject of casual conversation, most of us are only vaguely aware of the steps involved in settling an estate. This book sets out the probate process in a logical series of tasks that can be accomplished with relative ease.

The first step in probate is the appointment of the person responsible for settling the estate by the local court. This person, known as the Personal Representative, may be named as the Executor in the will, or can apply for the position of Administrator when there is no will. After appointment, the Personal Representative must collect, secure, and inventory the assets of the estate and notify creditors and potential heirs of his or her appointment. Next the estate must be valued, debts and claims checked for validity, and taxes due calculated. After taxes and debts have been paid, the Personal Representative distributes the estate as set out in the will or as required by state law. The Personal Representative files a final accounting, including receipts, with the probate court and is discharged from his or her duties.

The purpose of this book is to provide a practical guide to the probate process along with the information needed for responsible, cost-effective estate administration. A Personal Representative's checklist and a series of household and estate inventory sheets is included to help organize estate information. The various state requirements are discussed, and state by state summaries set out key information. Chapter 8 illustrates the settlement of an estate, using the fictitious Kent family situation as an example. This chapter also includes samples of completed tax forms and accounts for guidance.

In addition to serving as a step-by-step guide to probate, this book also addresses other aspects of practical estate settlement. Topics include what to do before probate begins, applying for benefits, and securing and disposing of property, as well as probate planning.

As you learn about the probate system, the importance of having a plan to guide distribution of your estate's assets will become apparent. Detachable will forms are provided so that you can act immediately to protect your beneficiaries and estate. Be sure to read the entire book and examine your options carefully before taking any action. The information presented will help you as the Personal Representative whether you perform all the tasks yourself or choose to supervise others. With preparation and knowledge you can confidently fulfill the duties required of the Personal Representative and minimize the cost and time involved in settling an estate.

F. BRUCE GENTRY
JENS C. APPEL, III

Salem, Virginia
1991

Contents

Introduction   1

The Language of Probate   5

CHAPTER *1* *Before Probate*   7

    Providing for Dependents, 8
    The Family Meeting, 8
    Sources of Living Expenses, 9
    Veterans Administration Benefits, 10
    Social Security Administration Benefits, 20

CHAPTER *2* *Opening Probate*   27

    Jurisdiction, 28
    Notice of Hearing, 28
    The Hearing, 29

Will Requirements, 30

Self-Proving, 30

Proof of a Will, 31

Will Probate—State Summary, 34

Small Estate Options, 42

Spouse's Elective Share, 42

CHAPTER 3 *Probate Administration*   *49*

Types of Administration, 49

Personal Representative Fees, 50

Nonresident Personal Representative, 51

Out-of-State Property, 52

Spouse's Automatic Share, 52

Notice to Creditors, 58

Insolvent Estates, 61

Collecting and Conserving Assets, 61

Farm and Business Operations, 63

Probate Administration—State Summary, 63

Probate Timetable, 82

Personal Representative's Checklist, 86

CHAPTER 4 *Inventory and Valuation*   *91*

Types of Ownership, 91

Real Property, 92

Personal Property, 93

Valuation, 94

Room-By-Room Inventory, 96

Estate Inventory Worksheets, 108

CHAPTER 5 *Before Distribution*   *121*

Liquidity, 121

Estate Auctions, 122

Debts and Claims, 124

Taxes, 126

Reports, 126
Estate Summary Worksheets, 127

CHAPTER **6** *Taxes*   **131**

Regular Taxes, 131
Estate-Related Taxes, 134
State Taxes—Summary, 134
State Tax Information and Forms, 136
Federal Tax Information and Forms, 143

CHAPTER **7** *Distribution and Closing*   **145**

Distribution with a Will, 145
Distribution without a Will, 146
Transferring Assets, 154
Dividing Personal Property, 154
Closing the Estate, 155

CHAPTER **8** *Settlement Sample*   **157**

The Estate of James Robert Kent, 157
Sample Forms, 165

CHAPTER **9** *Probate Planning*   **191**

The Importance of a Will, 191
Self-Proving, 192
Executor Data, 192
Joint Title, 193
Gifts, 193
Real Estate Options, 194
Life Insurance, 194
Trusts, 194
Living Wills, 196

Index   **197**

Record Set   *R-1*

Using the Detachable Forms, R-1
   Estate Summary
   Executor Data
      Immediate
      Contacts
      Personal
      Final Arrangements
      Beneficiaries
      Dependents/Guardians

Document Set   *D-1*

Using the Detachable Forms, D-1
   Last Will and Testament
   Codicil
   Will Self-Proving Certificate
   Codicil Self-Proving Certificate

Introduction

The tasks required to fulfill probate responsibilities vary with the extent and complexity of the estate. Many estates can be settled with very little time and effort. Adding, subtracting, and making lists may be the only skills needed to complete the entire process. More complex estates can involve extensive management of both real and personal assets. Capable individuals can usually handle most, if not all, of the tasks required in the probate process and can avail themselves of professional help when needed. In many cases the Executor named in the will, or Administrator appointed by the court (both known as the *Personal Representative*), is a primary beneficiary and directly gains the savings realized by performing estate administration tasks. A primary duty of the Personal Representative is the conservation of assets, regardless of the beneficiary.

The Complete Probate Kit serves as a practical guide to the process of settling an estate. The term *probate*, which literally means "to prove," is commonly used to describe all the steps that must be completed to close an estate. If the *decedent*, or deceased, left a will, the first step of probate is to *prove* the document to establish its validity. After the will is proved, the Executor is empowered by the court to act as the Personal Representative of the decedent. If the deceased died without a valid will *(intestate)*, probate begins with the court's appointment of an Administrator to act as Personal Representative. The Personal Representative is responsible for carrying out the duties prescribed by law and distributing the estate according to the terms of the will or, if there is no will, according to the state's law of intestate succession. After appointment, the Personal Representative must perform a series of tasks that end when a final account is submitted and the estate is declared closed by the court. Probate is overseen by the state court system to ensure that all valid interests of creditors and heirs are protected.

Because *The Complete Probate Kit* is a comprehensive guide, it presents material relevant to a broad variety of estates. The estate-related requirements for all 50 states and the District of Columbia are included. You will find this information useful both when settling an estate and in evaluating the effect of probate on your personal situation. The State Summaries provide extensive details regarding individual state requirements, rules, and tax information. If you do not have a current will, be sure to note the property distribution rules for intestate estates that are presented in Chapter 7. This information may serve as immediate motivation to prepare a will. Although the purpose of this book is to give you the knowlege needed to settle another person's estate, the information will also be helpful in preparing your own estate plan.

You will find the subject matter of this book easier to understand and more readable if you begin by gaining a clear understanding of *probate language,* the terms that are used in the probate process. You may already be familiar with many of these terms, but the definitions set forth in the next section of this book bear repeating. This probate language is unavoidable when settling an estate because it appears in many of the documents and forms that must be completed. As the Personal Representative your fluency in the language of probate will enable you to converse easily with court personnel and professionals regarding estate settlement.

Another point to consider as you learn more about the duties of the Personal Representative is the effect that probate could have on the estates of your family and friends. By sharing the information you gain from this book with those you love and care about, you can help them avoid potential estate problems.

Samples of completed tax forms are included in Chapter 8, illustrating the settlement of the fictitious Kent estate. The federal estate tax form (IRS Form 706) is the one appropriate to the sample. The federal estate tax form was revised in July 1990, and the revised form is to be used for all estates created after December 31, 1989. The content, layout, and numbering of items on the revised IRS Form 706 are the same as on the form shown in the sample. The changes in the revision were the deletion of Schedule N (regarding the deduction for the sale of employer securities to employee stock ownership plans [ESOPs]) and the elimination of the grandchild exclusion when calculating the Generation Skipping Transfer taxes.

If, after reading this book, you feel that settling an estate is too difficult or time consuming, don't hesitate to use the services of competent professionals. As you go through the probate process, appraisers, accountants, and attorneys may be needed to perform certain tasks that you consider beyond your skills. When choosing professionals, be sure to inquire about their experience in estate management and their fees. Often you may choose among several who have comparable skills and experience but vary greatly in the fees they charge. Becoming familiar with the probate system will enable you to make informed decisions based on your knowledge of the time and effort required for a particular task. As the Personal Representative, it is your responsibility to oversee any professionals you employ to ensure that the work they perform is satisfactory. You should always have a clear understanding of any probate task that you employ others to perform. The ultimate responsibility for all probate actions lies with the Personal Representative.

In most cases, the Executor named in the will or Administrator appointed by the court is the spouse or closest relative of the decedent. In this situation the Personal Representative should have intimate knowledge of the estate and be able to quickly organize the information and documents needed for probate. A Personal Representative who is related to the decedent should still conduct a thorough search for assets and records. Secrets are often kept from even the closest family members.

If you are named Executor of an estate by the will of a friend or distant relative, you should consider the appointment carefully. If deep family divisions exist, or close family members object to your appointment, you may find it difficult to manage the probate process. In these circumstances it is advisable to meet with the family of the decedent before accepting appointment to discuss the events that are to take place in settling the estate. Family members are important resources that the Personal Representative will rely on throughout the probate process, and the family meeting can make you aware of the attitude relatives hold toward the decedent, the estate, and your appointment. Your assessment of these family attitudes and whether they display a cooperative spirit can help you predict difficulties you may encounter in settling the estate.

Your appointment as Personal Representative is contingent upon your acceptance. If you refuse appointment, and an alternate Executor is named in the will, the position of Personal Representative will be offered to the alternate. If no alternate is named, the court will appoint an Executor for the estate. In either case the terms of the will, if it is accepted by the court, are unaffected.

The Language of Probate

This section presents a brief orientation to the specialized terms commonly used in the estate settlement process.

Probate, which literally means "to prove," refers both to the legal procedure for establishing the validity of a will and, in a more general sense, the entire process of settling an estate. An *estate* consists of everything a person owned at the time of death, as well as any outstanding obligations. If the liabilities exceed the assets, the estate is *insolvent.* The local court responsible for probate is determined by the domicile of the deceased. *Domicile* is defined as the permanent home or legal residence and is evidenced by where income and other taxes are paid and by where voter registration and bank accounts are maintained.

The person responsible for settling an estate, who is known as the *Personal Representative,* is either the *Executor* named in the will or an *Administrator* appointed by the local probate court. The Executor named in a will becomes the Personal Representative when he or she is confirmed by the court and issued *letters testamentary* as authorization to act on behalf of the decedent.

A will is a signed, witnessed document that sets out a person's directions for distribution of his or her estate. A will is *proved* by testimony or affidavit from one or more of the witnesses to its execution. An *affidavit* is a signed and notarized sworn statement. A *self-proving certificate* is an affidavit attached to the will that has been executed by the *Testator,* the person making the will, and the witnesses. The purpose of a self-proving certificate is to eliminate the need for the witnesses to be contacted during the probate process.

If there is no will, the estate is known as an *intestate* estate, and the court appoints an Administrator to act as the Personal Representative. The person appointed by the court to administer an intestate estate is empowered by *letters of administration* authorizing him or her to distribute the estate according to the *laws of intestate succession.* The laws of intestate succession are state laws that determine how the estate is to be divided on the basis of surviving spouse, descendants, and other relatives. A challenge to a will is called a *contest,* and if a will is successfully contested, the estate is administered as an intestate estate. Persons receiving intestate shares of an estate are called *heirs. Per stirpes* is a term referring to the right of direct descendants to receive a deceased parent's share. If there are no surviving relatives, the intestate estate is claimed by the state and this is termed *escheated.*

A surviving spouse is usually able to obtain an automatic share of the estate to assist with living expenses during probate. If there is a will and the surviving spouse receives only minimal bequests, the spouse may choose to take the *spouse's elective share* of the estate, which is defined by state law, rather than the bequest(s) in the will. The spouse's elective share is generally equal to or less than what his or her intestate share would have been.

Types of estate administration available to the Personal Representative vary from state to state and depend on the amount and type of property involved. One of three options is available for certain small estates. *Administration unnecessary* does not require formal administration, just a simple summary report; *administration by affidavit* reporting is similar, but also requires the completion of an affidavit affirming correctness; and *summary administration* involves a shortened form of that used for larger estates. Larger estates may be settled under *unsupervised* or *supervised* administration, with supervised administration requiring more approvals by the court before actions are taken.

All of the terms mentioned here are discussed further in the appropriate chapters that follow.

CHAPTER *1*

Before Probate

The legal duties of the Personal Representative begin with appointment by the court and the formal opening of the estate. As you read this chapter, it is extremely important that you bear in mind a few basic facts. For instance, if you are named Executor of the estate in the decedent's will, a court hearing to establish the validity of the document must be held before you can legally act on behalf of the estate. If there is no will and you wish to act as the Administrator of an intestate estate, you must apply to the court and be confirmed before you have any legal standing as Personal Representative. Any person taking actions involving the estate of the decedent before formal appointment may become personally liable for those actions.

Settling an estate includes many duties and responsibilities that require attention before the formal probate process has begun and thus before a Personal Representative has been designated. Organ donation, funeral arrangements, and application for certain benefits are typical responsibilities that must be attended to immediately after a person's death. If you are the spouse or closest relative of the decedent, you will most likely be responsible for these tasks and can perform them even though you are not legally acting as the Personal Representative.

Providing for Dependents

If the decedent has no surviving spouse but there are minor children, provisions for their immediate care must be made. This need usually can be best addressed at a meeting of the family members. Guardianship, which is officially determined by the court, has two aspects: guardianship of the child's person and guardianship of the child's assets. Until the court acts, guardianship of a child's person, which simply involves providing care, generally is handled by a relative living nearby.

The court will usually affirm guardianship provisions included in the will. If there is no will or it does not name a guardian, the court considers the home environment, financial position, and the child's wishes when appointing guardians of the child's person. The court will also determine who will be entrusted with the responsibility for management of assets belonging to a minor child, such as proceeds from life insurance policies and shares of the estate. Although often the guardian of the child's person is also named as guardian of the child's assets, the court may name separate guardians. In either case, the child's assets may be used, if needed, for care, medical expenses, costs of education, and other legitimate expenses incurred on the child's behalf.

Another concern that may have to be addressed is provision of care for a dependent adult, such as a partially incapacitated spouse. Family members sometimes are able to deal with this situation for a period of time, but often other arrangements must be made. Individual circumstances and estate resources will dictate whether semi-independent living with part-time nursing support, moving in with other family members, or moving to a nursing home is the most appropriate course.

Surviving minor children, disabled adults, and age-eligible spouses usually are entitled to Social Security income benefits that are based on the decedent's work record.

The Family Meeting

A meeting of close relatives of the deceased can be extremely helpful to both the Personal Representative and the family. The support and consolation of relatives is often essential to recovery from grief following the death of a family member. These meetings can also serve a functional purpose if they result in better understanding of the probate procedures by the surviving relatives and create a sense of unity.

Often the Personal Representative is the spouse of the decedent and is fully informed of the intimate details of the estate. When this situation exists, it may be unnecessary for the family to meet to discuss probate matters. Many times, however, the Personal Representative is a relative or friend who has only limited knowledge of the extent and nature of the decedent's estate, which can be a real obstacle to effective estate administration. When this occurs, the Personal Representative may find that a meeting of the decedent's family is the best way to obtain key estate information including the locations of assets, accounts, or important documents. The Personal Representative should ask family members about the decedent's eligibility for veterans' and Social Security benefits, outstanding loans, and other personal matters. If the decedent lived alone, arrangements for security of property and possessions should be planned.

Relatives of the decedent are usually the best source of information about the location of the decedent's records. Important papers and documents that need to be located quickly include the will and any related documents, life insurance policies, account agreements, deeds, titles, and income tax records. The Personal Representative will need these papers to speed the settlement process and make a preliminary estimate of the value of the estate.

The names, addresses, and telephone numbers of those who could share by intestate succession will be needed by the Personal Representative when the probate hearing date is set. Family members should be able to provide this information. Refer to Chapter 7 to find information about the rules for intestate estates in the decedent's state of residence.

In nine states, a meeting of beneficiaries or heirs is required to secure agreement for *unsupervised administration* of the estate, which means that fewer actions require prior court approval. If the estate meets the criteria for this type of administration, the Personal Representative should immediately confer with the family. In-kind gifts, family auctions, or other means of disposing of the deceased's property are also topics that may be discussed at such a meeting. If an estate auction or sale of assets is considered, the Personal Representative should consult with the family before making any commitments.

Even when not required, a meeting of the family can help avoid controversy that may arise over the disposition of the decedent's property. The Personal Representative should always inform the family of options for disposing of property or settling other matters regarding the estate. Their support and agreement can be of invaluable assistance in the efficient settlement of the estate.

Sources of Living Expenses

If the decedent was covered by life insurance, it is important to locate all policies immediately and apply for payment, which generally will be made between two and four weeks after an application has been filed. Often the surviving spouse is the beneficiary of the life insurance policy and needs the proceeds for living expenses. When no beneficiary is named, the face amount of the policy, less any loans, is paid directly to the estate. Because life insurance proceeds can significantly affect the value of the estate, it is important that the Personal Representative be aware of all policies and beneficiaries. The decedent's former employer should be contacted for information regarding company life insurance or other benefit programs. After being empowered by the court, the Personal Representative should collect any wages, vacation pay, or other benefits due the decedent.

Usually married people maintain joint bank accounts, with right of survivorship. In these cases the surviving spouse has unrestricted access to the funds in the accounts and can deal with living expenses as needed. Brokerage accounts for publicly traded securities can also be jointly owned, although sometimes they are held in the name of only one person. If such an account was held solely by the deceased, the assets must pass through probate and will not be available to the surviving spouse without court approval. ·

The titles of motor vehicles and the deeds of any real estate should be located and examined. If motor vehicles are titled jointly, the survivor can sell such personal property and use the proceeds to assist with living expenses. Real estate that is jointly titled with the right of survivorship passes directly to the survivor and is not subject to probate administration. After payment of any outstanding mortgages, taxes, and liens, such property can be sold without court involvement.

If after review of these options, the surviving spouse does not have access to sufficient assets for living expenses, refer to the section Spouse's Automatic Share in Chapter 3 and contact the local probate court.

Veterans Administration Benefits

When making final arrangements for an eligible veteran, you can obtain current information about veterans' benefits, and the necessary forms, by contacting the nearest Veterans Administration office. All persons who have received either a general or honorable discharge from the United States Armed Forces are entitled to a United States flag for burial purposes. The flag can be obtained from the nearest U.S. Post Office by filing a completed VA Form 90-2008—Application for United States Flag for Burial Purposes (Figure 1-1). The person filing the application, who may be a relative, the funeral director, or a friend involved with the funeral service, must provide the service serial number, the VA file number, and evidence of other than dishonorable discharge of the deceased. Only one flag will be issued, which can be draped over the casket. At the conclusion of the funeral service, the flag is folded and presented to the closest family member (Figure 1-2).

Once the VA receives notice of a veteran's death or a claim for benefits, the next of kin is provided with a memorial certificate expressing the nation's gratitude for the veteran's honorable service in the armed services and bearing the President's signature. Additional presidential memorial certificates for other family members or friends may be obtained upon written

VA Veterans Administration

APPLICATION FOR UNITED STATES FLAG FOR BURIAL PURPOSES

Postmaster or other issuing official: Submit this form to the nearest VA Regional Office. Be sure to complete the stub at the bottom.

LAST NAME - FIRST NAME - MIDDLE NAME OF DECEASED *(Print or type)*

Kent, James Robert

BRANCH OF SERVICE *(Check)*

[X] ARMY [ ] NAVY [ ] AIR FORCE [ ] MARINE CORPS [ ] COAST GUARD

[ ] OTHER *(Specify)*

VETERAN'S SERVICE *(Check)*

[ ] SPANISH AMERICAN [ ] WW I [X] WW II [ ] KOREAN CONFLICT [ ] AFTER 1-31-55 [ ] VIETNAM ERA

[ ] OTHER *(Specify)*

CONDITION UNDER WHICH VETERAN WAS RELEASED FROM SERVICE *(Check)*

[X] 1. VETERAN OF A WAR, MEXICAN BORDER SERVICE, OR OF SERVICE AFTER 1-31-55, DISCHARGED OR RELEASED FROM ACTIVE DUTY UNDER CONDITIONS OTHER THAN DISHONORABLE.

[ ] 2. DISCHARGED FROM, OR RELEASED FROM ACTIVE DUTY IN U.S. ARMED FORCES UNDER CONDITIONS OTHER THAN DISHONORABLE, AFTER SERVING AT LEAST ONE ENLISTMENT, OR DISCHARGED FOR DISABILITY INCURRED IN LINE OF DUTY.

[ ] 3. BY DEATH IN ACTIVE SERVICE AFTER MAY 27, 1941, AND FLAG NOT FURNISHED BY THE SERVICE DEPARTMENT.

[ ] 4. SEPARATED FROM PHILIPPINE MILITARY FORCES, UNDER CONDITIONS OTHER THAN DISHONORABLE, AFTER SERVING UNITED STATES IN SUCH FORCES UNDER PRESIDENT'S ORDER OF JULY 26, 1941, AND DIED ON OR AFTER APRIL 25, 1951.

NAME OF PERSON ENTITLED TO RECEIVE FLAG

Robert Lee Kent

RELATIONSHIP TO DECEASED

Son

ADDRESS OF PERSON ENTITLED TO RECEIVE FLAG

115 Gulf View Drive
Tampa, Florida   33601

PERSONAL DATA OF DECEASED *(To be completed if possible)*

VA FILE NUMBER	SOCIAL SECURITY NUMBER	SERVICE SERIAL NUMBER
C-75962	013-62-1458	RA-403958

DATE OF ENLISTMENT	DATE OF DISCHARGE	DATE OF BIRTH	DATE OF DEATH
1-15-41	6-20-45	12-10-22	2-21-89

DATE OF BURIAL	PLACE OF BURIAL *(Name of cemetery, city, and State)*
2-25-89	Sunset Memorial Gardens, Gainesville, Florida

REMARKS

I CERTIFY that, to the best of my knowledge and belief, the statements made above are correct and true, the deceased is eligible, in accordance with attached Instructions, for issue of a United States flag for burial purposes, and such flag has not previously been applied for or furnished.

SIGNATURE OF APPLICANT *(Sign in INK)*	ADDRESS	RELATIONSHIP TO DECEASED	DATE
Robert Lee Kent	115 Gulf View Drive Tampa, Florida 33601	Son	2-23-89

PENALTY--The law provides that whoever makes any statement of a material fact knowing it to be false shall be punished by a fine or by imprisonment or both.

ACKNOWLEDGMENT OF RECEIPT OF FLAG

I CERTIFY that the flag requested by the applicant will be used to drape the casket of the deceased in whose honor it is issued by the Veterans Administration; and that paragraph 7 of the attached Instructions will be complied with.

SIGNATURE OF PERSON RECEIVING FLAG *(Sign in INK)*	DATE FLAG RECEIVED
Robert Lee Kent	2-23-89

NAME AND ADDRESS OF POST OFFICE OR OTHER FLAG ISSUE POINT	FOR VA USE	
Gainesville Central Post Office 15 High Street, Gainesville, Florida 32601	DATE NOTIFICATION FORWARDED TO SUPPLY	INITIALS OF RESPONSIBLE VA EMPLOYEE

VA FORM
DEC 1985 **90-2008**

This stub is to be completed by the POSTMASTER or other issuing official. Upon receipt the VA Regional Office will detach and forward it to the appropriate Supply Officer.

NOTIFICATION OF ISSUANCE OF FLAG

DATE FLAG ISSUED	SIGNATURE OF POSTMASTER OR OTHER ISSUING OFFICIAL *(Sign in INK)*	ADDRESS

FOR VA USE ▶	DATE OF REPLACEMENT	

VA FORM
DEC 1985 **90-2008**

EXISTING STOCKS OF VA FORM 60-2008, 00-2008, AND 90-2008, FEB 1979, WILL BE USED.

EG3756

Figure 1-1

USE OF THE FLAG

1. This flag is issued on behalf of the Veterans Administration to honor the memory of one who has served our country.

2. When used to drape the casket, the flag should be placed as follows:

(a) Closed Casket.—When the flag is used to drape a closed casket, it should be so placed that the union (blue field) is at the head and over the left shoulder of the deceased.

(b) Half Couch (Open).—When the flag is used to drape a half-couch casket, it should be placed in three layers to cover the closed half of the casket in such a manner that the blue field will be the top fold, next to the open portion of the casket on the deceased's left.

(c) Full Couch (Open).—When the flag is used to drape a full-couch casket, it should be folded in a triangular shape and placed in the center part of the head panel of the casket cap, just above the left shoulder of the deceased.

3. During a military commitment ceremony, the flag which was used to drape the casket is held waist high over the grave by the pallbearers and, immediately after the sounding of "Taps," is folded in accordance with the paragraph below.

4. Folding the flag (see illustration):

CORRECT METHOD OF FOLDING THE UNITED STATES FLAG

(a) Fold the lower striped section of the flag over the blue field.

(b) Folded edge is then folded over to meet the open edge.

(c) A triangular fold is then started by bringing the striped corner of the folded edge to the open edge.

(d) Outer point is then turned inward parallel with the open edge to form a second triangle.

(e) Triangular folding is continued until the entire length of the flag is folded in the triangular shape of a cocked hat with only the blue field visible.

5. The flag should not be lowered into the grave or allowed to touch the ground. When taken from the casket, it should be folded as above.

6. The flag should form a distinctive feature of the ceremony of unveiling a statue or monument, but it should never be used as a covering for the statue or monument.

7. The flag should never be fastened, displayed, used, or stowed in such a manner as will permit it to be easily torn, soiled, or damaged in any way.

8. The flag should never have placed upon it, nor any part of it, nor attached to it, any mark, insignia, letter, word, figure, design, picture, or drawing of any nature.

9. The flag should never be used as a receptacle for receiving, holding, carrying, or delivering anything.

10. The flag, when badly worn, torn, or soiled should no longer be publicly displayed, but privately destroyed by burning in such a manner as to convey no suggestion of disrespect or irreverence.

Figure 1-2

INSTRUCTIONS

1. No flag may be issued unless a completed application form has been received (38 U.S.C. 901). The person filling out the application must state (under "relationship to deceased") whether he/she is: *(a)* A relative, and degree of relationship (e.g., "Brother"); *(b)* the funeral director; *(c)* a representative of veterans' or other organization having charge of the burial (e.g., "The American Legion"); *(d)* other person having a knowledge of the facts, and acting in the interest of the deceased or his/her family (e.g., "Friend"; "Det. Clerk").

2. One of the numbered conditions listed "under which deceased was separated from service" must be evidenced, normally by a document such as a discharge paper, before a flag may be issued.

(a) The phrase "veteran of a war" (No. 1) requires a showing that the deceased was in service in the United States armed forces during a war period. The phrase "Mexican border service" means active service during the period beginning on January 1, 1911, and ending on April 5, 1917, in Mexico, on the borders thereof, or in the waters adjacent thereto. The phrase "service after January 31, 1955" relates to veterans with active military, naval, or air service after that date.

(b) The phrase "under conditions other than dishonorable" requires a showing of discharge or release from active duty under honorable conditions ("Honorable" or "General") from the indicated period of service in the United States armed forces, or, in absence of such discharge or release from active duty, a determination by Veterans Administration that discharge or release from active duty, was under conditions other than dishonorable.

(c) The phrase "at least one enlistment" (No. 2) is construed to include service of a commissioned officer whose service, computed from date of entrance into commissioned status to date of separation from service, terminated under honorable conditions, and in all cases, relates to peacetime service before June 27, 1950.

(d) When the deceased was honorably discharged for disability, it may be assumed that the disability was "incurred in line of duty."

(e) Issue of flag in in-service cases (No. 3) is required only when deceased was interred outside the United States, or remains not recovered, or where service department cannot supply flag in time for burial. Explanation should be included under "Remarks."

3. When the applicant is unable to furnish documentary proof, such as a discharge under honorable conditions ("Honorable" or "General"), an application may be accepted and a flag issued when statement is made by a person of established character and reputation that he/she personally knows the deceased to have been a veteran of a war, the Mexican border service, or of service after January 31, 1955, discharged or released from active duty, under honorable conditions, or to have been a person discharged from, or released from active duty in the United States Army, Navy, Air Force, Marine Corps, or Coast Guard under honorable conditions after serving at least one complete peacetime enlistment, before June 27, 1950, or for disability incurred in line of duty; or that the deceased was in active service at the time of death and a flag was not obtainable from a military or naval establishment in time for burial.

4. The following classes of persons are ineligible for issue of a burial flag:

(a) A discharged or rejected draftee, or a member of the National Guard, who reported to camp in answer to the President's call for World War I service but who, when medically examined, was not finally accepted for military service.

(b) A person who was discharged from World War I service prior to November 12, 1918, on his/her own application or solicitation, by reason of being an alien, or any person discharged for alienage during a period of hostilities.

(c) A person who served with any of the forces allied with the United States in any war, even though a United States citizen, if he/she did not serve with the United States armed forces.

(d) A person inducted for training and service who, before entering upon such training and service, was transferred to the Enlisted Reserve Corps and given a furlough.

(e) A former temporary member of the United States Coast Guard Reserve.

(f) A reservist who served only on active duty for training unless he/she was disabled or died from a disease or injury incurred or aggravated in line of duty.

5. Flags will not be issued subsequent to burial, except where circumstances render it impossible to obtain a flag in time to drape the casket of a deceased veteran prior to final interment. The applicant must personally sign the application and include (under "Remarks") a statement explaining the circumstances preventing the requesting of a burial flag prior to final interment.

6. In no instance will flags be issued to funeral directors, organizations, or individuals to replace flags loaned or donated by them. Reimbursement may not be allowed for flags privately purchased by relatives, friends, or other parties, nor will any financial settlement be made in lieu of the issue of a flag.

7. *(a)* The flag will be disposed of as follows: When actually used to drape the casket of the deceased, it must be delivered to the next of kin (or to a close friend or associate when no claim is made by next of kin) following interment or inurnment. If there is no living relative, or one cannot be located, and no friend or associate requests the flag, it must be returned to the nearest Veterans Administration office.

(b) The phrase "next of kin," for the purpose of disposing of the flag, is defined as follows with preference to entitlement in the order listed below:

(1) Widow or widower.
(2) Children, according to age (minor child may be issued a flag on application signed by guardian).
(3) Parents, including adoptive, stepparents, and foster parents.
(4) Brothers or sisters, including brothers or sisters of the halfblood.
(5) Uncles or aunts.
(6) Nephews or nieces.
(7) Others—cousins, grandparents, etc.

(c) The phrase "close friend or associate" means any person who establishes by evidence that he/she was a close friend or an associate of the deceased.

★U.S.GPO:1987-0-181-822/57111

Figure 1-2 (continued)

request to any VA regional office by enclosing a copy of a document verifying honorable military service.

The Veterans Administration operates the National Cemetery System. Any veteran who entered military service before 1980 and was not dishonorably discharged is entitled to burial in any cemetery in the system that has available space. The spouse of the veteran is also eligible. Clearly, this benefit is most valuable at the time of the death of the veteran (or eligible spouse), and the next of kin must apply by contacting the local VA office or the director of the national cemetery where burial is desired. Although there is no charge for a grave in a national cemetery, transportation costs must be paid, unless the veteran died of a service-connected disability or was receiving or entitled to a disability pension.

A government monument to mark the grave of the veteran (or eligible spouse) is also furnished at no charge. VA form 40-1330 for obtaining a monument is shown in Figure 1-3; the third page of the form shows the four types of standard government monuments. Note that the government will pay for inscription of the following data:

- name
- branch of service
- year of birth
- year of death

and, if requested upon the application,

- military grade, rate, or rank
- month and day of dates of birth and death
- an emblem of religious belief
- purple heart (if applicable)

Additional items may be inscribed at private expense. Space may also be reserved for a spouse's inscription.

The Veterans Administration will also pay a $300 burial and funeral expense allowance if the veteran was entitled to receive pension or compensation at time of death. VA Form 21-530 is filed for this purpose (Figure 1-4). The second page of this form can be used to obtain an additional plot allowance of $150 if the veteran is not buried in a national cemetery. This allowance can be obtained on behalf of a veteran who

- was a veteran of any war
- was eligible to receive pension or compensation

or

- was discharged from active duty as a result of disability incurred in the line of duty

FOR DEPARTMENT OF VETERANS AFFAIRS USE ONLY MICROFILM ID NO.	IMPORTANT: Read the General Information sheet before completing this form Type or print clearly all information except for signatures. Incorrect spelling or illegible printing could result in an incorrect monument or delivery. All blocks NOT shaded must be completed or this application cannot be processed. SHADED blocks are optional inscription items or for cemetery completion. The copy of this application is for the applicant's use.

1. NAME OF DECEASED TO BE INSCRIBED ON MONUMENT (Do not show nickname or title)			2. ARE REMAINS OR CREMAINS AVAILABLE FOR BURIAL?
FIRST (Or Initial)	MIDDLE (Or Initial)	LAST	☐ YES ☐ NO (If "NO," explain in block 27.)

VETERAN'S SERVICE AND IDENTIFYING INFORMATION (Use numbers only, e.g., 05-15-41)

NOTE: Failure to provide correct numbers may delay receipt of monument

PERIODS OF ACTIVE MILITARY DUTY (For additional space use Block 27)

3A. SOCIAL SECURITY NO.	3B. SERVICE NO.	5A. DATE(S) ENTERED			5B. DATE(S) SEPARATED		
		MONTH	DAY	YEAR	MONTH	DAY	YEAR

4A. DATE OF BIRTH			4B. DATE OF DEATH					
MONTH	DAY	YEAR	MONTH	DAY	YEAR			

6. HIGHEST RANK ATTAINED	7. BRANCH OF SERVICE (Check box(es) - must be consistent with rank)

ARMY	NAVY	AIR FORCE	MARINE CORPS	COAST GUARD	ARMY AIR CORPS	OTHER (Specify)
☐ AR	☐ NA	☐ AF	☐ MC	☐ CG	☐ AC	

8. VALOR OR PURPLE HEART AWARD(S) (Check box(es) and provide documentation)	9. WAR SERVICE (Check applicable box(es))

MEDAL OF HONOR	DST SVC CROSS	NAVY CROSS	AIR FORCE CROSS	SILVER STAR	PURPLE HEART	WORLD WAR I	WORLD WAR II	KOREA	VIETNAM	OTHER (Specify)
☐ MOH	☐ DSC	☐ NC	☐ AFC	☐ SS	☐ PH	☐ WWI	☐ WWII	☐ KO	☐ VN	☐

10. TYPE OF MONUMENT REQUESTED (Check one)	11. DESIRED EMBLEM REFLECTIVE OF ONE'S BELIEF (Check one)

FLAT BRONZE	FLAT GRANITE	UPRIGHT MARBLE	FLAT MARBLE	LATIN CROSS (Christian)	WHEEL OF RIGHTEOUSNESS (Buddhist)	STAR OF DAVID (Jewish)	OTHER (Specify)
☐ B	☐ G	☐ U	☐ F	☐ 01	☐ 02	☐ 03	☐

12. APPLICANT'S NAME AND ADDRESS (No., street, city, State and ZIP Code)	13. RELATIONSHIP TO DECEASED
	14. DAYTIME TELEPHONE NO. (Include area code)

CERTIFICATION: I certify the monument will be installed on the deceased's unmarked grave at no expense to the Government and all statements made are true and correct to the best of my knowledge. I have not applied for and do not intend to apply for a cash reimbursement in lieu of a Government monument.

15. SIGNATURE OF APPLICANT	16. DATE

STATE VETERANS' CEMETERY AND GRAVE LOCATION (If applicable)			PRIVATE CEMETERY
17A. ID CODE	17B. SECTION	17C. GRAVE NO.	18. ID CODE (If applicable)

19. NAME AND ADDRESS OF PERSON, CEMETERY, OR OFFICIAL (CONSIGNEE) WHO WILL ACCEPT PREPAID DELIVERY (No. and street, city, State and ZIP Code); P.O. BOX IS NOT SUFFICIENT	20. TELEPHONE NO. (Include Area Code)	21. NAME AND LOCATION OF CEMETERY (City and Street)

CERTIFICATION: I agree to accept the monument on behalf of the applicant.

22. SIGNATURE OF PERSON TO ACCEPT DELIVERY (CONSIGNEE)	23. DATE

CERTIFICATION: I certify the type of monument checked in block 10 is permitted on the unmarked grave of the deceased.

24. SIGNATURE OF CEMETERY OFFICIAL	25. DAYTIME TELEPHONE NO. (Include Area Code)	26. DATE

27. REMARKS (For additional space continue on reverse)

VA FORM APR 1990 **40-1330**   **APPLICATION FOR STANDARD GOVERNMENT MONUMENT**

Figure 1-3

APPLICATION FOR STANDARD GOVERNMENT MONUMENT
FOR INSTALLATION IN A PRIVATE OR STATE VETERANS' CEMETERY

RESPONDENT BURDEN - Public reporting burden for this collection of information is estimated to average one-fourth hour per response, including the time for reviewing instructions, searching existing data sources, gathering and maintaining the data needed, and completing and reviewing the collection of information. Send comments regarding this burden estimate or any other aspect of this collection of information, including suggestions for reducing this burden to VA Clearance Officer (723), 810 Vermont Avenue, NW, Washington, DC 20420; and to the Office of Management and Budget, Paperwork Reduction Project (2900-0222), Washington, DC 20503.

BENEFIT PROVIDED

a. MONUMENT - Furnish upon application for the **unmarked grave** of any deceased veteran. Applicant must certify the grave is **unmarked** and a Government monument is preferred to a privately purchased monument. This restriction does not apply to a family monument which identifies more than one gravesite. Applicant may be anyone having knowledge of the deceased.

b. MEMORIAL MONUMENT - Furnished upon application by a relative recognized as the next of kin for installation in a private, State veterans' or national cemetery to commemorate any veteran whose remains have not been recovered or identified, were buried at sea, donated to science, or cremated and the remains scattered. Check box in block 2 and explain in block 27.

c. BRONZE NICHE MARKER - See illustration for standard bronze niche marker if entombment is in a columbarium or mausoleum, and if desired so indicate in block 27.

WHO IS ELIGIBLE - Any deceased veteran discharged under conditions other than dishonorable. To expedite processing, attach a copy of the deceased veteran's discharge certificate or a copy of other official document(s) pertaining to military service, if available. **Do not send original documents.** Persons whose only active duty service is training while in the National Guard or Reserves are not eligible unless there are special circumstances, e.g., death while on, or as a result of training. Service after September 7, 1980, must be for a minimum of 24 months or be completed under special circumstances, e.g., death on active duty. Service prior to World War I requires detailed documentation, e.g., muster rolls, extracts from State files, military or State organization where served, pension or land warrant, etc.

HOW TO APPLY - Mail the original of the completed application (VA Form 40-1330) to:

> Monument Service (42)
> Department of Veterans Affairs
> 810 Vermont Avenue, NW.
> Washington, DC 20420

The copy is for your records. No Government monument may be furnished unless a fully completed application form has been received (38 U.S.C. 906).

SIGNATURES REQUIRED - The applicant, next of kin or other responsible person, signs in block 15, obtains the signature of consignee in block 22 and cemetery official in block 24. If there is no official on duty at the cemetery write "NONE" in block 24. State Veterans' Cemeteries are not required to complete blocks: 15, 16, 22 and 23.

ASSISTANCE NEEDED - If assistance is needed to complete this application, contact the nearest VA Regional Office, national cemetery, or a local veterans' organization. No fee should be paid in connection with the preparation of this application. Use block 27 for any clarification or information you wish to provide.

INSTALLATION - All costs to install the monument must be paid from private funds.

TRANSPORTATION - The monument is shipped without charge to the consignee, designated in block 19 of the application. The consignee must have a full street address; **delivery cannot be made to a Post Office Box.** An address showing Rural Delivery must show a telephone number in block 20 to obtain delivery.

DUPLICATION OF BENEFITS PROHIBITED - The applicant has the option of requesting a monetary allowance instead of a Government monument. **An application may be filed for only one benefit.** Application for the monetary allowance must be submitted on VA Form 21-8834, Application for Reimbursement of Headstone or Marker Expenses, which may be obtained from, and submitted to the nearest VA Regional Office.

CAUTION - After completing the application, please check carefully to be sure you have accurately furnished all required information, thereby avoiding delays in marking the gravesite. Mistakes cannot be corrected after a monument has been ordered. Monuments furnished remain the property of the United States Government and cannot be used for any purpose other than to honor the memory of the decedent for whom the monument is issued.

DETACH AND RETAIN THIS GENERAL INFORMATION SHEET AND THE COPY OF THE APPLICATION

VA FORM **40-1330**
APR 1990

EXISTING STOCKS OF VA FORM 40-1330, JUL 1980,
WILL BE USED.

Figure 1-3 (continued)

ILLUSTRATIONS OF STANDARD GOVERNMENT MONUMENTS

NOTE: In addition to monuments pictured, two special styles of upright marble monuments are available upon request - one for eligible deceased who served with the Union Forces, Civil War, or during the Spanish-American War; and the other for eligible deceased who served with the Confederate Forces, Civil War. Request should be made in block 27 of the application. Submit detailed documentation.

UPRIGHT WHITE MARBLE

This monument is 42 inches long, 13 inches wide, and 4 inches thick. Weight is approximately 230 pounds. Variations may occur in stone color, and the marble may contain light to moderate veining.

FLAT TYPES
BRONZE

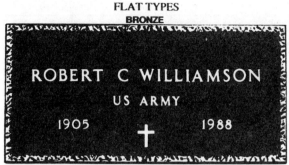

This marker is 24 inches long, 12 inches wide, with 3/4 inch rise. Weight is approximately 18 pounds. Anchor bolts, nuts and washer for fastening to a base are furnished with the marker. The base is not furnished by the Government.

LIGHT GRAY GRANITE OR WHITE MARBLE

This marker is 24 inches long, 12 inches wide, and 4 inches thick. Weight is approximately 130 pounds. Variations may occur in stone color; the marble may contain light to moderate veining.

BRONZE NICHE

This niche marker is 8-1/2 inches long, 5-1/2 inches wide, and 7/16 inches thick. Weight is approximately 3 pounds and mounting bolts and washers are furnished with the marker.

INSCRIPTION INFORMATION

MANDATORY ITEMS of inscription at Government expense are: Name, Branch of Service, Year of Birth, and Year of Death. Branches of Service are: U.S. Army, U.S. Navy, U.S. Air Force, U.S. Marine Corps, U.S. Coast Guard, and by exception, U.S. Army Air Corps, and other parent organizations authorized for certain periods of time. The formats of the inscriptions are illustrated above; deviations are not permitted.

OPTIONAL ITEMS which may be inscribed at Government expense are: military grade, rate or rank, war service, month and day of the dates of birth and death, an emblem reflective of one's belief, and the valor awards and the Purple Heart listed in block 8. If any of these items are desired the information must be shown clearly in the shaded blocks.

RESERVED SPACE for future inscription such as spousal or dependent data may be authorized below the standard inscription if requested in block 27. Only two lines of space may be reserved on flat granite and marble markers. Reserved space is unnecessary on upright marble headstones as the reverse side is available for future inscriptions.

MEMORIAL MONUMENTS (remains are not buried). The words "In Memory of" are mandatory and precede the authorized inscription data.

ADDITIONAL ITEMS may be inscribed at private expense, **subject to VA approval**, below the standard inscription. Such items may be terms of endearment, nicknames (not unseemly in nature) in expressions such as OUR BELOVED POPPY, LOVINGLY CALLED DUTCH, representations of military and civilian participation or accomplishment, and titles such as DOCTOR, REVEREND, etc. These requests should be made in block 27. The manufacturer will bill the applicant for the cost of the additional inscription.

INCOMPLETE OR INACCURATE INFORMATION ON THE APPLICATION MAY RESULT IN ITS RETURN TO THE APPLICANT, A DELAY IN RECEIPT OF THE MONUMENT, OR AN INCORRECT MONUMENT.

Figure 1-3 (continued)

OMB Approved No. 2900-0003
Respondent Burden: 1/3 Hour

VA Department of Veterans Affairs

(DO NOT WRITE IN THIS SPACE)
VA DATE STAMP

APPLICATION FOR BURIAL BENEFITS
(Under 38 U.S.C., Chapter 23)

IMPORTANT – Read instructions carefully before completing form. YOUR COMPLIANCE WITH ALL INSTRUCTIONS WILL AVOID DELAY. Type or print all information.

1. FIRST, MIDDLE, LAST NAME OF DECEASED VETERAN
James Robert Kent

2. SOCIAL SECURITY NO. OF VETERAN
013-62-1458

3. VA FILE NO.
C- 75962

4A. FIRST, MIDDLE, LAST NAME OF CLAIMANT
Gainesville Funeral Home, Inc.

4B. MAILING ADDRESS OF CLAIMANT (Number and street or rural route, city or P.O., State and ZIP Code)
342 Cypress Street
Gainesville, Florida 32601

PART I – INFORMATION REGARDING VETERAN

5A. DATE OF BIRTH
12-10-22

5B. PLACE OF BIRTH
Jacksonville, Florida

6A. DATE OF DEATH
2-21-89

6B. PLACE OF DEATH
Gainesville, Florida

6C. DATE OF BURIAL
2-25-89

SERVICE INFORMATION (The following information should be furnished for the periods of the VETERAN'S ACTIVE SERVICE)

7A. ENTERED SERVICE		7B. SERVICE NO.	7C. SEPARATED FROM SERVICE		7D. GRADE, RANK OR RATING, ORGANIZATION AND BRANCH OF SERVICE
DATE	PLACE		DATE	PLACE	
1-15-41	Jacksonville Florida	RA-403958	6-20-45	Jacksonville Florida	Sergeant, Army

8. IF VETERAN SERVED UNDER NAME OTHER THAN THAT SHOWN IN ITEM I, GIVE FULL NAME AND SERVICE RENDERED UNDER THAT NAME

9. ARE YOU CLAIMING THAT THE CAUSE OF DEATH WAS DUE TO SERVICE?
☐ YES ☒ NO

PART II – CLAIM FOR BURIAL BENEFITS AND/OR INTERMENT ALLOWANCE IF PAID BY CLAIMANT

NOTE – If claiming Plot Allowance Only, do not complete Part II, but complete Parts III and IV on reverse.

10. PLACE OF BURIAL OR LOCATION OF CREMAINS
Sunset Memorial Gardens
Gainesville, Florida

11. WAS BURIAL (WITHOUT CHARGE FOR PLOT OR INTERMENT) IN A STATE OWNED CEMETERY, OR SECTION THEREOF, USED SOLELY FOR PERSONS ELIGIBLE FOR BURIAL IN A NATIONAL CEMETERY?
☐ YES ☒ NO (If "NO," complete Items 13 and 14)

12. WAS BURIAL IN A NATIONAL CEMETERY OR CEMETERY OWNED BY THE FEDERAL GOVERNMENT?
☐ YES ☒ NO (If "NO," complete Items 13 and 14)

13. BURIAL PLOT, MAUSOLEUM VAULT, COLUMBARIUM NICHE, ETC. COST IS:
(CHECK ONE)
☐ PAID BY ANOTHER PERSON(S)
☐ PAID BY CLAIMANT FOR BURIAL
☒ DUE FUNERAL DIRECTOR
☐ NONE
☐ DUE CEMETERY OWNER

14. IF PLOT/INTERMENT EXPENSES ARE UNPAID, WHO WILL FILE CLAIM FOR EXPENSES? (Name and Address)

15. TOTAL EXPENSE OF BURIAL, FUNERAL, TRANSPORTATION AND IF CLAIMED, BURIAL PLOT (This includes cremation, cost of burial urn, and placement of cremains)
$ 3,675.00

16. AMOUNT PAID
$ 3,675.00 ADVANCE

17. WHOSE FUNDS WERE USED?
Gainesville Funeral Home, Inc.

18A. HAS PERSON WHOSE FUNDS WERE USED BEEN REIMBURSED?
☐ YES ☒ NO (If "YES," complete Items 18B and 18C)

18B. AMOUNT OF REIMBURSEMENT
$

18C. SOURCE OF REIMBURSEMENT

19A. HAS OR WILL ANY AMOUNT BE ALLOWED ON EXPENSES BY LOCAL, STATE OR FEDERAL AGENCY?
☐ YES ☒ NO (If "YES," complete Items 19B and 19C)

19B. AMOUNT
$

19C. SOURCE

20. WAS THE VETERAN A MEMBER OF A BURIAL ASSOCIATION OR COVERED BY BURIAL INSURANCE?
☐ YES ☒ NO (Before answering, read and comply with Instruction 11)

VA EOHM FEB 1990 **21-530**

EXISTING STOCKS OF VA FORM 21-530, NOV 1985, WILL BE USED.

Figure 1-4

PART III – CLAIM FOR PLOT COST ALLOWANCE

IMPORTANT – Complete only if burial was NOT in a national cemetery or cemetery owned by the Federal Government.

21. WAS BURIAL (WITHOUT CHARGE FOR PLOT OR INTERMENT) IN A STATE OWNED CEMETERY, OR SECTION THEREOF, USED SOLELY FOR PERSONS ELIGIBLE FOR BURIAL IN A NATIONAL CEMETERY	22. PLACE OF BURIAL OR LOCATION OF CREMAINS	
23A. COST OF BURIAL PLOT *(Individual Grave Site, Mausoleum Vault, or Columbarium Niche)* $	**23B.** DATE OF PURCHASE	**23C.** DATE OF PAYMENT

24A. HAVE BILLS BEEN PAID IN FULL? ☐ YES ☐ NO *If "NO," complete Item 24B)*	24B. AMOUNT PAID $	25. WHOSE FUNDS WERE USED?
26A. HAS PERSON WHOSE FUNDS WERE USED BEEN REIMBURSED? ☐ YES ☐ NO *(If "YES," complete Items 26B and 26C)*	**26B.** AMOUNT OF REIMBURSEMENT $	**26C.** SOURCE OF REIMBURSEMENT
27A. HAS OR WILL ANY AMOUNT BE ALLOWED ON EXPENSES BY STATE OR FEDERAL AGENCY? ☐ YES ☐ NO *(If "YES," complete Items 27B and 27C)*	**27B.** AMOUNT $	**27C.** SOURCE

PART IV – CERTIFICATION AND SIGNATURE

I CERTIFY THAT the foregoing statements made in connection with this application on account of the named veteran are true and correct to the best of my knowledge and belief.

28A. SIGNATURE OF CLAIMANT *(If signed by mark, complete Items 34A. thru 35B)* *(If signing for firm, corporation, or State agency, complete Items 28B thru 29)* *David G. Stone*	28B. OFFICIAL POSITION OF PERSON SIGNING ON BEHALF OF FIRM, CORPORATION OR STATE AGENCY Secretary-Treasurer

29. FULL NAME AND ADDRESS OF THE FIRM, CORPORATION, OR STATE AGENCY FILING AS CLAIMANT

Gainesville Funeral Home, Inc.
342 Cypress Street
Gainesville, Florida 32601

NOTE – Where the claimant is a firm or other unpaid creditor, Items 30A thru 33 MUST be completed by the individual who authorized services.

I CERTIFY THAT the foregoing statements made by the claimant are correct to the best of my knowledge and belief.

30A. SIGNATURE OF PERSON WHO AUTHORIZED SERVICES *(If signed by mark, complete Items 34A thru 35B)* *Robert Lee Kent*	30B. NAME OF PERSON AUTHORIZING SERVICES *(Type or Print)* Robert Lee Kent

31. ADDRESS *(Number and street or rural route, City or P.O., State and Zip Code)*

115 Gulf View Drive
Tampa, Florida 33601

32. DATE 2-23-89	33. RELATIONSHIP TO VETERAN Son

WITNESS TO SIGNATURE IF MADE BY "X" MARK

NOTE: Signature made by mark must be witnessed by two persons to whom the person making the statement is personally known, and the signatures and addresses of such witnesses must be shown below.

34A. SIGNATURE OF WITNESS	34B. ADDRESS OF WITNESS
35A. SIGNATURE OF WITNESS	35B. ADDRESS OF WITNESS

PENALTY – The law provides severe penalties which include fine or imprisonment, or both, for the willful submission of any statement or evidence of a material fact, knowing it to be false.

DEPARTMENT OF VETERANS AFFAIRS HEADSTONES AND MARKERS

The Department of Veterans Affairs will furnish, upon request, a Government headstone or marker at the expense of the United States for the unmarked graves of certain individuals eligible for burial in a national cemetery, but not buried there. These individuals include any veteran with an other than dishonorable discharge who dies after service or any serviceman or servicewoman who dies on active duty. Certain other individuals may also be eligible for the headstone or marker. Headstones or markers for all individuals in a national or post cemetery are furnished automatically without request from the family.

The Department of Veterans Affairs may make a limited reimbursement for the cost of a privately purchased headstone or marker, or for additional engraving on a headstone or marker purchased prior to the veteran's death. If a veteran is buried in a national cemetery, or is provided a Government headstone or marker, this benefit is not payable. The amount of reimbursement is payable to the purchaser but not the seller and the amount payable will not exceed the actual average cost of a Government headstone or marker.

For additional information and an application, contact the nearest VA office. Please state whether you wish to apply for a Government headstone or marker or whether you wish to apply for limited reimbursement for costs incurred in acquiring a non-Government headstone or marker.

*U.S. GPO:1990-262-755/06710

Figure 1-4 (continued)

If no government monument is requested, an additional monetary allowance equal to the average actual cost of a government monument will be paid to reimburse a portion of costs of a privately purchased monument. Currently this allowance is $85 and can be obtained by filing VA Form 21-8834 (Figure 1-5).

For veterans who die of a service-connected disability, a burial allowance up to $1,500 can be chosen in lieu of other burial benefits.

Social Security Administration Benefits

Social Security survivors' benefits are cash benefits paid to the family of a deceased worker that are based on the earnings record of the deceased. Survivors who may be eligible are a surviving spouse, or a divorced spouse if the marriage lasted at least 10 years, and minor children. Benefits to a spouse will be paid when the spouse attains the age of eligibility (60 to 65) or immediately if the spouse is caring for minor children of the deceased. Family members who are eligible to receive survivors' benefits may also receive a lump sum death payment of $255. If there is no surviving spouse or minor children, this payment is not made. A divorced spouse entitled to income benefits is not eligible to receive the lump sum death benefit.

Eligibility for Social Security is established by work credits from employment or self-employment that is subject to Social Security (FICA) taxes. In 1990, each $520 in earnings provided one work credit, with a maximum of four credits per year. A minimum of 40 work credits is required for survivors' benefits to be payable. Under a special rule, survivors' benefits can be paid to a deceased worker's minor children and spouse even though the worker died with few work credits, provided that the worker had worked under Social Security for 18 months in the last three years before death.

Work credits establish eligibility, but actual payment amounts depend on the deceased worker's earnings. The higher the income was, the higher the benefits will be, up to the maximum, subject to restrictions based on other sources of income. The other factor affecting the amount of Social Security payments is the age at which the surviving spouse elects to start receiving them. The payments are permanently reduced if taken before age 65. Because these calculations are rather complex and vary with each individual's work and earnings record, it is important to contact the Social Security Administration promptly if there are survivors eligible for benefits. In some cases benefits may not be payable for the months preceding the month in which an application is filed.

Application for survivors' benefits can be made at any Social Security office. You can find the location and telephone number of the nearest office in the United States Government section of the phone book, or you can call (800) 234-5772 for assistance. The documentation you will need to present

Form Approved
OMB No. 2900-0266

Veterans Administration

APPLICATION FOR REIMBURSEMENT OF HEADSTONE OR MARKER EXPENSES

1. NAME OF DECEASED VETERAN (First, middle, last)	2. SOCIAL SECURITY NUMBER	3. VA FILE NUMBER
James Robert Kent	013-62-1458	C-75962

4. DATE OF BIRTH	5. PLACE OF BIRTH	6. DATE OF DEATH	7. PLACE OF DEATH
12-10-22	Jacksonville, Florida	2-21-89	Gainesville, Florida

8. DATE OF BURIAL	9. PLACE OF BURIAL OR MEMORIAL (Name and location)	10. WAS VETERAN BURIED OR MEMORIALIZED IN A NATIONAL CEMETERY?
2-25-89	Sunset Memorial Gardens Gainesville, Florida	☐ YES ☒ NO

II. SERVICE INFORMATION

A. ENTERED SERVICE DATE	PLACE	B. SERVICE NUMBER	C. SEPARATED FROM SERVICE DATE	PLACE	D. GRADE AND ORGANIZATION	E. BRANCH OF SERVICE
1-15-41	Jacksonville Florida	RA-403958	6-20-45	Jacksonville Florida	Sergeant	ARMY

12. NAME OF CLAIMANT (First, middle, last)	13. RELATIONSHIP TO VETERAN
Robert Lee Kent, Executor	Son

14. MAILING ADDRESS OF CLAIMANT	15. AMOUNT PAID
Estate of James Robert Kent c/o Robert Lee Kent 115 Gulf View Drive Tampa, Florida 33601	A. HEADSTONE OR MARKER $ 1,800.00 B. ENGRAVING OF EXISTING STONE OR MARKER $

16. DATE PURCHASED (Mo., day, yr.)
A. HEADSTONE OR MARKER 3-15-89 B. ENGRAVING

I CERTIFY THAT the foregoing statements made in connection with this application on account of the named veteran are true and correct to the best of my knowledge and belief and that I have NOT filed a separate application for a headstone.

FOR VA USE ONLY

The above application has been received and is pending payment

17. SIGNATURE OF CLAIMANT	18. DATE	DATE RECEIVED	DATE FORWARDED	RO NO.
Robert Lee Kent	4-20-89			

INFORMATION AND INSTRUCTIONS FOR
COMPLETING APPLICATION FOR REIMBURSEMENT OF HEADSTONE OR MARKER EXPENSES
IN LIEU OF A GOVERNMENT FURNISHED HEADSTONE OR MARKER

HOW TO APPLY — Forward this application to the Veterans Administration Regional Office nearest you.

1. Privacy Act Information. No reimbursement of headstone or marker expense may be granted unless this form is completed and returned as required by law (38 U.S.C. Chapter 23). The information requested by this form is considered relevant and necessary to determine maximum benefits provided under the law. Responses may be disclosed outside the VA only if the disclosure is authorized under the Privacy Act, including the routine uses identified in VA system of records, 58VA21/22/28, Compensation, Pension, Education and Rehabilitation Records — VA, published in the Federal Register.

2. Benefits Payable. In lieu of a headstone or marker furnished at government expense, an amount, not to exceed the average government cost, or the actual cost, whichever is less, of privately procured headstones or markers (excluding base) or the additional engraving of an existing headstone or marker already in place to include the deceased's data may be paid on a reimbursable basis when the veteran is buried or memorialized in other than a National Cemetery. NOTE: Reimbursement applies only to headstone, marker, or engraving expenses incurred and paid subsequent to the veterans death.

CAUTION — This is a limited benefit and is not intended to reimburse the total cost of the selected headstone or marker.

Figure 1-5

at the Social Security office to verify information on your application for benefits includes:

- your Social Security number
- the deceased worker's Social Security number
- proof of age (birth certificate, driver's license, passport)
- proof of marriage (marriage license)
- death certificate for deceased worker
- children's birth certificates and Social Security numbers (if minors or disabled)
- most recent federal income tax return or W-2 forms of the deceased
- proof of divorce (final decree), if applying for divorced spouse benefits
- your checkbook (for direct deposit information)

Discuss your situation with the local Social Security office on the telephone to establish the documentation that will be needed in your case. The forms you may need when applying for Social Security survivors' benefits include:

- Form SSA-10-BK—Application for Widow's or Widower's Insurance Benefits
- Form SSA-4-BK—Application for Child's Insurance Benefits
- Form SSA-8-F4—Application for Lump-Sum Death Payment

The last of these forms is shown here (Figure 1-6).

APPLICATION FOR LUMP-SUM DEATH PAYMENT*

I apply for all insurance benefits for which I am eligible under Title II (Federal Old-Age, Survivors, and Disability Insurance) of the Social Security Act, as presently amended, on the named deceased's Social Security record.
(This application must be filed within 2 years after the date of death of the wage earner or self-employed person.)

*This may also be considered an application for insurance benefits payable under the Railroad Retirement Act.

1.	(a) PRINT name of Deceased Wage Earner or Self-Employed Person ⟶ (herein referred to as the "deceased")	FIRST NAME, MIDDLE INITIAL, LAST NAME
	(b) Check (✓) one for the deceased ⟶	☐ Male ☐ Female
	(c) Enter deceased's Social Security Number ⟶	__ __ __ / __ __ / __ __ __ __
2.	PRINT your name ⟶	FIRST NAME, MIDDLE INITIAL, LAST NAME
3.	Enter date of birth of deceased (Month, day, year) ⟶	
4.	(a) Enter date of death (Month, day, year) ⟶	
	(b) Enter place of death (City and State) ⟶	
5.	(a) Did the deceased ever file an application for Social Security benefits, a period of disability under Social Security, supplemental security income, or hospital or medical insurance under Medicare? ⟶	☐ Yes ☐ No ☐ Unknown (If "Yes," answer (b) and (c).) (If "No" or "Unknown," go on to item 6.)
	(b) Enter name(s) of person(s) on whose Social Security record(s) other application was filed. ⟶	FIRST NAME, MIDDLE INITIAL, LAST NAME
	(c) Enter Social Security Number(s) of person(s) named in (b). (If unknown, so indicate) ⟶	__ __ __ / __ __ / __ __ __ __
6.	ANSWER ITEM 6 **ONLY** IF THE DECEASED WORKED WITHIN THE PAST 2 YEARS.	
	(a) About how much did the deceased earn from employment and self-employment during the year of death? ⟶	AMOUNT $
	(b) About how much did the deceased earn the year before death? ⟶	AMOUNT $
7.	ANSWER ITEM 7 **ONLY** IF THE DECEASED DIED PRIOR TO AGE 66 AND WITHIN THE PAST 4 MONTHS	
	(a) Was the deceased unable to work because of a disabling condition at the time of death? ⟶	☐ Yes (If "Yes," answer (b).) ☐ No (If "No," go on to item 8.)
	(b) Enter date disability began (Month, day, year) ⟶	
8.	(a) Was the deceased in the active military or naval service (including Reserve or National Guard *active* duty or active duty for training) after September 7, 1939 and before 1968? ⟶	☐ Yes (If "Yes," answer (b) and (c).) ☐ No (If "No," go on to item 9.)
	(b) Enter dates of service. ⟶	From: (Month, Year) To: (Month, Year)
	(c) Has anyone (including the deceased) received, or does anyone expect to receive, a benefit from any other Federal agency?	☐ Yes ☐ No
9.	Did the deceased work in the railroad industry for 7 years or more? ⟶	☐ Yes ☐ No

Form **SSA-8-F4** (1-87)

Page 1

Figure 1-6

10.	(a)	Did the deceased ever engage in work that was covered under the social security system of a country other than the United States? ⟶	☐ Yes ☐ No _(If "Yes," answer (b).) (If "No," go on to item 11.)_
	(b)	If "Yes," list the country(ies). ⟶	

11.	Is the deceased survived by a spouse or ex-spouse? (If "No," go on to item 12. If "Yes," give the following information about all marriages of the deceased including marriage in effect at time of death.) (If you need more space, use "Remarks" section on back page or attach a separate sheet.)		☐ Yes ☐ No

	To whom married _(Name at Birth)_	When _(Month, day, year)_	Where _(Enter name of City and State)_
Last marriage of the deceased	How marriage ended	When _(Month, day, year)_	Where _(Enter name of City and State)_
	Marriage performed by: ☐ Clergyman or public official ☐ Other _(Explain in Remarks)_	Spouse's date of birth (or age)	
	Spouse's Social Security Number _(If none or unknown, so indicate)_ __ __ __ / __ / __ __ __ __		

	To whom married	When _(Month, day, year)_	Where _(Enter name of City and State)_
Previous marriage of the deceased If none, write "None."	How marriage ended	When _(Month, day, year)_	Where _(Enter name of City and State)_
	Marriage performed by: ☐ Clergyman or public official ☐ Other _(Explain in Remarks)_	Spouse's date of birth (or age)	If spouse deceased, give date of death
	Spouse's Social Security Number _(If none or unknown, so indicate)_ __ __ __ / __ / __ __ __ __		

12.	The deceased's surviving children (including natural children, adopted children, and stepchildren) or dependent grandchildren (including stepgrandchildren) may be eligible for benefits based on the earnings record of the deceased.

List below ALL such children who are now or were in the past 12 months UNMARRIED and:
- UNDER AGE 18
- AGE 18 TO 19 AND ATTENDING SECONDARY SCHOOL
- DISABLED OR HANDICAPPED (age 18 or over and disability began before age 22)

(If none, write "None.")

Full Name of Child	Full Name of Child

13.	Is there a surviving parent (or parents) of the deceased who was receiving support from the deceased either at the time the deceased became disabled under the Social Security law or at the time of death? ⟶	☐ Yes ☐ No _(If "Yes," enter the name and address of the parent(s) in "Remarks".)_
14.	Have you filed for any Social Security benefits on the deceased's earnings record before? ⟶	☐ Yes ☐ No

NOTE: If there is a surviving spouse, continue with item 15. If not, skip items 15 through 18.

15.	If you are not the surviving spouse, enter the surviving spouse's name and address here

16.	(a)	Were the deceased and the surviving spouse living together at the same address when the deceased died?	☐ Yes ☐ No _(If "Yes," go on to item 17.) (If "No," answer (b).)_
	(b)	If either the deceased or surviving spouse was away from home (whether or not temporarily) when the deceased died, give the following:	

Who was away? ⟶	☐ Deceased ☐ Surviving spouse

Date last home	Reason absence began	Reason they were apart at time of death

If separated because of illness, enter nature of illness or disabling condition.

Figure 1-6 (continued)

If you are the surviving spouse, and if you are under age 66, answer 17.

| 17. | (a) Are you so disabled that you cannot work or was there some period during the last 14 months when you were so disabled that you could not work? ──────▶ | ☐ Yes ☐ No |
| | (b) If "Yes," enter the date you became disabled. ──────▶ | *(Month, day, year)* |

Answer 18 ONLY if you are the surviving spouse.

18. Were you married before your marriage to the deceased?
(If "Yes," give the following about each of your previous marriages. If you need more space, use "Remarks" section on back page or attach a separate sheet.) ──────▶   ☐ Yes   ☐ No

To whom married		When *(Month, day, year)*	Where *(Enter name of City and State)*
Your previous marriage	How marriage ended	When *(Month, day, year)*	Where *(Enter name of City and State)*
	Marriage performed by: ☐ Clergyman or public official ☐ Other *(Explain in Remarks)*	Spouse's date of birth (or age)	If spouse deceased, give date of death
	Spouse's Social Security Number *(If none or unknown, so indicate)* __ __ __ / __ __ / __ __ __ __		

Remarks: *(You may use this space for any explanation. If you need more space, attach a separate sheet.)*

I know that anyone who makes or causes to be made a false statement or representation of material fact in an application or for use in determining a right to payment under the Social Security Act commits a crime punishable under Federal law by fine, imprisonment or both. I affirm that all information I have given in this document is true.

SIGNATURE OF APPLICANT	Date *(Month, day, year)*
Signature *(First name, middle initial, last name) (Write in ink)* ▶	Telephone Number(s) at which you may be contacted during the day Area Code

Mailing Address *(Number and street, Apt. No., P.O. Box, or Rural Route)*

City and State	ZIP Code	Enter Name of County (if any) in which you now live

Witnesses are required ONLY if this application has been signed by mark (X) above. If signed by mark (X), two witnesses to the signing who know the applicant must sign below, giving their full addresses.

1. Signature of Witness	2. Signature of Witness
Address *(Number and street, City, State, and ZIP Code)*	Address *(Number and street, City, State, and ZIP Code)*

Form **SSA-8-F4** (1-87)   Page 3

Figure 1-6 (continued)

CHAPTER 2

Opening Probate

The formal opening of probate begins with a scheduled hearing in the court that has jurisdiction over the decedent's estate. This hearing may be requested by the Executor named in the will or by a close relative of the decedent who is qualified to become Administrator of the estate. Before holding the hearing and opening the estate for probate, the court will establish that proper notice has been given to the beneficiaries named in the will and any relatives not named who could receive a share under the laws of intestate succession. This notice is required so that persons who have, or may have, an interest in the estate can be present at the hearing. If no will is presented when the hearing is opened, the court may require proof that a diligent search for one has been made. When a will is presented, the court determines whether it has been properly executed and rules on its validity. After the Executor named in the will or the person applying for appointment as Administrator is confirmed by the court, he or she will become the legal Personal Representative of the decedent. Official documents are then issued to allow the Personal Representative to act on behalf of decedent and the estate.

This chapter discusses the steps in opening probate for both testate and intestate estates. The process is very similar for both, the major difference being in the notice requirements. Two state-by-state summaries that contain information referenced in the text are included. The first of these, the Will

Probate Summary, lists the notice requirements for the opening of probate, the name of the court of jurisdiction, and information about each state's requirements for a valid will. The second State Summary sets out the Spouse's Elective Share, which is the amount of the estate the decedent's spouse is entitled to regardless of the provisions of the will. Samples of a will and self-proving form are included for reference.

Jurisdiction

The court that has jurisdiction over the decedent's legal residence is responsible for probate of the entire estate unless there is real property located in another state. If there are homes in different states, each is subject to probate in the jurisdiction where it is located. The court that has jurisdiction over the primary estate is determined by establishing the decedent's *domicile,* or primary residence. Factors that determine domicile, in addition to the amount of time the decedent spent at the residence, are what address was used on the decedent's federal income tax forms and where the decedent was registered to vote. The address listed on a driver's license and bank accounts, particularly checking accounts, are also determining factors. Except for out-of-state property, the court having jurisdiction over the legal residence will be responsible for probate of the entire estate. The local court that has jurisdiction over out-of-state real property will oversee the transfer of that real property and any related tangible personal property, such as furnishings.

The Will Probate State Summary on pages 34–43 lists the name of the local court having jurisdiction over probate in all 50 states and the District of Columbia. Note that in Colorado, Indiana, Maryland, and Tennessee, the court having jurisdiction depends on the locality of last residence; the localities for which the court of jurisdiction differs from that for the rest of the state are given in parentheses, along with the name of their court of jurisdiction.

Notice of Hearing

Generally, all persons named in the will, and any relatives not named who could receive a share under the laws of intestate succession, must be given notice prior to the court hearing. Notice is delivered in person or mailed by the Personal Representative or clerk of the court, and in many cases public notice is also required. Public notice is usually demanded by the court if the address of any potential heir is unknown. When required, public notice of the opening of probate is run in the local newspaper, usually for several weeks, to allow those who have an interest in the estate to be aware of the time and date of the hearing. The exact wording of this notice is available from the court, but it normally states the date and time of the hearing and often advises anyone with an interest in the estate to be present.

Notice requirements vary significantly from state to state. In Connecticut, Delaware, Iowa, Maine, and Pennsylvania, notice is provided at the discretion of, or by direction of, the probate court. No prior notice is required in Louisiana, Mississippi, Missouri, New Hampshire, Oregon, Virginia, Washington, West Virginia, and Wyoming; in these states, notice to those who are named in the will or who could receive an intestate share is required after appointment of the Personal Representative. In New York, published prior notice is not required if all who could share in the estate agree. In Tennessee, prior notice is not required for an informal hearing. The notice required before opening an estate is listed in the Will Probate State Summary on pages 34–43. If notice is required in your state and you apply to be named Personal Representative, contact the local probate court to set a hearing date and obtain the required wording for the notice.

The Hearing

The original of the last will and testament and the self-proving certificate (if there is one) and a copy of the death certificate will be needed at the probate court hearing. If there are several wills, take them all to the hearing. The most recent will is the one that governs distribution of the estate's assets if it is properly executed. When a person executes a new will, he or she revokes all prior wills. However, if the latest will is improperly executed and hence declared invalid, a prior will may have been executed properly and hence be acceptable to the court. This situation is rare because a person usually destroys the original of a prior will after executing a new one. A copy is not acceptable; the original will bearing all signatures must be presented.

If no will has been located by the time of the hearing, the court must be assured that a diligent search was carried out. The decedent's bank safety deposit box or personal safe and personal financial papers should be examined. Inquiries to friends of the deceased may also help locate the will. Often the original of the will is entrusted to the person named as the Executor, but it may be held by an attorney or even, in some states, pre-filed with the court.

The probate court will rule on the validity of the will submitted. If it is accepted, the Executor named will become the Personal Representative and will be issued *letters testamentary,* the documents that empower him or her to act on behalf of the estate. The Executor is required to distribute the estate as set out in the will.

Because so many people die without a properly executed will, each state has developed its own rules for distribution of intestate estates. These rules are known as the *laws of intestate succession* and specify those surviving relatives who may be entitled to a share of the estate. (A summary of the state laws of intestate succession is included in Chapter 7.) If there is no will, or the will presented is not accepted, the court appoints an Administrator for the intestate estate and issues *letters of administration* to confirm the appointment. The Administrator must distribute the estate according to the state's laws of intestate succession. A close relative of the decedent usually applies for appointment as Administrator, although others with an interest in the estate may apply. If no applicants are accepted by the court or no one applies, the court often appoints a local attorney as Administrator.

After you are appointed as the Personal Representative, you usually have to post a surety bond, available through a local bonding company, to protect the assets of the estate. Bond may not be required if specifically waived in the will. Before you leave the court, request several certified copies of the will (if there is one) and letters empowering you as the Personal Representative. These documents will be needed as you proceed to settle the estate.

Will Requirements

To prepare a valid will, a person must be a legal adult who is of sound mind and not acting under threat, duress, or undue influence of others. The will document sets out the plan for disposition of the Testator's assets. A will must be *executed,* that is signed and dated, by the Testator in the presence of two or more disinterested witnesses, who then also sign the document.

All 50 states, with the exceptions of Louisiana and Vermont, and the District of Columbia require two witnesses to the signing of a will. Vermont requires three witnesses for a valid will. Louisiana recognizes three types of wills: a *statutory* will, which requires two witnesses (three if the Testator is visually impaired) and a notary; a *mystic* will, which requires three witnesses to notarization when the will is sealed in an envelope; a *noncupative* will, a written will that is read aloud before three or five witnesses and a notary, or privately executed before five or seven witnesses and a notary. The lower number of witnesses is accepted if they are all of the same locality as the Testator; the higher number is required if they are from other localities.

Self-Proving

When a will is presented to the court, the witnesses may be required to sign an affidavit or personally appear to verify (prove) their signatures. Because witnesses may move or die before the will is presented to the probate court, they may be difficult, if not impossible, to locate. A self-proving certificate allows the witnesses to prove, in advance, their signatures on the will. A *self-*

proving certificate is a form signed by the Testator and the witnesses to the will, before a notary, affirming that the Testator signed the will in their presence together. The self-proving certificate is then signed and sealed by the notary and affixed to the will, resulting in a self-proved will. When a will is self-proved, the witnesses do not have to appear in court or submit an affidavit. Currently, Vermont and Wisconsin are the only states that do not recognize self-proved wills.

Figures 2-1 and 2-2 show a properly executed will and a completed self-proving certificate for that will.

Proof of a Will

Probate used as a legal term literally means "to prove." As such, it refers to the court's standards involved in determining the validity of a document presented as a person's last will and testament. Because a will is a document that contains instructions regarding transfer of property, the court will hold a hearing to establish that it is genuine and properly executed.

When a will has not been self-proved, the probate court must rely on other proof of authenticity. Generally the court will require testimony or an affidavit from one or more signing witnesses affirming that they did indeed witness the signing of the document by the Testator. A property executed will must be proved at the court hearing in almost all cases. Exceptions are properly executed, uncontested wills in Massachusetts, South Dakota, Vermont, and Wisconsin, when agreed to by all who could receive a share of the estate under the laws of intestate succession. Proof of a properly executed will is not required in Illinois if the estate is less than $25,000.

If a will is contested, or challenged, states generally require more proof than if it is uncontested. For example, in some states an affidavit by one signing witness is sufficient to prove an uncontested will, but testimony of all witnesses may be required if the will is contested. When witnesses are unavailable, the court generally requires testimony and/or evidence to verify the signatures of the Testator and one or more of the witnesses. Signed letters, checks, or tax returns of the decedent and witnesses can usually be located for use as such evidence if needed.

The standards of proof for a will in each state are listed in the Will Probate State Summary that follows this section.

If a will is successfully contested, the document is not accepted by the court and the estate is dealt with on the basis that there is no will. Since wills can be contested only on the grounds that the Testator was not of sound mind or was acting under threat, duress, or undue influence or that the document was not properly executed, successful contests are rare. Proving that the deceased was of unsound mind or not acting freely when he or she executed the will is extremely difficult.

LAST WILL AND TESTAMENT

I, __James Robert Kent__ , resident of the County of __Alachua__ in the State of __Florida__ , being of sound mind, do make and declare the following to be my LAST WILL AND TESTAMENT and expressly revoke all my prior wills and codicils and certify that I am not acting under undue influence, duress or menace.

I. EXECUTOR

I appoint __Robert Lee Kent, my son,__ EXECUTOR of this, my LAST WILL AND TESTAMENT. If this EXECUTOR is unable to serve for any reason, then I appoint __James Byrd Kent, my son,__ EXECUTOR.

The EXECUTOR is empowered to carry out all provisions of this WILL.

The EXECUTOR shall pay from the Estate all taxes due thereon and shall pay all just debts, excepting mortgages.

The EXECUTOR named shall not be required to post surety bond. I direct that no outside appraisal be made of my Estate, unless required for estate tax purposes.

II. BEQUESTS

I leave my entire estate to my two beloved sons, Robert Lee Kent and James Byrd Kent, in equal shares, per stirpes. This concludes my entire last will and testament.

IN WITNESS WHEREOF, I have hereunto set my hand this _twentieth_ day of _March_ , 19_87_ .

_____
(Signature)

III. WITNESSED

This LAST WILL AND TESTAMENT of __James Robert Kent__ was signed and declared to be his/~~her~~ LAST WILL AND TESTAMENT in our presence at his/~~her~~ request and in his/~~her~~ presence as witnesses on this __twentieth__ day of __March__ , 19_87_ .

Samuel Irving Green _____ Gainesville, Florida
(Witness signature) _____ (Address)

Peter Carr Wood _____ 16 Crest Hill Drive, Gainesville Fla.
(Witness signature) _____ (Address)

_____ _____
(Witness signature) _____ (Address)

Figure 2-1

32

SELF-PROVING CERTIFICATE

State of _____Florida_____

County/City of _____Alachua_____

                 Before me, the undersigned authority, on this day personally appeared

_____James Robert Kent_____

Testator _Samuel Irving Green_

Witness _Peter Carr Wood_

Witness _____

Witness _____

known to me to be the Testator and Witnesses, respectively, whose names are signed to the attached or foregoing instrument and, all of these persons being by me first duly sworn, _____James_____

_____Robert Kent_____ , the testator, declared to me and to the witnesses in my presence that said instrument is his/her LAST WILL AND TESTAMENT and that he/she had willingly signed or directed another to sign the same for him/her, and executed it in the presence of said witnesses as his/her free and voluntary act for the purposes therein expressed; that said witnesses stated before me that the foregoing will was executed and acknowledged by the testator as his/her LAST WILL AND TESTAMENT in the presence of said witnesses who, in his/her presence and at his/her request, and in the presence of each other, did subscribe their names thereto as attesting witnesses on the day of the date of said will, and that the testator, at the time of the execution of said will was over the age of eighteen years and of sound and disposing mind and memory.

_____
(Testator signature)

_____
(Witness signature)

_____
(Witness signature)

_____
(Witness signature)

Subscribed, sworn and acknowledged before me by

_____James Robert Kent_____ , the Testator,

and subscribed and sworn before me by _____Samuel Irving Green_____

_____and Peter Carr Wood_____

_____ , Witnesses,

this _twentieth_ day of _March_ , 19 _87_ A.D.

Signed: _____

Notary Public

My Commission Expires: _____2-15-91_____

(Seal)

**Figure 2-2**

33

Will Probate—State Summary

The following table shows the court of jurisdiction and the probate requirements for all 50 states and the District of Columbia.

Will Probate—State Summary

State	Court Having Probate Jurisdiction	Witness Signatures Required	Self-Proved Wills Accepted
Alabama	Probate Court—Code of Alabama, Title 43	Two	Yes
Alaska	Superior Court—Alaska Statutes, Title 13	Two	Yes
Arizona	Superior Court—Arizona Statutes, Title 14	Two	Yes
Arkansas	Probate Court—Arkansas Code, Title 28	Two	Yes
California	Superior Court/Probate Division—California Probate Code Sections 1–1700	Two	Yes
Colorado	District Court—Colorado Statutes, Title 15 (Denver—Probate Court)	Two	Yes
Connecticut	Probate Court—Connecticut General Statutes, Title 45	Two	Yes
Delaware	Chancery/Register of Wills—Delaware Code, Title 12	Two	Yes
District of Columbia	Superior Court/Probate Division and Register of Wills—District of Columbia Code, Titles 18–20	Two	Yes
Florida	Circuit Court—Florida Statutes, Chapters 731–738	Two	Yes

Notice Required Before Opening Estate	Requirements for Proving a Will
At least 10 days to spouse and those who could share by will or intestacy; if address(es) unknown, weekly notice published for 3 consecutive weeks before hearing	Testimony of one signing witness or, if unavailable, proof of handwriting of Testator and one signing witness
At least 14 days to spouse and those who could share by will or intestacy; if address(es) unknown, weekly notice published for 3 consecutive weeks, with last publication at least 10 days before hearing	Testimony or affidavit of one signing witness or, if unavailable, other evidence
At least 14 days to spouse and those who could share by will or intestacy; if address(es) unknown, notice published three times, with first notice at least 14 days before hearing	Testimony or affidavit of one signing witness; if unavailable, other evidence
At least 15 days to spouse and those who could share by will or intestacy; if address(es) unknown, weekly notice published for 2 consecutive weeks, with first publication at least 15 days before hearing	Testimony of two signing witnessess or, if unavailable, testimony of two witnesses proving handwriting of Testator and unavailable signing witness(es)
At least 15 days to spouse and those who could share by will or intestacy and notice published three times with at least 5 days between first and last notice, with first publication at least 15 days before hearing	Testimony of one signing witness (uncontested) or, if unavailable, by affidavit; or testimony of each signing witness (contested) or, if unavailable, proof of handwriting of Testator
At least 10 days to spouse and those who could share by will or intestacy; if address(es) unknown, weekly notice published for 3 consecutive weeks, with last publication at least 10 days before hearing	Testimony (contested) or affidavit (uncontested) of one signing witness; if unavailable, other evidence
To those who could share by will or intestacy, as the court directs	Court sets hearing and receives evidence
As court directs	Testimony of two signing witnesses; if one unavailable, testimony and affidavit; if both unavailable, testimony proving signature of Testator
Promptly to those who could share by will or intestacy and weekly notice published for 2 consecutive weeks before hearing	Affidavit by signing witnesses; if unavailable, affidavit from someone with personal knowledge of execution of will
To those with same or greater right to be Personal Representative	Testimony of one signing witness; if unavailable, testimony from someone with knowledge of execution of will

Will Probate—State Summary (*continued*)

State	Court Having Probate Jurisdiction	Witness Signatures Required	Self-Proved Wills Accepted
Georgia	Probate Court—Code of Georgia, Title 53	Two	Yes
Hawaii	Circuit Court—Hawaii Statutes, Title 29–30A	Two	Yes
Idaho	District Court/Magistrates' Division—Idaho Code Titles 14–15	Two	Yes
Illinois	Circuit Court—Illinois Statutes, Chapter 110-1/2, Articles 1–27	Two	Yes
Indiana	Circuit Court, Superior Court—Indiana Statutes, Title 29 (St. Joseph's County—Probate Court)	Two	Yes
Iowa	District Court—Iowa Code, Title 32, Chapter 633	Two	Yes
Kansas	District Court—Kansas Statutes, Chapter 59	Two	Yes
Kentucky	District Court—Kentucky Statutes, Title 32, Chapters 391–397	Two	Yes
Louisiana	District Court—Louisiana Statutes, Code of Civil Procedure Articles 2811–3462, Civil Code, Articles 871–1465	Three	Yes
Maine	Probate Court—Maine Statutes, Title 18A, Sections 5–614	Two	Yes
Maryland	Orphans' Court—Code of the Public General Laws of Maryland, Estates and Trusts, Titles 1–12 (Hartford and Montgomery Counties—Circuit Court)	Two	Yes
Massachusetts	District Court, Probate and Family Departments—Laws of Massachusetts, Part II, Title II, Chapters 189–206	Two	Yes

Notice Required Before Opening Estate	Requirements for Proving a Will
At least 10 days to spouse and others who could share by will or intestacy; if address(es) unknown, weekly notices published for 4 consecutive weeks before hearing	Testimony of one signing witness (uncontested) or testimony of all signing witnesses (contested); if unavailable, affidavit proving Testator's signature
At least 14 days to spouse and those who could share by will or intestacy and weekly notice published for 3 consecutive weeks, with last publication at least 10 days before hearing	Testimony (contested) or affidavit (uncontested) of one signing witness; if unavailable, other evidence
At least 14 days to those who could share by will or intestacy; if address(es) unknown, weekly notice published for 3 consecutive weeks, with last publication at least 10 days before hearing	Testimony (contested) or affidavit (uncontested) of one signing witness; if unavailable, other evidence
At least 30 days to anyone with the same or greater right to be appointed Personal Representative; after appointment as Personal Representative, notice to all who could share by will or intestacy within 14 days; if address(es) unknown, weekly notice published for 3 consecutive weeks	Not required for estates of less than $25,000; testimony or affidavit of two signing witnesses; if unavailable, testimony or affidavit of someone proving handwriting of witnesses
At least 14 days to those who could share by will or intestacy and weekly notice published for 2 consecutive weeks	Testimony or affidavit of one signing witness; if unavailable, proof of handwriting of Testator or two signing witnesses
At court's discretion	Testimony or affidavit of one signing witness; if unavailable, two witnesses proving handwriting of Testator and signing witnesses
At least 7 days to those who could share by will or intestacy	Testimony or affidavit of two signing witnesses; if unavailable, testimony to signatures of Testator and witnesses
At least 5 days to those state residents who could share by will or intestacy; weekly notice published for 6 consecutive weeks before appointment as Personal Representative if administration is unnecessary	Testimony and affidavit of one signing witness or, if unavailable, testimony of two persons proving handwriting of Testator (uncontested); court's discretion if will is contested
None required	Testimony of three signing witnesses; if unavailable, testimony of two persons proving handwriting of Testator (or notary)
Court determines notice to those who could share by will or intestacy	Testimony or affidavit (uncontested) of one signing witness; if unavailable, other evidence
By registrar to those who could share by will or intestacy and weekly notice published for 2 consecutive weeks before hearing	Affidavit or testimony of anyone with knowledge of will execution; if unavailable, the court determines method
At least 14 days to those who could share by will or intestacy and weekly notice published for 2 consecutive weeks before hearing; no notice necessary if no will	Testimony or affidavit of one signing witness; no proof required if all who could share by will or intestacy agree

Will Probate—State Summary (continued)

State	Court Having Probate Jurisdiction	Witness Signatures Required	Self-Proved Wills Accepted
Michigan	Probate Court—Michigan Statutes, Chapter 27.5001–27.5993	Two	Yes
Minnesota	Probate or County Court—Minnesota Statutes, Chapters 524–528	Two	Yes
Mississippi	Chancery Court—Mississippi Code, Title 91	Two	Yes
Missouri	Circuit Court/Probate Division—Missouri Statutes, Chapter 472–474	Two	Yes
Montana	District Court—Montana Code, Title 72	Two	Yes
Nebraska	County Court—Statutes of Nebraska, Chapter 30	Two	Yes
Nevada	District Court—Nevada Statutes, Title 12, Chapters 132–156	Two	Yes
New Hampshire	Probate Court—New Hampshire Statutes, Titles 56–57, Chapters 547–569	Two	Yes
New Jersey	Surrogate or Superior Court—New Jersey Statutes, Title 3B 1–29	Two	Yes
New Mexico	District and Probate Courts—New Mexico Statutes, Chapter 45	Two	Yes
New York	Surrogate's Court—Surrogate's Court Procedure Act	Two	Yes
North Carolina	Superior Court—General Statutes of North Carolina, Volume 2A Part 1, Chapters 28–41	Two	Yes
North Dakota	District and County Courts—North Dakota Code, Title 30	Two	Yes

Notice Required Before Opening Estate	Requirements for Proving a Will
At least 14 days to those who could share by will or intestacy; if address(es) unknown, notice published at least 14 days before hearing	Testimony or affidavit of one signing witness; if unavailable, testimony proving handwriting of Testator and witnesses
At least 14 days to those who could share by will or intestacy and weekly notice published at least 10 days before hearing for 2 consecutive weeks	Testimony or affidavit (uncontested) of one signing witness; if unavailable, other evidence
None required	Testimony by one signing witness; if unavailable, proof of handwriting of Testator and signing witnesses
None required	Testimony of two signing witnesses; if unavailable, testimony of one signing witness and proof of handwriting of other witness; if unavailable, other evidence
At least 14 days to those who could share by will or intestacy; if address(es) unknown, weekly notice published for 3 consevutive weeks (with at least 10 days between first and last notice) before hearing	Testimony or affidavit (uncontested) by one signing witness; if unavailable, other evidence
At least 14 days to those who could share by will or intestacy and weekly notice published by clerk for 3 consecutive weeks before hearing	Testimony or affidavit (uncontested) of one signing witness; if unavailable, other evidence
At least 10 days to those who could share by will or intestacy and published weekly for 3 consecutive weeks (with at least 10 days between first and last notice) before hearing	Testimony or affidavit of two signing witnesses (contested) or testimony or affidavit of one signing witness (uncontested); if unavailable, proof of handwriting of Testator or other evidence
None required; notice within 60 days of proving will to those who could share by will or intestacy	Testimony of one or two signing witnesses; if unavailable, other evidence
At least 10 days (in state) or 60 days (out of state) to those with same or greater right to be Personal Representative	Testimony of one signing witness; court may require two
At least 14 days to those who could share by will or intestacy; if address(es) unknown, weekly notice published for 2 consecutive weeks before hearing	Testimony or affidavit (uncontested) by one signing witness; if unavailable, other evidence
None required if those who could share by will or intestacy agree; otherwise, court summons served at least 20 days before hearing to all who could share by will or intestacy	Testimony of one signing witness; if unavailable, proof of handwriting of Testator and one witness
Court serves summons to those who could share by will or intestacy	Testimony of two signing witnesses or, if unavailable, testimony of one signing witness and proof of handwriting of other witness; if unavailable, other evidence
At least 14 days to those who could share by will or intestacy; if address(es) unknown, weekly notice published for 3 consecutive weeks, with last notice at least 10 days before hearing	Testimony or affidavit (uncontested) by one signing witness; if unavailable, other evidence

Will Probate—State Summary (*continued*)

State	Court Having Probate Jurisdiction	Witness Signatures Required	Self-Proved Wills Accepted
Ohio	Court of Common Pleas/Probate Division—Ohio Code, Title 21	Two	Yes
Oklahoma	District Court—Oklahoma Statutes, Titles 58, 84	Two	Yes
Oregon	Circuit and County Courts—Oregon Statutes, Title 12	Two	Yes
Pennsylvania	Common Pleas Court/Orphan's Court Division and Registrar of Wills—Pennsylvania Statutes, Title 20	Two	Yes
Rhode Island	Probate Court—General Laws of Rhode Island, Title 33	Two	Yes
South Carolina	Probate Court—Codes of South Carolina, Title 62	Two	Yes
South Dakota	Circuit Court—South Dakota Laws, Chapters 29, 30	Two	Yes
Tennessee	Chancery Court—Tennessee Code, 30-1-101–32-5-110 (Davidson and Shelby Counties—Probate Court)	Two	Yes
Texas	County or Statutory Probate Court—Civil Statutes of the State of Texas, Probate Code	Two	Yes
Utah	District Court—Utah Code, Probate Code	Two	Yes
Vermont	Probate Court—Vermont Statutes, Title 14	Three	No
Virginia	Circuit Court—Code of Virginia, Titles 26-32.1, 63.1-65.1	Two	Yes
Washington	Superior Court/Probate Division—Code of Washington, Title 11	Two	Yes

Notice Required Before Opening Estate	Requirements for Proving a Will
At least 7 days to those who could share by will or intestacy	Testimony or affidavit of two signing witnesses; if unavailable, other evidence
At least 10 days to those who could share by will or intestacy; if address(es) unknown, published notice in county newspaper	Testimony or affidavit of one signing witness (uncontested) or testimony of all signing witnesses (contested); if unavailable, affidavit of signing and other witnesses
None required; notice to those who could share by will or intestacy within 30 days of appointment of Personal Representative and weekly notice published for 3 consecutive weeks	Testimony or affidavit (uncontested) of one signing witness; if unavailable, evidence of signature of Testator or one signing witness
Court may publish	Testimony of two signing witnesses; if unavailable, proof of signature of Testator or signing witnesses
At least 10 days to those who could share by will or intestacy	Testimony of two signing witnesses or, if unavailable, testimony of two persons to prove handwriting of Testator; if unavailable, other evidence
At least 20 days to those who could share by will or intestacy	Testimony or affidavit (uncontested) of one signing witness; if unavailable, other evidence
At least 14 days to those who could share by will or intestacy and notice published weekly for 3 consecutive weeks, with last notice at least 15 days before hearing; this notice is also the creditors' notice	If copies of properly witnessed will are mailed to all who could share by will or intestacy and no one contests, no further proof is required; if contested, then testimony of all signing witnesses or, if unavailable, proof of handwriting of Testator and witnesses
None required for informal hearing; at least 30 days before formal hearing to those who could share by will or intestacy	Testimony or affidavit of one signing witness for informal hearing; for formal hearing, testimony of all signing witnesses or, if unavailable, testimony of one signing witness proving signature of Testator
Clerk posts in courthouse 10 days before hearing	Testimony or affidavit of one signing witness; if unavailable, two persons proving handwriting of Testator and signing witnesses
At least 10 days to those who could share by will or intestacy; if address(es) unknown, weekly notice published by clerk for 3 consecutive weeks before hearing	Testimony or affidavit (uncontested) by one signing witness; if unavailable, other evidence
At least 14 days to those who could share by will or intestacy; if address(es) unknown, weekly notice published for 2 consecutive weeks before hearing	Will accepted without further evidence if those who could share by intestacy agree; if contested, testimony of one signing witness or, if unavailable, testimony of two persons proving handwriting of Testator, sanity, and proper execution
None required; notice to those who could share by will or intestacy within 20 days of appointment of Personal Representative	Testimony of one signing witness or, if unavailable, testimony proving signatures of witnesses; if unavailable, court presumes valid
None required; notice to those who could share by will or intestacy within 20 days of appointment of Personal Representative	Testimony of two signing witnesses or, if unavailable, by deposition; if unavailable, by proof of handwriting of Testator and witnesses or other evidence

Will Probate—State Summary (*continued*)

State	Court Having Probate Jurisdiction	Witness Signatures Required	Self-Proved Wills Accepted
West Virginia	County Commission—West Virginia Code, Chapters 41–44	Two	Yes
Wisconsin	Circuit Court—Wisconsin Statutes, Chapter 851–879	Two	No
Wyoming	District Court—Wyoming Statutes, Title 2	Two	Yes

Small Estate Options

If the estate is small, it is advisable to prepare a preliminary estimate of its total value. All 50 states and the District of Columbia have special provisions for settling small estates under certain conditions. Often these options, *administration unnecessary* and *administration by affidavit*, and *summary administration* are available if the estate consists only of personal property worth less than a specified amount and if a minimum period of time has passed since the date of death. These options are usually available only when no application for appointment as Personal Representative is pending with the probate court. The Probate Administration State Summary in the next chapter lists the general requirements that an estate must meet to qualify for administration unnecessary, administration by affidavit, or summary administration. Note that in Rhode Island, South Carolina, and Utah small estate options must be selected within a specified number of days after the date of death. If review of the Probate Administration State Summary indicates that one of these options may apply, contact the local probate court for more specific information before the scheduled hearing date. Since several states take into account allowances, exemptions, costs, and even the spouse's automatic share when calculating the estate threshold, it is important to know the basis of calculation to be used for the specific small estate involved. Discuss these administrative options with the clerk of the probate court as it may mean that a formal hearing will not be required.

Spouse's Elective Share

If a will has been presented and accepted by the probate court and the surviving spouse is omitted, disinherited, or receives only a minor share, most

Notice Required Before Opening Estate	Requirements for Proving a Will
None required	Testimony of signing witnesses; if unavailable, proof of signature of Testator or witnesses, other evidence
At least 20 days to those who could share by will or intestacy and weekly notice published for 3 consecutive weeks before hearing	Not required if properly executed and uncontested; if contested, testimony or affidavit of one signing witness or, if unavailable, testimony proving handwriting of Testator and witness
None required; notice to those who could share by will or intestacy and creditors published weekly for 3 consecutive weeks after appointment of Personal Representative	Testimony or affidavit of one signing witness; if unavailable, testimony of two persons proving handwriting of Testator and witnesses

states provide protection to the surviving spouse by giving him or her the right of election. An outgrowth of dower (wife) and curtsey (husband) rights to property held by married persons, the right of election allows the surviving spouse to reject the share left by the will and elect to take the state's elective share instead. The elective share is generally equal to or less than the spouse's share of an intestate estate.

All but nine states—Arizona, California, Georgia, Louisiana, Nevada, New Mexico, Texas, Washington, and Wisconsin—provide a right of election to the surviving spouse. Community property states do not provide a right of election because the surviving spouse already has one-half ownership of all community property. Idaho does allow the surviving spouse the right of election related to quasi-community property, that is, property that was acquired during the marriage while the couple was not resident in Idaho. The spouse's elective share is available only if a will has been accepted by the probate court; if the will presented is contested and found to be invalid, the surviving spouse receives the intestate share.

If the surviving spouse chooses to take the elective share, the balance of the estate is divided among the remaining heirs in accord with the state's laws of intestate succession. The claim of an elective share must be made within a stated period of time and, once made, cannot be revoked. Following is a summary of the surviving spouse's elective share for each state. Recently an increasing number of states further protect the surviving spouse's elective share by calculating it on the basis of the "augmented" estate, rather than the probate estate. The "augmented" estate consists of specified additions to the probate estate such as certain jointly held property, gifts, and some trust arrangements that exclude the surviving spouse. If review of the surviving spouse's share under the will shows it to be less than the elective share listed for your state in the following table, do not hesitate to get complete, detailed information from the local probate court on current elective share provisions and filing requirements.

Spouse's Elective Share—State Summary

State	Share	Election
Alabama	One-third of estate	Within 6 months of acceptance of will
Alaska	One-third of estate	Within 6 months of acceptance of will or within 9 months of death, whichever is later
Arizona	No provision—community property state	
Arkansas	A. If living issue and married over 1 year: One-third of estate B. If no living issue: One-third of estate before creditors One-half of estate before heirs C. If real estate owned by family for two or more generations: Lifetime use of one-third of real estate before creditors Lifetime use of one-half of real estate before heirs One-half of personal property	Within approximately 4 months of acceptance of will (30 days after creditor claims due) or within 1 month of resolution of will contest
California	No provision—community property state	
Colorado	One-half of estate	Within 6 months of first creditor notice or within 1 year of death, whichever is earlier
Connecticut	Lifetime use of one-third of estate	Within 7 months (210 days) of appointment of Executor
Delaware	One-third of adjusted gross estate (per IRS Form 706)	Within 6 months of appointment of Executor (court may grant extension)
District of Columbia	A. If living issue: one-third of estate, after debts B. If no living issue: one-half of estate, after debts or C. Lifetime use of one-third of real estate, after debts and Lifetime use of one-half of other property, after debts	Within 6 months of acceptance of will
Florida	Thirty percent of fair market value of estate property in Florida, after debts, excluding jointly held savings and trusts	Within 4 months of appointment of Executor or within 40 days of resolution of will contest
Georgia	No provision	
Hawaii	One-third of estate	Within 6 months of acceptance of will or within 9 months of death, whichever is later
Idaho	Community property state; one-half of quasi-community property (property acquired during marriage when Idaho not permanent residence)	Within 6 months of first creditor notice (court may grant extension)
Illinois	A. If living issue: one-third of estate, after debts	Within 7 months of acceptance of will; court may extend if will is contested

Spouse's Elective Share—State Summary (*continued*)

State	Share	Election
	B. If no living issue: one-half of estate, after debts	
Indiana	A. If not first spouse, with no children by deceased and other issue of deceased from previous marriage(s): lifetime use of one-third of real estate and one-third of personal property, after debts B. Otherwise: one-half of estate	Within 5 months and 10 days of first creditor notice or within 30 days of resolution of will contest
Iowa	One-third of real estate and one-third of personal property, after debts, or lifetime use of home	Within 4 months of second creditor notice
Kansas	A. If living issue: one-half of estate B. If no living issue: entire estate	Within 6 months of acceptance of will
Kentucky	One-half of community property, one-half of separate personal property, one-third of real estate owned, lifetime use of one-third of other real estate, and living expense up to $7,500, less last illness, funeral, and administration costs	Within 6 months of acceptance of will
Louisiana	No provision—community property state	
Maine	One-third of estate	Within 6 months of acceptance of will or within 9 months of death, whichever is later
Maryland	A. If living issue: one-third of estate B. If no living issue: one-half of estate	Within 7 months of acceptance of will (30 days after claims are due)
Massachusetts	A. If living issue: one-third of estate B. If no living issue, but relatives: $25,000 plus one-half of balance of personal property plus lifetime use of one-half of real estate C. If no living issue and no living relatives: $25,000 plus one-half of estate	Within 6 months of acceptance of will
Michigan	One-half of estate or lfetime use of one-third of real estate	Within 60 days of deadline for claims or inventory, whichever is later (minimum of 4 months)
Minnesota	One-third of estate	Within 6 months of acceptance of will or within 9 months of death, whichever is later
Mississippi	A. If living issue: one-third of estate B. If no living issue: one-half of estate NOTE: If surviving spouse's property equals intestate share below, then share is nothing 1. If living issue: equal share with children 2. If no living issue: entire estate	Within 90 days of acceptance of will
Missouri	A. If living issue: one-third of estate B. If no living issue: one-half of estate	Within 6 months and 10 days of acceptance of will

Spouse's Elective Share—State Summary (*continued*)

State	Share	Election
Montana	One-third of estate	Within 6 months of acceptance of will or within 9 months of death, whichever is later
Nebraska	One-half of estate	Within 6 months of acceptance of will or within 9 months of death, whichever is later
New Hampshire	A. If living issue: one-third of estate B. If no living issue, but living parents or siblings: $10,000 of personal property and $10,000 of real estate plus one-half of balance of estate C. If no living issue and no living parents or siblings: $10,000 and $2,000 for each year of marriage plus one-half of balance of estate	Within 6 months of appointment of Executor
New Jersey	One-third of estate or lifetime use of one-half of real estate owned between 1929 and 1980 (dower)	Within 6 months of appointment of Executor
New Mexico	No provision—community property state	
New York	A. If living issue: one-half of estate B. If no living issue: one-third of estate	Within 6 months of appointment of Executor
North Carolina	Lifetime use of home or one-third of real estate, whichever is greater	May elect if share by will is less than intestate share, within 12 months of death
North Dakota	One-third of estate	Within 6 months of acceptance of will or within 9 months of death, whichever is later
Ohio	A. If one living issue: one-half of estate B. Otherwise: one-third of estate	Within 1 month of acceptance of will or within 3 months of notice, if will is contested
Oklahoma	One-half of property acquired by "joint industry"	Prior to date for final distribution hearing
Oregon	One-fourth of estate, in addition to inherited share, up to a total of one-half of estate	Within 90 days of acceptance of will
Pennsylvania	One-third of estate	Within 6 months of acceptance of will
Rhode Island	Lifetime use of real estate	Within 6 months of acceptance of will
South Carolina	One-third of estate	Within 6 months of acceptance of will or within 8 months of death, whichever is later
South Dakota	$100,000 or one-third of property in will, whichever is greater	Within 6 months of appointment of Executor or before decree of distribution, whichever is earlier
Tennessee	One-third of estate	Within 6 months of appointment of Executor or within 9 months of death, whichever is later
Texas	No provision—community property state	

Spouse's Elective Share—State Summary (*continued*)

State	Share	Election
Utah	One-third of estate	Within 6 months of acceptance of will or within 12 months of death, whichever is later
Vermont	A. If only one living issue, by surviving spouse: one-half of real estate B. Otherwise: one-third of real estate	Within 8 months of acceptance of will
Virginia	A. If living issue: one-third of estate B. If no living issue: one-half of estate	Within 1 year of acceptance of will
Washington	No provision—community property state	
West Virginia	One-third of estate or lifetime use of one-third of real estate	Within 8 months of acceptance of will or within 2 months of resolution of will contest
Wisconsin	No provision—community property state	
Wyoming	A. If one or more living issue are not by surviving spouse: one-fourth of estate B. If all living issue are by surviving spouse or if no living issue: one-half of estate	Within 3 months of acceptance of will

CHAPTER *3*

Probate Administration

The issuance of letters testamentary or letters of administration formally authorizes the Personal Representative to carry out administration of the estate. At this point the Personal Representative may legally collect the assets of the deceased, including any unpaid wages or vacation pay and debts owed to the deceased. The nature of the assets will have an effect on the type and amount of administration involved. One of the first duties of the Personal Representative is to determine the type of administration for the estate.

Types of Administration

As mentioned in the preceding chapter, many states make provision for simplified forms of probate administration if certain requirements are met. In addition to the *administration unnecessary* and *administration by affidavit* options, another form of simplified administration known as *summary administration* may be available. Summary administration requires only the submission of a summary of assets and their values, taxes, and claims paid, along with the distribution of the estate balance to close the estate. Summary administration is available for certain small estates that are under the state's threshold. The Probate Administration State Summary on pages 64–83 gives these thresholds for the states that make such a provision.

There are two basic types of probate administration: *unsupervised administration,* which requires only periodic reporting to the probate court, and supervised administration, which requires court approval before every step of the probate process. Under unsupervised administration, decisions to sell assets and pay debts, given sufficient funds, can generally be made and implemented by the Personal Representative without obtaining specific court approval in advance. Unsupervised administration is less formal and more convenient than supervised administration. Unless one of the previous administration options is chosen, unsupervised administration is the norm in 20 states—Alaska, Arizona, California, Colorado, Idaho, Illinois, Kansas, Maine, Michigan, Minnesota, Montana, Nebraska, New Jersey, New Mexico, New York, North Dakota, South Dakota, Texas, Utah, and Washington (if solvent). Unsupervised administration is also available for solvent estates in Georgia, Indiana, Missouri, Pennsylvania, and Wisconsin if all who share agree. In all of these states, unsupervised administration can be denied and supervised administration imposed if the probate court is petitioned by someone with a share in the estate and the court determines that supervised administration is needed to protect the interest of the petitioner.

Hawaii requires supervised administration for estates over $40,000. In Hawaii, as well as the remaining 24 states and the District of Columbia, supervised administration is required for all estates not being administered under the administration unnecessary, administration by affidavit, or summary administration options. The tasks that the Personal Representative must complete under supervised administration are no different from those required for settling an estate under the other forms of administration; however, approval of the local probate court must be secured before any major steps, transfers, payments, or distributions are made. In all cases the Personal Representative should discuss his or her administrative options with the local probate court. Selecting the least restrictive option available can speed settlement by reducing the amount of consultation time for both the Personal Representative and the probate court. A general description of the types of administration available and the qualifying estate characteristics is presented in the Probate Administration State Summary on pages 64–83.

Personal Representative Fees

Any empowered Personal Representative is entitled to receive compensation for settling the estate if he or she wishes to do so. In most cases in which the Personal Representative is the sole or primary beneficiary or heir there is no advantage in charging a fee for carrying out the settlement of the estate. Personal Representative fees are an administration cost and hence result in a smaller balance available for distribution to those who share in the estate. Fees received as a Personal Representative are considered ordinary income and must be reported as such on the individual's income tax return.

Because fulfilling the duties of Personal Representative involves time and effort, all states allow compensation, if requested. Most states stipulate a maximum fee that can be paid for the services of the Personal Representative, taking into account the size and complexity of the estate being settled. These maximum amounts vary from state to state and may be calculated on a sliding scale related to assets or simply be identified as "reasonable compensation." Generally, maximum Personal Representative fees allowed will amount to 3 to 5 percent of the probate estate's assets.

In some cases the will specifies an amount for compensation of the Executor. The Executor may elect not to collect it or, if he or she finds the stated compensation inadequate, may petition the probate court for a higher amount. In all cases, a Personal Representative may petition the local probate court to determine and allow fair compensation in accord with state law.

Fees paid to the Personal Representative are for the oversight, coordination, and reporting related to settling the estate. These fees do not include the cost of hiring professional assistance such as accounting, legal, and appraisal services. Also court fees, copy fees, and filing and transfer fees are separate expenses. These costs are paid out of the estate's assets prior to their distribution. In many states, legal fees that can be charged to the estate are subject to the same maximums as the fees for the Personal Representative. An attorney may, however, petition the probate court for a fee higher than the maximum generally available, by citing unusual complexity or circumstances in the settlement of the estate. The local probate court will rule on the acceptability of all fees related to settlement of the estate.

Clearly, these fees can add up to a substantial amount. Since properly documented out-of-pocket expenses of the Personal Representative can be directly reimbursed, it is usually more beneficial for a family member to forgo receiving compensation. Use of professional services should be targeted to specific tasks, and payment for a group of activities on a percentage basis should be avoided.

Nonresident Personal Representative

The person named as Executor or seeking appointment as Administrator may not be a resident of the same state as the deceased. All 50 states and the District of Columbia allow a nonresident to serve as a Personal Representative, although requirements as to relationship, posting bond, securing a state resident as agent or co-Personal Representative, or providing power of attorney to the probate court may apply. These nonresident Personal Representative requirements are shown in the Probate Administration State Summary on pages 64–83.

In 19 states—Arkansas, Illinois, Indiana, Iowa, Kansas, Louisiana, Maryland, Massachusetts, Missouri, New Hampshire, North Carolina, Oklahoma, South Dakota, Tennessee, Texas, Virginia, Washington, Wisconsin, and Wyoming—a nonresident Personal Representative is required to secure a resident agent. A resident agent is an adult resident of the state and usually lives within the jurisdiction of the court overseeing probate. The resident agent is generally required to ensure that any needed legal notices can be readily served by the court. A resident who consents to serve as the agent of a nonresident Personal Representative must have all information necessary to contact the nonresident Personal Representative quickly when needed. Often another family member or friend of the deceased serves as a resident agent. Unless a professional is retained, a resident agent generally serves with little or no compensation, since the responsibilities are few.

Because a nonresident Personal Representative will incur greater travel costs, particularly for supervised administration, the decision whether or not to take compensation may be affected. Remember that the Personal Representative can request reasonable compensation from the probate court if desired.

Out-of-State Property

If the deceased owned real estate in another state, that property will be subject to the probate system of that state. Obviously the Personal Representative will be a nonresident of one of the states involved and will have to deal with the nonresident Personal Representative requirements discussed above. Administration of property located out of the state of primary residence and primary administration is known as ancillary administration. The degree of cooperation and coordination between different states varies, although usually the local probate court overseeing ancillary administration will accept a certified copy of the will (if there is one) and recognize certified copies of the letters testamentary or letters of administration issued to the Personal Representative by the probate court overseeing primary administration. Whenever the estate includes out-of-state real property, be sure to contact the probate court that has jurisdiction where such property is located as soon as possible to determine what documentation will be required and to coordinate hearing dates. Any estate or inheritance taxes on the property has to be paid to the state where the real estate is situated. Taxes are discussed in detail in Chapter 6.

Spouse's Automatic Share

Recognizing that settling an estate takes time, most state probate laws make some provisions for a surviving spouse to withdraw reasonable living expenses from the estate during administration prior to settlement. The six states that do not specifically address living expenses—Indiana, Kansas, Louisiana, New York, South Carolina, and West Virginia—grant a portion of the deceased's personal property or estate to the surviving spouse. These shares of an estate pass automatically to the surviving spouse, although he or she may be required to file a petition with the local probate court. Generally the spouse's automatic share is available without offset and is not subject to claims of creditors of the estate; in some cases, however, the costs of last illness, funeral arrangements, and administration must be paid first.

The intent of the spouse's automatic share is to prevent the surviving spouse from being financially ruined immediately, as a result of creditors' claims against the deceased. In fact, 17 states authorize payment of reasonable living expenses to the surviving spouse for up to one year, even if the estate is insolvent. Further, depending on state of residence, the spouse's automatic share may include use or protection of the home, automobile, and portions of community and/or personal property in addition to living expenses. The spouse's automatic share protects a basic portion of the estate from creditors' claims for a period of time so that suitable alternative arrangements can be worked out.

The spouse's automatic share is separate and distinct from the spouse's elective share or the spouse's intestate share, except in the states of New Hampshire, Ohio, and Virginia, where all or a portion is deducted from the surviving spouse's final inherited share.

The following table provides a brief summary of the surviving spouse's automatic share in each state. Clearly a surviving spouse, or a person representing the interests of a surviving spouse, should contact the local probate court without delay to obtain full details.

Spouse's Automatic Share—State Summary

State	Provisions Granted	Limitations
Alabama	Homestead	Up to $6,000
	Personal property	Up to $3,500
	Living expenses	During administration; for insolvent estate, up to 1 year
Alaska	Homestead	Up to $27,000
	Personal property	Up to $10,000
	Living expenses	During administration; for insolvent estate, up to 1 year
Arizona	Homestead	Up to $12,000
	Personal property	Up to $7,000
	Community property	One-half
	Living expenses	During administration; for insolvent estate, up to 1 year
Arkansas	Homestead	Up to $2,500
	Personal property	Up to $1,000 before creditors; up to $2,000 before others
	Community property	One-half

Spouse's Automatic Share—State Summary (continued)

State	Provisions Granted	Limitations
	Living expenses	Up to $500 per month for 2 months; furnishings necessary for family
California	Use of home	Until 60 days after filing inventory
	Community property	One-half
	Quasi-community property	One-half
	Living expenses plus intestate share	During administration
Colorado	Personal property	Up to $7,500
	Community property	One-half
	Living expenses	During administration; for insolvent estate, up to 1 year
Connecticut	Use of car	During administration, if permitted by court
	Living expenses	During administration as set by court
Delaware	Living expenses	Up to $2,000
District of Columbia	Living expenses	Up to $10,000, less $750 funeral costs
Florida	Homestead	Lifetime use
	Personal property	Up to $10,000
	Personal effects	Up to $1,000
	Living expenses	During administration, up to $6,000
Georgia	Living expenses	No less than $1,600, no less than 1 year, determined by court
Hawaii	Homestead	Up to $5,000
	Personal property	Up to $5,000
	Living expenses	During administration; for insolvent estate, up to 1 year
Idaho	Homestead	
	No dependent issue	Up to $4,000
	With dependent issue living with surviving spouse	Up to $10,000
	Personal property	Up to $3,500
	Community proprty	One-half
	Living expenses	During administration; for insolvent estate, up to 1 year
Illinois	Homestead	Up to $7,500, if spouse remains on property
	Living expenses	Up to 9 months, up to $10,000 plus $2,000 per dependent
Indiana	Personal property	Up to $8,500
	Real estate	To make up difference if less than $8,500 of personal property
Iowa	Personal property	Certain items
	Living expenses	For 1 year

Spouse's Automatic Share—State Summary (*continued*)

State	Provisions Granted	Limitations
Kansas	Homestead:	
	Within municipal limits	Lifetime use of up to 1 acre
	Outside	Lifetime use of up to 60 acres
	Personal property	Up to $7,500
Kentucky	Real estate	One-half owned at death Lifetime use of one-third of other real estate
	Personal property	One-half
	Community property	One-half
	Living expenses	Up to $7,500 after costs of funeral, last illness, and administration
Louisiana	Community property	One-half
	If decedent died rich relative to surviving spouse, then:	
	No child	One-half of estate
	3 or fewer children	Lifetime use of one-fourth of estate, until remarriage
	4 or more children	Lifetime use of share of estate equal to that of child, until remarriage
Maine	Homestead	Up to $5,000
	Personal property	Up to $3,500
	Living expenses	During administration; for insolvent estate, living expenses up to 1 year
Maryland	Living expenses	Up to $2,000, plus $1,000 for each unmarried child under 18
Massachusetts	Use of home	For 6 months
	Living expenses	For 6 months
	Homestead	Lifetime use up to $100,000, until remarriage, in certain cases
Michigan	Homestead	Up to $10,000
	Personal property	Up to $3,500
	Living expenses	During administration; for insolvent estate, living expenses up to 1 year
Minnesota	Homestead	Homestead or lifetime use of homestead, if living children or issue
	Personal property	Up to $9,000 and one automobile
	Living expenses	Up to 18 months; for insolvent estate, living expenses up to 1 year
Mississippi	Homestead	Lifetime use up to $30,000 and 150 acres
	Living expenses	Up to 1 year
Missouri	Homestead	Up to one-half of estate or $7,500, whichever is less
	Personal property	Certain personal property
	Living expenses	Up to 1 year

Spouse's Automatic Share—State Summary (*continued*)

State	Provisions Granted	Limitations
Montana	Homestead	Up to $20,000
	Personal property	Up to $3,500
	Living expenses	During administration; for insolvent estate, living expenses up to 1 year
Nebraska	Homestead	Up to $7,500
	Personal property	Up to $5,000
	Living expenses	During administration; for insolvent estate, living expenses up to 1 year
Nevada	Homestead	Homestead
	Personal property	Certain personal property
	Community property	One-half
	Living expenses	At court discretion
New Hampshire	Use of home	40 days after death
	Living expenses	40 days after death
	Living expenses	During administration, deducted from share
New Jersey	Living expenses	During administration, if applied for
New Mexico	Homestead	Up to $100,000, in certain cases
	Personal property	Up to $3,500
	Community property	One-half
	Living expenses	Up to $10,000
New York	Personal property:	
	Homestead	Up to $5,000
	Farm machines	Up to $10,000
	Other	Up to $1,000, if not needed for funeral expenses
North Carolina	Living expenses	Between $5,000 and one-half of decedent's annual income for 1 year at court's discretion
North Dakota	Homestead	Lifetime use
	Personal property	Up to $5,000
	Living expenses	During administration; for insolvent estate, up to 1 year
Ohio	Use of home	1 year
	Living expenses	Up to $5,000, deducted from share
Oklahoma	Homestead	As long as occupant
	Personal property	Certain personal property
	Living expenses	At court's discretion; for insolvent estate, up to 1 year
Oregon	Use of home	1 year
	Living expenses	Up to 2 years, at court's discretion
Pennsylvania	Living expenses	Up to $2,000
Rhode Island	Personal property	Certain personal property
	Living expenses	6 months
South Carolina	Personal property	Certain personal property and $5,000 (must file within

Spouse's Automatic Share—State Summary (continued)

State	Provisions Granted	Limitations
		8 months of death or 6 months of opening estate, whichever is later)
South Dakota	Homestead	Lifetime use
	Personal property	Up to $1,500
	Living expenses	During administration; for insolvent estate, up to 1 year
Tennessee	Homestead	Lifetime use up to $5,000
	Personal property	Up to $5,000
	Living expenses	1 year, based on previous standard of living
Texas	Homestead:	
	In city	Lifetime use of home and up to 1 acre, at court's discretion
	Outside	Lifetime use of home and up to 200 acres, at court's discretion
	No home	$10,000
	Personal property	Certain personal property or $1,000
	Community property	One-half
	Living expenses	1 year
Utah	Homestead	Up to $10,000
	Personal property	Four vehicles up to $25,000 Certain personal property up to $5,000
	Living expenses	During administration; for insolvent estate, up to 1 year
Vermont	Homestead	Up to $30,000
	Living expenses	During administration; for insolvent estate, living expenses up to 8 months
Virginia	Homestead	Up to $5,000, deducted from share
	Personal property	Up to $3,500
	Living expenses	During administration; for insolvent estate, up to 1 year
Washington	Homestead	Up to $30,000 after debts and cost of funeral, last illness, and administration, at court's discretion
	Community property	One-half
	Living expenses	During administration
West Virginia	Use of home	Until children are 21 or dower share taken
	Personal property	Up to $1,000
Wisconsin	Homestead	Lifetime use or ownership up to $10,000, at court's discretion
	Personal property	Up to $1,000
	Community property	One-half of all property acquired after January 1, 1986
	Living expenses	During administration
Wyoming	Homestead	Up to $30,000 in certain cases
	Use of home	Until inventory
	Living expenses	At court's discretion

Notice to Creditors

Settlement of an estate involves payment of just debts of the deceased. When the Personal Representative reviews the financial papers, checking accounts, and mail of the deceased, most of these debts will be evident. The Personal Representative should prepare a list of the debts and record the amount, the creditor with address, payment terms, and date payment was last made. The debts should be classified as funeral expenses, last illness costs, mortgages, installment loans, credit cards, taxes due, and other debts. If any of the debts are related to expenses involved for income-producing property, they should be categorized separately.

The Personal Representative or probate court must usually notify known creditors after administration of the estate has begun. No formal notice to creditors is required in Massachusetts if the estate is solvent, that is, its assets exceed its liabilities. In New York no formal notice is required unless the court directs it, and in Connecticut and Louisiana creditor notice is at probate court's discretion and direction. Notice to creditors is handled by the local probate court in Kentucky, Ohio, Rhode Island, Tennessee, Utah, and West Virginia. In all other states and the District of Columbia, providing notice to creditors is the responsibility of the Personal Representative. Known creditors may be contacted by mail, and a legal notice is required to be published, usually for several consecutive weeks, in a local newspaper so that creditors not known to the Personal Representative can present claims. A notice to creditors, when required, must be published within a specified time after appointment as Personal Representative. This time frame and the number of times the notice is to be published are listed for each state and the District of Columbia in the Probate Administration State Summary on pages 64–83. Also shown are the time limits within which all creditor claims must be filed. If a required creditor notice is not provided, claims may have to be honored for several years after the date of death. Contact the local probate court soon after your appointment as Personal Representative to confirm the notice publication schedule required and to obtain an example of the wording of the notice. An example of California's Notice to Creditors form is shown in Figure 3-1. The cost of the advertisements is an administration cost and is paid from the estate's assets.

Although valid claims can be paid by the Personal Representative at almost any time after appointment (subject to court approval under supervised administration), it is usually best to wait until all claims have been received and evaluated before paying any of them. Exceptions may include utility bills (where the estate is best served by continuing service), installment payments on valuable personal property, real estate and personal property taxes (to avoid additional penalty fees), mortgages, and expenses related to income-producing property. These payment decisions should be made with common sense and good judgment by the Personal Representative. If there are any questions, or if the estate is subject to supervised administration, be sure to contact the probate court before disbursing any funds.

NOTICE OF ADMINISTRATION*
OF THE ESTATE OF

_____

(NAME)
DECEDENT

NOTICE TO CREDITORS

1. _(Name)_:
   (Address):

   is the **personal representative** of the **ESTATE OF** _(name)_: , who is deceased.

2. The personal representative HAS BEGUN ADMINISTRATION of the decedent's estate in the

   a. **SUPERIOR COURT OF CALIFORNIA, COUNTY OF**

       STREET ADDRESS:

       MAILING ADDRESS:

       CITY AND ZIP CODE:

       BRANCH NAME:

   b. Case Number _(specify)_:

3. You must FILE YOUR CLAIM with the court clerk (address in item 2a) AND mail or deliver a copy to the personal representative before the **later** of the following dates as provided in section 9100 of the California Probate Code:

   a. **four months** after _(date)_: [_____] , the date letters (authority to act for the estate) were first issued to the personal representative, OR

   b. **thirty days** after _(date)_: [_____] , the date this notice was mailed or personally delivered to you.

You may obtain a **CREDITOR'S CLAIM FORM** from any superior court clerk. _(Judicial Council form No. DE-172, Creditor's Claim.)_ **A letter is not sufficient.**

If you use the mail to file your claim with the court, for your protection you should send your claim by certified **mail, with return receipt requested. If you mail a copy of your claim to the personal representative, you should also use certified mail.**

(Proof of Service on reverse)

---

* Use this form in estates begun on or after July 1, 1988.

Form Approved by the
Judicial Council of California
DE-157 [New July 1, 1988]

NOTICE OF ADMINISTRATION TO CREDITORS
(Probate)

Probate Code, §§ 9050, 9052

Figure 3-1

PROOF OF SERVICE BY MAIL

1. I am over the age of 18 and not a party to this cause. I am a resident of or employed in the county where the mailing occurred.
2. My residence or business address is *(specify)*:

3. I served the foregoing **Notice of Administration to Creditors** on each person named below by enclosing a copy in an envelope addressed as shown below AND
   a. ☐ **depositing** the sealed envelope with the United States Postal Service with the postage fully prepaid.
   b. ☐ **placing** the envelope for collection and mailing on the date and at the place shown in item 4 following our ordinary business practices. I am readily familiar with this business' practice for collecting and processing correspondence for mailing. On the same day that correspondence is placed for collection and mailing, it is deposited in the ordinary course of business with the United States Postal Service in a sealed envelope with postage fully prepaid.

4. a. Date of deposit: b. Place of deposit *(city and state)*:

   I declare under penalty of perjury under the laws of the State of California that the foregoing is true and correct.

Date:

▶

. . . .   _____
              (TYPE OR PRINT NAME)   (SIGNATURE OF DECLARANT)

NAME AND ADDRESS OF EACH PERSON TO WHOM NOTICE WAS MAILED

Figure 3-1 (continued)

Insolvent Estates

In some situations, the Personal Representative may know beforehand or discover as claims are filed that the estate is insolvent. Usually this is known before administration begins, although if the estate is complex or highly leveraged, it may take some time to determine. Supervised administration is required for insolvent estates almost everywhere and is a good idea in any case, as the probate court will have to determine the priority and amount of payment for claims. Wherever possible the request for any spouse's automatic share should be accelerated, and Personal Representative fees should be requested as well. Unless co-signed, the debts of the deceased will have to be written off by creditors after the estate is exhausted.

If the estate is not sufficient to pay all its debts, each state establishes the priority of claims against the estate. Generally, payment of expenses and debts is in the following order:

1. Court fees and costs
2. Funeral and burial or cremation expenses
3. Estate administration costs, fees, and expenses (legal fees, Personal Representative compensation, and real estate brokerage commissions from sale of the estate's real property)
4. Spousal and family allowances
5. Taxes
6. Reasonable expenses for last illness (medical, hospital, nursing)
7. Last three months of rent in arrears
8. Last three months of wages, salaries, or commissions due to be paid
9. All other claims

Given insufficient funds remaining after priorities 1–8 (above) have been paid, all claims listed under priority 9 must be paid proportionally. If all these costs have been paid, bequests will be honored in the following sequence:

1. Specific and monetary bequests
2. A general (not source or item-specific) bequest to the surviving spouse
3. General bequests to others
4. Residual bequest(s)

Collecting and Conserving Assets

The primary task in the first phase of estate administration is collecting and conserving the assets that make up the estate. A complete inventory will need to be filed with the probate court, usually within a few months of appointment as Personal Representative. The due date for filing the initial estate inventory is contained in the Probate Administration State Summary on pages 64–83 and varies from as little as 30 days after appointment in Hawaii, Kansas, Missouri, Ohio, Rhode Island, and Vermont to up to nine months from the date of death in Minnesota, North Dakota, Pennsylvania, and South Dakota. Louisiana and New Jersey do not require an estate inventory unless the court directs that one be made.

It is the duty of the Personal Representative to exercise reasonable diligence in locating all estate assets. If the Personal Representative is the spouse or primary beneficiary or heir, the type, location, and approximate value of all assets are usually known. If the Personal Representative is unfamiliar with the estate, a complete search for all real and personal property assets will be necessary. A thorough search of records and receipts can reveal bank deposits, brokerage accounts, bonds, rental storage units, and other assets of the deceased. Inquiries of relatives and friends can also help ensure that all assets are collected. Room-by-room household inventory forms for tangible personal property and estate inventory forms are included in the next chapter to simplify this activity and help ensure that no estate assets are omitted.

As estate assets are collected, they must be conserved and protected. Be sure that hazard insurance on improved real estate is in force. A separate bank account, with its own Employer Identification Number, should be opened in the name of the estate as soon as is practical. An example of an application for an Employer Identification Number is included in the Settlement Sample in Chapter 8. Any monies, proceeds from liquidated assets, or benefits due the deceased should be deposited in the estate bank account and legitimate estate expenses should be paid from that account. The Personal Representative should never commingle estate assets in his or her personal account. The separate account simplifies record-keeping and protects the Personal Representative. If substantial cash assets are available, the Personal Representative should consider placing the bulk of them in an interest-bearing account. The estate is considered to be a separate entity for income tax purposes, and estate interest income may be taxable by both the state and federal governments. When administering an estate it is worthwhile to separately track estate income, including interest, dividends, and rents received, as well as any expenses related to the income-producing assets such as utilities and bank, brokerage, or property management fees. The principal of the estate is the amount that may be subject to estate taxes, while the estate's net income may be subject to income taxes. Because of this, some states require that estate inventory and status reports show the principal and income portions of the estate separately. Whether required by the probate court or not, this is a useful practice that will simplify preparation of tax returns. If income in excess of $600 is expected to be received before the estate is closed, use of a separate bank account for estate income is strongly recommended.

Farm and Business Operations

The Personal Representative must take special care if the estate includes a working farm or business operation. Usually business or farm ownership interests are transferred by an arrangement set up in advance, such as a buy–sell agreement or stock transfer with management authority assigned. If this is not the case, the Personal Representative should discuss the powers granted in the will, as they relate to the business or farm operation, with the probate court. Since the Personal Representative is personally liable for decisions made, it is imperative that the situation be discussed with everyone involved and available options identified. In many cases, the Personal Representative will be required to conserve the business for only as long as is required to liquidate it. Under most circumstances, any continuation of the business operation will require court approval. Operation of a business can be time-consuming, and preparing for the most effective sale may become a high priority. The ultimate value of the business can be strongly affected by the speed with which it is sold. Other family members or persons owning a share of or employed by the business may be the best potential purchasers. Further, an installment sale or some other form of private financing may be necessary for a sale of the concern. Clearly, this type of situation will require consultation with those involved in the operation and the beneficiaries or heirs of the estate to develop the best transfer plan. It is essential that the probate court is fully informed and authorizes steps to be taken prior to action by the Personal Representative.

Probate Administration—State Summary

The following summary lists the types of administration available, nonresident Personal Representative requirements, creditor notice and claim information, and filing deadlines for the estate inventory in all 50 states and the District of Columbia. This material is presented for general guidance and planning purposes; for specific details that apply to the estate being settled, always contact the local probate court, which was identified in the Will Probate State Summary in Chapter 2.

Probate Administration—State Summary

State	Administration Options	Supervised Administration
Alabama	Summary administration: Available to estates of less than $3,000, after debts, if closest relative applies	Required for all other estates

Alaska	Administration by affidavit:
	  Available to estates of less than $15,000, if inheritor applies after 30 days from date of death and no application for Personal Representative is pending
	Summary administration:
	  Available to estates totaling less than spouse's exemption plus funeral, last illness, and administration costs
		Upon petition to court only

Arizona	Administration by affidavit:
	  Available for vehicles and earnings owed up to $5,000, if inheritor applies. Available for personal property and debts owed to estate up to $30,000, if inheritor applies after 30 days from date of death and no application for Personal Representative is pending. Available for real estate if estate is less than $15,000, if inheritor applies after 6 months from date of death, all funeral, last illness, unsecured debts, and tax costs are paid, and no application for Personal Representative is pending
	Summary administration:
	  Available to estates totaling less than exemptions and allowances plus funeral, last illness, and administration costs
	Unsupervised administration:
	  Available to all other estates
		Upon petition to court only

Arkansas	Administration unnecessary: Available to solvent estates of less than $50,000 after debts and spouse's exemption after 45 days from date of death, if no application for Personal Representative is pending	Required for all other estates

California	Non-probate transfer:
	  Available to estates where surviving spouse collects all property
	Summary administration:
	  Available for estates of less than $60,000 (excluding life insurance, vehicles, salary of $5,000, and real estate gifts to spouse) including less than $10,000 of California real estate, after 40 days from date of death, if close relative applies
	Unsupervised administration:
	  All other estates	

Nonresident as Personal Representative	Notice to Creditors and Creditor Claims Due	Estate Inventory Due	Selection of Appraisers
Only if named in will	Notice to creditors: Within 1 month of appointment as Personal Representative; published weekly for 3 consecutive weeks Creditor claims due within 6 months of appointment of Personal Representative	Within 2 months of appointment as Personal Representative	By Personal Representative
Permitted	Notice to creditors: Published weekly for 3 consecutive weeks Creditor claims due within 4 months of first published notice	Within 3 months of appointment as Personal Representative	By Personal Representative
Permitted	Notice to creditors: Promptly published weekly for 3 consecutive weeks Creditor claims due within 4 months of first published notice	Within 3 months (90 days) of appointment as Personal Representative	By Personal Representative
Only if named in will and secures resident agent	Notice to creditors: Published weekly for 2 consecutive weeks Creditor claims due within 3 months of first creditor notice	Within 2 months of appointment as Personal Representative (unless waived by those named in the will)	By Personal Representative
Permitted	Notice to creditors: Within 4 months of appointment as Personal Representative; published three times, with at least 5 days between first and last notice Creditor claims due within 4 months of appointment or 30 days after last creditor notice, whichever is later	Within 3 months of appointment as Personal Representative	By Personal Representative

Probate Administration—State Summary (*continued*)

State	Administration Options	Supervised Administration
Colorado	Administration by affidavit: Available to estates of less than $20,000, if inheritor applies after 10 days from date of death and no application for Personal Representative is pending Summary administration: Available to estates totaling less than exemptions and spouse's allowances plus funeral, last illness, and administration costs Unsupervised administration: Available to all other estates	Upon petition to court only
Connecticut	Administration unnecessary: For estates consisting only of personal property less than $20,000, after debts, if closest relative applies	Required for all other estates
Delaware	Administration unnecessary: For estates consisting only of personal property less than $12,500, after debts, if closest relative applies after 30 days from date of death and no application for Personal Representative is pending	Required for all other estates
District of Columbia	Administration unnecessary: For estates of only one or two cars Summary administration: For estates of less than $10,000	Required for all other estates
Florida	Administration unnecessary: For estates consisting only of personal property less than funeral and last 60 days of illness costs Summary administration: Available to estates less than $25,000 after exemptions Unsupervised administration: For estates with personal property less than $60,000, if all claims are determined and those who could receive major shares are spouse, descendants, or ancestors	Required for all other estates

Nonresident as Personal Representative	Notice to Creditors and Creditor Claims Due	Estate Inventory Due	Selection of Appraisers
Permitted	Notice to creditors: Published weekly for 3 consecutive weeks Creditor claims due within 4 months of first creditor notice or 1 year from date of death, whichever is earlier	Within 3 months of appointment as Personal Representative	By Personal Representative
Only if named in will; must grant power of attorney to Connecticut secretary of state	Notice to creditors: Publish as directed by court Creditor claims due within 3 to 12 months of notice, as set by court	Within 2 months of appointment as Personal Representative	By Personal Representative
Yes, if named in will. As Administrator, after 60 days from date of death if no resident application for Personal Representative pending. Nonresidents must grant power of attorney to register of wills	Notice to creditors: Within 40 days of appointment as Personal Representative; published weekly for 4 consecutive weeks by register of wills Credit claims due within 8 months of death	Within 3 months of appointment as Personal Representative	By Personal Representative
Permitted; must give power of attorney to register of wills	Notice to creditors: Within 20 days of appointment as Personal Representative; published weekly for 3 consecutive weeks Creditor claims due within 6 months of first creditor notice	Within 3 months of appointment as Personal Representative	Must be approved by court
Permitted, if close relative	Notice to creditors: Published weekly for 2 consecutive weeks promptly after appointment Creditor claims due within 3 months of first creditor notice	Within 2 months (60 days) of appointment as Personal Representative	By Personal Representative

Probate Administration—State Summary (*continued*)

State	Administration Options	Supervised Administration
Georgia	Administration unnecessary: For solvent estates if all property is in Georgia and those who could share by will or intestacy agree	Required for all other estates
Hawaii	Administration by affidavit: Available to estates less than $5,000, if no application for Personal Representative is pending Summary administration: Available for estates of less than $20,000 Unsupervised administration: Available for estates of less than $40,000	Required for all other estates
Idaho	Administration by affidavit: For estates less than $5,000 if inheritor applies after 30 days from date of death and no application for Personal Representative is pending Summary administration: Available for estates passing wholly to spouse and for estates totaling less than spouse's automatic share plus funeral, last illness, and administration costs Unsupervised administration: Available to all other estates	Upon petition to court only
Illinois	Administration unnecessary: If all who share by will or intestacy agree and pay taxes and creditors	If court finds necessary
Indiana	Summary administration: Available to estates totaling less than spouse's automatic share plus funeral and administration costs Unsupervised administration: Available for all solvent estates if all who share by will or intestacy agree	If requested or court finds necessary
Iowa	Administration unnecessary: Available for solvent estates of less than $50,000 if those who share by will or intestacy are spouse, children, and parents and no application for Personal Representative is pending	Required for all other estates

Nonresident as Personal Representative	Notice to Creditors and Creditor Claims Due	Estate Inventory Due	Selection of Appraisers
Permitted, with posted bond equal to twice value of estate	Notice to creditors: Published weekly for 4 consecutive weeks, starting within 60 days of appointment as Personal Representative Creditor claims due within 3 months of last creditor notice	Within 4 months of appointment as Personal Representative	Personal Representative may appraise, unless court appoints appraiser after receiving request within 90 days of filing inventory
Permitted	Notice to creditors: Promptly published weekly for 3 consecutive weeks Creditor claims due within 4 months of first creditor notice	Within 30 days of appointment as Personal Representative of supervised estate; otherwise at close of administration	Registrar of wills may hire, if value in doubt
Permitted	Notice to creditors: Published weekly for 3 consecutive weeks Creditor claims due within 4 months of first creditor notice	Within 3 months of appointment as Personal Representative	By Personal Representative
Only if named in will and secures resident agent	Notice to creditors: Published weekly for 3 consecutive weeks, starting within 14 days of appointment as Personal Representative Creditor claims due within 6 months of creditor notice	Within 2 months (60 days) of appointment as Personal Representative	By Personal Representative
Permitted, if bond filed and secures resident agent	Notice to creditors: Weekly notice published for 2 consecutive weeks after appointment as Personal Representative Creditor claims due within 5 months of first creditor notice	Within 2 months of appointment as Personal Representative	By Personal Representative
Permitted, but generally must have resident as co-Personal Representative	Notice to creditors: Published weekly for 2 consecutive weeks promptly after appointment as Personal Representative Creditor claims due within 4 months of second notice	Within 3 months (90 days) of appointment as Personal Representative	Needed only upon request

Probate Administration—State Summary (*continued*)

State	Administration Options	Supervised Administration
Kansas	Administration unnecessary: For all estates if taxes are paid and court finds administration unnecessary Unsupervised administration: For all other estates	Only upon petition or at court's discretion
Kentucky	Administration unnecessary: For estates less than $5,000 if surviving spouse applies and for solvent estates if all who share by will or intestacy agree	Required for all other estates
Louisiana	Administration unnecessary: For all estates if creditors consent and all who share by will or intestacy accept liability for debts; for all estates less than $50,000 if only to spouse, siblings, and issue	Required for all other estates
Maine	Administration by affidavit: Available for estates less than $10,000 after 30 days from date of death, if no application for appointment as Personal Representative is pending Summary administration: Available for estates totaling less than spouse's automatic share plus funeral, last illness, and administration costs Unsupervised administration: For all other estates	Upon petition to court only
Maryland	Summary administration: Available for estates less than $20,000	Required for all other estates
Massachusetts	Summary administration: Available for estates consisting only of personal property less than $15,000 (excluding automobile) if relatives apply after 30 days from date of death and no application for appointment as Personal Representative is pending	Required for all other estates

Nonresident as Personal Representative	Notice to Creditors and Creditor Claims Due	Estate Inventory Due	Selection of Appraisers
Only if named in will and secures resident agent	Notice to creditors: Published weekly for 3 consecutive weeks starting within 10 days of filing for appointment as Personal Representative Creditor claims due within 4 months of first creditor notice; within 6 months for estates where administration is unnecessary	Within 1 month (30 days) of appointment as Personal Representative	Court-approved, if court requests
Permitted, if related to deceased	Notice to creditors: Published monthly by clerk Creditor claims due within 1 year of appointment of Personal Representative	Within 2 months of appointment as Personal Representative	By Personal Representative
Permitted, if secures resident agent	Notice to creditors: At court's discretion Creditor claims due before or at final hearing (can be submitted up to 5 years later in most cases)	Only if requested	Court may order three public appraisers
Permitted	Notice to creditors: Weekly notice published for 2 consecutive weeks after appointment as Personal Representative Creditor claims due within 4 months of first creditor notice	Within 3 months of appointment as Personal Representative	By Personal Representative
Permitted, if secures resident agent	Notice to creditors: Published weekly by registrar for 3 consecutive weeks to start within 20 days after appointment as Personal Representative Creditor claims due within 6 months of appointment of Personal Representative	Within 3 months of appointment as Personal Representative	Appointed by court
Permitted, if secures resident agent	Notice to creditors: None, unless estate is insolvent (letter to court) Creditor claims due within 4 months of Personal Representative posting bond	Within 3 months of appointment as Personal Representative	By Personal Representative

Probate Administration—State Summary (*continued*)

State	Administration Options	Supervised Administration

Michigan	Summary administration:
	    Available for estates less than $5,000, if spouse (or next inheritor, if no surviving spouse) applies and for estate totaling less than spouse's automatic share plus funeral, last illness, and administration costs
	Unsupervised administration:
	    For all other estates
		Upon petition or at court's discretion

Minnesota	Administration by affidavit:
	    Available for estates less than $5,000, if inheritor applies over 30 days after date of death and no application for appointment as Personal Representative is pending
	Administration unnecessary:
	    Available for estates less than $30,000 (excluding homestead) and for insolvent estates
	Unsupervised administration:
	    For all other estates
		Upon petition to court only

Mississippi	Administration by affidavit: Available for estates less than $10,000, if spouse (or next inheritor, if no surviving spouse) applies at least 30 days after date of death and no application for appointment as Personal Representative is pending	Required for all other estates

Missouri	Administration unnecessary:
	    For estates totaling less than spouse's automatic share if spouse or unmarried minor children apply and for estates less than $15,000 if inheritor applies after 30 days from date of death and no application for appointment as Personal Representative is pending
	Unsupervised administration:
	    Available for estates if will directs or these who share agree
		Upon petition to court only

Montana	Administration by affidavit:
	    Available if estate is less than $7,500 and inheritor applies after 30 days from the date of death and no application for appointment as Personal Representative is pending
	Summary administration:
	    Available for estates less than $7,500 and for estates totaling less than exempt property, living expenses, funeral, last illness, and administration costs
	Unsupervised administration:
	    For all other estates
		Upon petition to court only

Nonresident as Personal Representative	Notice to Creditors and Creditor Claims Due	Estate Inventory Due	Selection of Appraisers
Permitted	Notice to creditors: 　Published once at least 4 months before closing estate Creditor claims due within 2 to 4 months of creditor notice	Within 3 months (90 days) after appointment as Personal Representative	By Personal Representative
Permitted	Notice to creditors: 　Published weekly for 2 consecutive weeks after appointment as Personal Representative (as directed by clerk) Creditor claims due within 4 months of first creditor notice	Within 6 months of appointment as Personal Representative or 9 months of date of death, whichever is later	By Personal Representative
Permitted	Notice to creditors: 　Published weekly for 3 consecutive weeks, to start within 90 days of appointment as Personal Representative Creditor claims due within 3 months (90 days) of first creditor notice	Within 3 months (90 days) of appointment as Personal Representative	Appointed by court
Permitted, if secures resident agent	Notice to creditors: 　Published weekly for 4 consecutive weeks by clerk Creditor claims due within 6 months of first creditor notice	Within 30 days of appointment as Personal Representative	By Personal Representative
Permitted	Notice to creditors: 　Published weekly for 3 consecutive weeks after appointment as Personal Representative Creditor claims due within 4 months of first creditor notice	Within 3 months of appointment as Personal Representative	By Personal Representative

Probate Administration—State Summary (*continued*)

State	Administration Options	Supervised Administration
Nebraska	Administration by affidavit: 　Available for estates less than $10,000, if inheritor applies over 30 days from date of death and no application for appointment as Personal Representative is pending Summary administration: 　Available for estates totaling less than allowance plus funeral, last illness, and administration costs Unsupervised administration: 　For all other estates	Upon petition to court only
Nevada	Administration by affidavit: 　Available for estates consisting only of personal property less than $10,000 if close relative applies after 40 days from date of death and no application for appointment as Personal Representative is pending Administration unnecessary: 　Available at court's discretion for estates less than $25,000 if spouse or child applies Summary administration: 　Available for estates less than $100,000 if court agrees	Required for all other estates
New Hampshire	Summary administration: 　Available for estates less than $5,000	Required for all other estates
New Jersey	Administration unnecessary: 　Available for estates less than $10,000 if spouse applies and for estates less than $5,000 if no surviving spouse and inheritor applies with consent of all others Unsupervised administration: 　For all other estates	None required
New Mexico	Administration by affidavit: 　Available for estates less than $20,000 if inheritor applies over 30 days from date of death and no application for appointment as Personal Representative is pending Summary administration: 　Available for estates totaling less than spouse's automatic share plus funeral, last illness, and administration costs Unsupervised administration: 　For all other estates	Upon petition to court only

Nonresident as Personal Representative	Notice to Creditors and Creditor Claims Due	Estate Inventory Due	Selection of Appraisers
Permitted	Notice to creditors: Published weekly by clerk for 3 consecutive weeks, starting within 30 days of appointment as Personal Representative Creditor claims due within 2 months of first creditor notice	Within 2 months of appointment as Personal Representative	By Personal Representative
Permitted, if close relative	Notice to creditors: Published weekly for 3 consecutive weeks after appointment as Personal Representative Creditor claims due within 2 months (60 days) of first creditor notice if estate is less than $100,000; otherwise within 3 months (90 days) of first creditor notice	Within 2 months (60 days) of appointment as Personal Representative	By Personal Representative
Permitted, if secures resident agent	Notice to creditors: Published weekly by registrar for 2 consecutive weeks, starting within 15 days of appointment of Personal Representative Creditor claims due within 6 months of appointment of Personal Representative	Within 3 months of appointment as Personal Representative	Appointed by court
Permitted, if posts bond	Notice to creditors: Published weekly for 2 consecutive weeks, starting within 20 days of appointment as Personal Representative Creditor claims due within 6 months of first creditor notice	Not required unless court directs	By Personal Representative
Permitted	Notice to creditors: Published weekly for 2 consecutive weeks after appointment as Personal Representative Creditor claims due within 2 months of first creditor notice	Within 3 months of appointment as Personal Representative	By Personal Representative

Probate Administration—State Summary (*continued*)

State	Administration Options	Supervised Administration

New York	Administration unnecessary:
	    Available for estates consisting only of personal property less than $10,000 (excluding spouse's automatic share) if spouse (or if no surviving spouse, next inheritor) applies
	Unsupervised administration:
	    For all other estates
		Upon petition to court only

North Carolina	Administration by affidavit: Available for estates consisting only of personal property less than $10,000, if inheritor applies after 30 days from date of death	Required for all other estates

North Dakota	Administration by affidavit:
	    Available for estates less than $15,000 after 30 days from date of death if no application for appointment as Personal Representative is pending
	Summary administration:
	    Available for estates totaling less than homestead and spouse's automatic share plus funeral, last illness, and administration costs
	Unsupervised administration:
	    For all other estates
		Upon petition to court only

Ohio	Summary administration: Available to estates less than $25,000	Required for all other estates
Oklahoma	Summary administration: Available for estates less than $60,000	Required for all other estates

Oregon	Administration unnecessary:
	    Available for estates with less than $15,000 of personal property and less than $35,000 of real estate if inheritor applies over 30 days from date of death
	Summary administration:
	    Available for estates necessary to support spouse and children as determined by court
		Required for all other estates

Nonresident as Personal Representative	Notice to Creditors and Creditor Claims Due	Estate Inventory Due	Selection of Appraisers
Permitted	Notice to creditors: Not required unless court directs Creditor claims due within 7 months of appointment of Personal Representative	Within 6 months of appointment as Personal Representative	By Personal Representative
Permitted, if secures resident agent	Notice to creditors: Published weekly for 4 consecutive weeks, starting within 20 days of appointment as Personal Representative Creditor claims due within 6 months of first creditor notice	Within 3 months of appointment as Personal Representative	By Personal Representative
Permitted	Notice to creditors: Published weekly for 3 consecutive weeks, starting upon appointment as Personal Representative Creditor claims due within 3 months of first creditor notice	Within 6 months of appointment as Personal Representative or 9 months of date of death	By Personal Representative
Permitted, only if named in will and close relative	Notice to creditors: Published weekly by probate judge for 3 consecutive weeks after appointment of Personal Representative Creditor claims due within 3 months of appointment of Personal Representative	Within 1 month of appointment as Personal Representative	By Personal Representative
Permitted, if secures resident agent	Notice to creditors: Published weekly for 2 consecutive weeks and mailed to known creditors, within 2 months of appointment as Personal Representative Creditor claims due within 2 months of first creditor notice	Within 2 months of appointment as Personal Representative	Appointed by court
Permitted	Notice to creditors: Published weekly for 3 consecutive weeks, to start within 30 days of appointment as Personal Representative Creditor claims due within 12 months of first published notice or before final accounting, whichever comes first	Within 2 months (60 days) of appointment as Personal Representative	By Personal Representative

Probate Administration—State Summary (*continued*)

State	Administration Options	Supervised Administration
Pennsylvania	Administration unnecessary: Available for estates consisting only of real estate and less than $10,000 of personal property Unsupervised administration: Available for estates if all who share by will or intestacy agree	Required for all other estates
Rhode Island	Administration unnecessary: Available for estate less than $10,000 if spouse applies within 45 days from date of death and no application for appointment as Personal Representative is pending	Required for all other estates
South Carolina	Administration by affidavit: Available for estates less than $10,000 if inheritor applies within 30 days of date of death and no application for appointment as Personal Representative is pending	Required for all other estates
South Dakota	Administration by affidavit: Available for estates with personal property less than $5,000 if inheritor applies after 30 days from date of death and no application for appointment as Personal Representative is pending Summary administration: Available for estates less than $60,000 if any inheritor applies with estimated inventory Unsupervised administration: For all other estates	Upon petition to court only
Tennessee	Summary administration: Available for estates consisting only of personal property less than $10,000 if inheritor applies after 45 days from the date of death and no application for appointment as Personal Representative is pending	Required for all other estates
Texas	Administration unnecessary: A. Available for estates consisting only of personal property less than $50,000 (after spouse's automatic share) if inheritor applies after 30 days from date of death and no application for appointment as Personal Representative is pending B. Available if inheritor posts bond twice the estate's appraised value C. Available for estates totaling less than spouse's living expenses (after homestead and personal property) if spouse applies Unsupervised administration: For all other estates	Upon petition to court only

Nonresident as Personal Representative	Notice to Creditors and Creditor Claims Due	Estate Inventory Due	Selection of Appraisers
Permitted, if approved by registrar	Notice to creditors: Published weekly for 3 consecutive weeks after appointment as Personal Representative. Creditor claims due within 1 year of death	Within 9 months of date of death or filing of final account, whichever is later	By Personal Representative
Permitted, at court discretion	Notice to creditors: Published by clerk, as court directs. Creditor claims due within 6 months of published notice	Within 1 month (30 days) of appointment as Personal Representative	Court may appoint, upon request
Permitted	Notice to creditors: Published weekly for 3 consecutive weeks, to start within 30 days of appointment as Personal Representative. Creditor claims due within 8 months of first creditor notice	Within 2 months (60 days) of appointment as Personal Representative	Appointed by court
Permitted, if secures resident agent	Notice to creditors: Published weekly for 3 consecutive weeks with last notice at least 15 days before hearing that opens estate. Creditor claims due within 2 months of first published notice	Within 9 months of date of death	By Personal Representative
Permitted, if resident appointed as co-Personal Representative	Notice to creditors: Published weekly by clerk for 2 consecutive weeks within 30 days of appointment of Personal Representative. Creditor claims due within 6 months of first creditor notice	Within 2 months (60 days) of appointment as Personal Representative	By Personal Representative
Permitted, if secures resident agent	Notice to creditors: Published within 1 month of appointment as Personal Representative and sent by registered mail to anyone presenting a claim. Creditor claims due within 6 months of appointment of Personal Representative	Within 3 months (90 days) of appointment as Personal Representative	Appointed by court

Probate Administration—State Summary (*continued*)

State	Administration Options	Supervised Administration

Utah	Administration by affidavit:
	  Available for estates less than $25,000 if inheritor applies within 30 days of date of death and no application for appointment as Personal Representative is pending
	Summary administration:
	  Available for estates totaling less than homestead and spouse's automatic share plus funeral, last illness, and administration costs
	Unsupervised administration:
	  For all other estates
		Only upon petition to the court

Vermont	Summary administration: Available for estates consisting of only personal property less than $10,000 if spouse or adult children apply	Required for all other estates
Virginia	Administration by affidavit: Available for estates consisting only of personal property less than $5,000 if inheritor applies after 60 days from date of death and no application for appointment as Personal Representative is pending	Required for all other estates

Washington	Administration by affidavit:
	  Available for solvent estates less than $30,000 if inheritor applies after 40 days from date of death and no application for appointment as Personal Representative is pending
	Unsupervised administration:
	  For all other solvent estates
		For insolvent estates or if requested by will or petition to court

West Virginia	Summary administration: A. Available for estates with only one inheritor B. Available for insolvent estates less than $50,000 C. Available in Braxton, Kanawha, Marion, Putnam, and Summers Counties for solvent estates less than $100,000	Required for all other estates

Wisconsin	Administration by affidavit:
	  Available for estates of less than $5,000 and five motor vehicles if spouse applies
	Summary administration:
	  Available for estates less than $10,000 if spouse or sole inheritor applies
		Upon petition to the court

Nonresident as Personal Representative	Notice to Creditors and Creditor Claims Due	Estate Inventory Due	Selection of Appraisers
Permitted	Notice to creditors: 　Published weekly by clerk for 3 consecutive weeks promptly after appointment of Personal Representative Creditor claims due within 3 months of first creditor notice	Within 3 months of appointment as Personal Representative	By Personal Representative
Permitted, at court's discretion; may require resident agent	Notice to creditors: 　Published twice at least 7 days apart, starting within 30 days of appointment as Personal Representative Creditor claims due within 4 months of first creditor notice	Within 1 month (30 days) of appointment as Personal Representative	By Personal Representative
Permitted, if secures resident agent	Notice to creditors: 　Published weekly for 4 consecutive weeks, with last notice at least 2 weeks before closing Creditor claims due within 1 year of creditor notice or at "show cause" hearing if requested by Personal Representative 6 months after appointment	Within 4 months of appointment as Personal Representative	By Personal Representative, subject to court approval
Permitted, if secures resident agent	Notice to creditors: 　Published weekly for 3 consecutive weeks after appointment as Personal Representative Creditor claims due within 4 months of first creditor notice	Within 3 months of appointment as Personal Representative	By Personal Representative
Only if sole inheritor or close family member, and posts bond and appoints county commissioner as service agent	Notice to creditors: 　Published weekly by county clerk for 2 consecutive weeks before final accounting Creditor claims due within 2 to 3 months of notice	Within 8 months of appointment as Personal Representative	County appoints
Permitted, if secures resident agent	Notice to creditors: 　Published three times beginning within 15 days of registrar ordering claims due Creditor claims due within 3 months of court order	Within 6 months of appointment as Personal Representative	By Personal Representative; court may appoint

Probate Administration—State Summary (*continued*)

State	Administration Options	Supervised Administration
	Unsupervised administration: If all who share agree or requested in will	
Wyoming	Administration unnecessary: Available for estates less than $30,000 if inheritor applies after 30 days from date of death and no appli- cation for appointment as Personal Representative is pending or Personal Representative is sole inheritor	Required for all other estates

Probate Timetable

Publication of notice, filing of the estate inventory, and cutoffs for filing creditor claims and filing of taxes on the estate are subject to different deadlines.
It is the responsibility of the Personal Representative to meet all the deadlines established under the state's probate laws. Most of these deadlines are
related to a previous step in the probate process. For example, the initial
estate inventory due date is typically calculated as a number of days or
months after the probate hearing and appointment of a Personal Representative. The probate hearing is usually scheduled subject to the requirement
for published notice to those who could share in the estate. It is advisable

Nonresident as Personal Representative	Notice to Creditors and Creditor Claims Due	Estate Inventory Due	Selection of Appraisers
Permitted, if serves with resident	Notice to creditors: Published weekly for 3 consecutive weeks after appointment as Personal Representative Creditor claims due within 3 months of first published notice	Within 4 months (120 days) of appointment as Personal Representative	By Personal Representative

to calculate the due dates that apply to the estate to ensure that these deadlines are complied with. The following worksheet can assist the Personal Representative in outlining the estate's probate timetable. Due dates that will apply for each state are listed in the Will Probate State Summary in Chapter 2, the preceding Probate Administration State Summary, and the filing due column in the list of State Tax Information and Forms in Chapter 6. Two copies of the worksheet are provided, in case probate must be carried out in two states.

The worksheets are followed by a checklist that sets forth typical duties of the Personal Representative. Reviewing this checklist as you proceed through the probate process will help you avoid overlooking anything.

P R O B A T E   T I M E T A B L E

─────────────────────── **KEY DATE OUTLINE** ───────────────────────

Date of Death (DOD)   Date: _____

Special Administration Options (Administration Unnecessary,
Administration by Affidavit, Summary Administration)
    Must apply within _____ days of DOD   Date: _____
     or
    Must apply after _____ days of DOD   Date: _____

Notice of Hearing
    Delivered/mailed to those who could share   Date: _____
    Published—First Notice   Date: _____
    Published—Last Notice   Date: _____

Hearing Date   Date: _____

Appointment as Personal Representative   Date: _____

Notice to Creditors
    Published—First Notice   Date: _____
    Published—Last Notice   Date: _____

Estate Inventory Due
    Within _____ days or _____ months after appointment
    as Personal Representative   Date: _____
     or
    Within _____ months from DOD   Date: _____

Creditor Claims Due
    Within _____ months of first creditor notice   Date: _____
     or
    Within _____ months of last creditor notice   Date: _____
     or
    Within _____ months of DOD   Date: _____

State Tax Filing Due
    Within _____ months of DOD   Date: _____

Federal Estate Tax Filing Due (estates over $600,000 only)
    Within 9 months of DOD   Date: _____

Estimated Distribution   Date: _____

Estimated Closing of Estate   Date: _____

Decedent's Last Year Income Tax Return Due
    Federal   Date: _____
    State   Date: _____

Estate Income Tax Return Due
    Federal   Date: _____
    State   Date: _____

P R O B A T E   T I M E T A B L E

_____ **KEY DATE OUTLINE** _____

Date of Death (DOD)   Date: _____

Special Administration Options (Administration Unnecessary,
Administration by Affidavit, Summary Administration)
    Must apply within _____ days of DOD   Date: _____
       or
    Must apply after _____ days of DOD   Date: _____

Notice of Hearing
    Delivered/mailed to those who could share   Date: _____
    Published—First Notice   Date: _____
    Published—Last Notice   Date: _____

Hearing Date   Date: _____

Appointment as Personal Representative   Date: _____

Notice to Creditors
    Published—First Notice   Date: _____
    Published—Last Notice   Date: _____

Estate Inventory Due
    Within _____ days or _____ months after appointment
    as Personal Representative   Date: _____
       or
    Within _____ months from DOD   Date: _____

Creditor Claims Due
    Within _____ months of first creditor notice   Date: _____
       or
    Within _____ months of last creditor notice   Date: _____
       or
    Within _____ months of DOD   Date: _____

State Tax Filing Due
    Within _____ months of DOD   Date: _____

Federal Estate Tax Filing Due (estates over $600,000 only)
    Within 9 months of DOD   Date: _____

Estimated Distribution   Date: _____

Estimated Closing of Estate   Date: _____

Decedent's Last Year Income Tax Return Due
    Federal   Date: _____
    State   Date: _____

Estate Income Tax Return Due
    Federal   Date: _____
    State   Date: _____

Personal Representative's Checklist

_____ Assist with funeral arrangements.

_____ Obtain several copies of the death certificate.

_____ Locate the original of the last will of the deceased and any related documents.

_____ If no will is found, determine who should and can serve as Personal Representative.

_____ Prepare a list of all beneficiaries or heirs, including their addresses and telephone numbers.

_____ Prepare a preliminary estimate of value of estate.

_____ Review financial records and recent tax returns of the deceased.

_____ File claims for life insurance.

_____ Contact employer of deceased for any unpaid salary and benefits.

_____ Contact the local court having jurisdiction over probate in the locality where the deceased was a legal resident. Refer to the Will Probate State Summary for the name of this court.

Court: _____

Address: _____

_____

Clerk: _____

Telephone: (   ) _____

_____ Discuss the availability of administrative options with the probate court staff.

    _____ Administration unnecessary

    _____ Administration by affidavit

    _____ Summary administration

    _____ Unsupervised administration

    _____ Supervised administration

Personal Representative's Checklist (continued)

_____ Follow the procedures required for the type of administration involved and submit documents to set the probate hearing date and open the probate process.

_____ Notify all interested persons of the opening of probate and the hearing date.

_____ Place notice of opening of probate in the newspaper as required by the local probate court.

_____ If the deceased owned out-of-state property, complete the preceding five steps with the local probate court that has jurisdiction where the property is located.

_____ If there is a will, contact witnesses for availability.

_____ Attend probate court hearing.

_____ If nonresident of state, secure resident personal agent, if required.

Personal agent: _____

Address: _____

_____

Telephone: ( ) _____

_____ Have court confirm appointment as Personal Representative.

_____ Request that court confirm appointment of guardian(s), if required.

_____ Post surety bond, if required.

_____ Obtain letters testamentary or letters of administration from court and request additional certified copies.

_____ Arrange for notice to creditors as required.

_____ Apply for Federal Employer Identification Number for estate by filing form SS-4.

_____ Open bank account(s) for estate.

_____ If there is a will, assess the surviving spouse's right of election.

Personal Representative's Checklist (continued)

_____ File for any Social Security, Civil Service, Veterans Administration, or other death and pension benefits.

_____ Inspect all real estate and review mortgages, leases, property insurance policies, etc.

_____ Identify and expedite transfer of property not subject to probate (trusts, jointly held property).

_____ Provide funds for allowable living expenses to surviving spouse and dependents with approval of local court.

_____ Notify utilities, post office, creditors, etc., of death, and transfer accounts to survivors or estate as appropriate.

_____ Open and inventory all safe deposit boxes; transfer contents to estate safe deposit box, if necessary.

NOTE: Some states require that a representative of the state be present at the opening of the decedent's safe deposit box.

_____ Appraise estate assets for a "date of death" valuation.

_____ Engage professional appraisers, if required by court or for tax purposes.

_____ Arrange for management of real property located in other states.

_____ Make arrangements for such special concerns as business interests and ongoing farming operations.

_____ Collect all property belonging, or owed, to the estate.

_____ Prepare complete detailed inventory and appraisal of entire estate and file it with the court, with copies to major beneficiaries.

_____ Review all debts and claims for validity and accuracy; if any questions, contact local probate court.

_____ Prepare and file decedent's personal federal and state income tax returns for portion of last year of life.

Personal Representative's Checklist (continued)

NOTE: Qualified widow/widower status is available if dependent children live with surviving spouse.

_____ Determine cash needs of estate.

_____ Arrange sale of estate property, if required.

_____ Pay all valid claims, bills, and expenses, with court approval if required.

_____ Prepare and file federal and state estate income tax returns for period of administration.

_____ File federal and state estate-related tax returns, if applicable.

NOTE: A certified copy of the will must be attached to estate tax returns.

_____ Obtain court authorization to pay professional fees, if applicable.

_____ Distribute all assets as set out in the will or required by the laws of intestate succession.

_____ Prepare a final account of estate assets and distribution with receipts, and file it with the court.

_____ Close estate, and obtain documents from court indicating completion of Executor's duties.

_____ Retain copies of all records in a personal file for at least three years. If there is a surviving spouse and state estate-related taxes were paid, retain tax records for 10 years.

CHAPTER *4*

Inventory and Valuation

After notices to creditors have been placed, the next task to complete is the preparation of an inventory of the assets of the estate. The gross estate consists of everything owned by the deceased. The portion of the gross estate that is subject to the probate process is affected by the way the property is titled and, in the case of life insurance, how the policy is payable. Estates are adjusted to net values by offsetting their debts and liabilities. The remaining net probate estate, after administration expenses and various deductions, yields the taxable estate, which may be subject to state and federal estate-related taxes, depending on its size. It is important to keep this sequence in mind when examining the title terms of real property and any titled personal property included in the estate.

Types of Ownership

Real property may be owned solely by the deceased or may be owned jointly with a spouse or another person. If property is owned solely by the deceased, the entire interest becomes a portion of the probate estate. Whether or not jointly owned property becomes part of the estate depends on the type of ownership. The forms of joint ownership are *joint tenancy, tenancy by the entirety,* and *tenancy in common.* Upon the death of one of the joint tenants with right of survivorship, or a tenant by the entirety, the property ownership transfers to the other joint tenant with no action required by the Personal Representative and the property is not part of the probate estate. A property interest held as a tenant in common is owned individually and must be transferred by the Personal Representative in the distribution of the estate. Similarly, a community property interest is held individually and also must be distributed under probate.

Although joint property interests held with a right of survivorship or as tenants by the entirety are not subject to probate administration, the value of the decedent's share is included when determining the taxable estate. Thus, even though the type of ownership determines whether or not jointly held property is considered a probate asset, it does not affect its inclusion in the assets that may be subject to estate-related taxes. The Personal Representative should examine the deeds of real property involved, to determine the shares that are subject to estate-related taxation.

Bank accounts, stocks, and bonds can also be held jointly, with right of survivorship. Such accounts and securities pass directly to the surviving joint owner and do not have to pass through the probate process. Jointly held personal property such as motor vehicles, boats, and airplanes transfer in a similar manner. It is important to recognize that joint titling options can bypass the need for probate administration, but the Personal Representative should note the value of these assets as they will have to be included when calculating the taxable estate.

Real Property

Real estate and real property interests make up the bulk of the assets of many estates. In addition to the primary residence, an estate may include whole or partial interests in rental property, commercial buildings, and vacation property. After determining the type of ownership involved, the Personal Representative can determine those real estate assets that are his or her responsibility. All such property should be listed by its address and tax identification number. An initial value can be taken from the assessed value listed on the real estate property tax bill.

Property that passes outside of probate to a surviving joint owner is transferred when the surviving joint owner presents a copy of the death certificate and pays the title transfer and recordation fees. The Personal Representative needs only to list the property identification and valuation information. If a valid contract for the sale of the property had been signed by the deceased, the Personal Representative must act on his or her behalf in completing the sale and collecting the proceeds.

After ascertaining the real property that is subject to probate, the Personal Representative must check for liabilities related to that property. Such liabilities can include first and second mortgages, secured lines of credit, home equity loans, reverse mortgages, and taxes. Another form of encumbrance that may be encountered is a *life estate interest,* which is the right to occupy and use property whose title passes to another for the lifetime of the life estate holder. If a life estate interest has been granted, it is recorded on or with the deed. The creation of a life estate interest affects the property's value because it usually means that the property cannot be sold for an indefinite period of time. A life estate can be established before death by amending the deed, or can be created under the laws of intestate succession for a surviving spouse in Arkansas, Delaware, Indiana, Kentucky, Louisiana, Rhode Island, West Virginia, and the District of Columbia. Review of liabilities and encumbrances will allow the Personal Representative to estimate the amount that could be realized by sale of the real estate, and to estimate the net value that will be included in the taxable estate.

Personal Property

Personal property consists of all other property that is not real estate. Personal property is further classified as *tangible* and *intangible.* Tangible personal property includes actual items such as clothing, furniture, automobiles, and jewelry. Intangible personal property is representative in nature and includes cash, notes receivable, stocks, and bonds. A category of intangible personal property known as *intellectual property* may include copyrights and patents and their royalties and residual performance rights. Every estate will include some personal property.

Since most tangible personal property is located at a person's primary residence, a room-by-room inventory is generally the best place to start. A set of worksheets is provided at the end of the next section to assist you. When reporting to the probate court, general categories are usually sufficient, such as household furnishings and personal effects. Items with significant value should be identified, such as silver, jewelry, antiques, art, and collections. Although only summary categories will need to be reported to the probate court, a detailed inventory is useful to the Personal Representative in assessing value and determining a disposition strategy. The Personal Representative should carry out a thorough inventory, being alert for items in unexpected places, such as cash in books and stock certificates under mattresses. Another benefit of a careful search and inventory of personal property is the location of items of special significance to those who share in the estate. Items of personal property with little cash value are often treasured by survivors for the positive memories they evoke. When carrying out the room-by-room inventory, do not neglect the basement, attic, garage, and any rental storage units. As you assign value to these types of personal property, be conservative. The value of this property is considered to be its market value, not its purchase or replacement cost. For example, clothing usually has almost no resale value.

Most titled personal property is subject to local personal property taxes. The basis of this taxation, such as the blue books that list values of automobiles, provides a reasonable guide to valuation. Titled personal property can also be subject to liens that affect the net equity position.

The value of most intangible personal property is usually easy to establish. In the case of cash accounts, certificates of deposit, independent retirement accounts, and money market funds, the amount of the account balance is the value. The value of publicly traded securities, such as stocks and bonds, fluctuates but is available in the daily market reports in most newspapers. The value of private stock may be established by a preexisting buy–sell agreement or may have to be determined by review of the company's net worth. Previous business income may not be a factor in valuation, if the deceased was actively involved in the business and did not make arrangements for continuance of the business. The value of intellectual property rights can be estimated on the basis of previous royalty income received, tempered with the anticipated period of time that such royalties can be expected to be paid.

Life insurance payable to a named beneficiary is not part of the probate estate and is not reported to the court. However, life insurance payable to the deceased's estate is included and must be administered by the Personal Representative. Examples of life insurance that may be paid to the estate include mortgage and credit card life insurance coverage. Life insurance payable to the Executor of an estate is included with the estate's assets when calculating the taxable estate.

Although not subject to probate administration, the value of pensions or annuities payable to survivors is included in the taxable estate. Farm and business interests will usually include both real and personal property. These interests should be listed and evaluated separately because they may qualify for special tax treatment.

Immediately following the room-by-room inventory worksheets at the end of the next section is a series of estate inventory worksheets, which cover the same categories that are used in filing estate-related taxes. The totals from the room-by-room inventory and other estate assets are listed there as well. Completion of these worksheets will provide the Personal Representative with the background information needed for both probate reporting and calculation of estate-related tax liability.

Valuation

The inventory of estate assets should list a value for each item, which represents the market value of the asset at the date of death. The total value of the estate has an impact on the estate-related tax liability. A general knowledge of the value of the estate will be needed at the probate hearing. After appointment of a Personal Representative, a more specific value will have to be determined. In some cases, the Personal Representative will assign values to all elements of the estate. If the estate includes real property or substantial personal property assets (other than cash or stocks and bonds), the Personal Representative may need to obtain a professional appraisal. Be sure to check with the local probate court to ascertain which property must be so appraised. Selection of appraisers is generally up to the Personal Representative, although in some states court-appointed or court-approved appraisers must be used. The Probate Administration State Summary in Chapter 3 lists each state's requirements regarding the selection of appraisers. Appraisers fees vary, as does their experience in estate appraisal work, so it is usually advisable to contact several before making a selection.

If the estate is near or exceeds $600,000, the appraised values may have significant implications for the estate-related tax. An estate value of more than $600,000 means that a federal estate tax return must be filed and the estate will also be subject to a *federal credit* estate tax that is collected by the state. Two valuation options may apply to federally taxable estates. *Alternate valuation* is the calculation of the value of the estate at six months from the date of death. This option is used only if the later valuation shows an overall reduction in the value of the taxable estate. Examples of how this might occur are the difference between an appraised value and a subsequent actual sale price for real or personal property and a decline in market value of publicly traded securities. The other option, *special use valuation,* is available when farm or business operations constitute a substantial portion of the estate. Under special use valuation, the assets of the farm or business may be valued on the basis of their use, rather than their fair market value if sold. As an example, the valuation of a working farm would be based on its income as a farm rather than the value of the land for another use, such as a subdivision. Another provision allows payment of federal estate tax due on an estate valued under special use valuation to be spread over a period of 10 years.

A surviving spouse receiving a large estate is eligible for an unlimited *marital deduction.* This deduction has the effect of deferring federal estate taxation until after the death of the surviving spouse. The Personal Representative of a large estate should review the federal publications and forms set out in Chapter 6 to take full advantage of these provisions.

———— VALUABLES: ANTIQUES, JEWELRY, SILVER, COLLECTIONS ————

Item/description	Valuation	Sale price
_____	$_____	$_____
_____	$_____	$_____
_____	$_____	$_____
_____	$_____	$_____
_____	$_____	$_____
_____	$_____	$_____
_____	$_____	$_____
_____	$_____	$_____
_____	$_____	$_____
_____	$_____	$_____
_____	$_____	$_____
_____	$_____	$_____
_____	$_____	$_____
_____	$_____	$_____
_____	$_____	$_____
_____	$_____	$_____

Second Home/Additional Items

_____	$_____	$_____
_____	$_____	$_____
_____	$_____	$_____
_____	$_____	$_____
_____	$_____	$_____

———————————————— **LIVING ROOM** ————————————————

Item/description	Valuation	Sale price
	$	$
	$	$
	$	$
	$	$
	$	$
	$	$
	$	$
	$	$
	$	$
	$	$
	$	$
	$	$
	$	$
	$	$
	$	$
	$	$
	$	$

Second Home/Additional Items

	$	$
	$	$
	$	$
	$	$
	$	$

———————————— FAMILY ROOM/DEN ————————————

Item/description	Valuation	Sale price
	$	$
	$	$
	$	$
	$	$
	$	$
	$	$
	$	$
	$	$
	$	$
	$	$
	$	$
	$	$
	$	$
	$	$
	$	$
	$	$

Second Home/Additional Items

	$	$
	$	$
	$	$
	$	$
	$	$

DINING ROOM

Item/description	Valuation	Sale price
	$	$
	$	$
	$	$
	$	$
	$	$
	$	$
	$	$
	$	$
	$	$
	$	$
	$	$
	$	$
	$	$
	$	$
	$	$
	$	$

Second Home/Additional Items

	$	$
	$	$
	$	$
	$	$
	$	$

———————————————————— **KITCHEN/PANTRY** ————————————————————

Item/description	Valuation	Sale price
	$	$
	$	$
	$	$
	$	$
	$	$
	$	$
	$	$
	$	$
	$	$
	$	$
	$	$
	$	$
	$	$
	$	$
	$	$
	$	$

Second Home/Additional Items

	$	$
	$	$
	$	$
	$	$
	$	$

————— MASTER BEDROOM —————

Item/description	Valuation	Sale price
	$	$
	$	$
	$	$
	$	$
	$	$
	$	$
	$	$
	$	$
	$	$
	$	$
	$	$
	$	$
	$	$
	$	$
	$	$
	$	$

Second Home/Additional Items

	Valuation	Sale price
	$	$
	$	$
	$	$
	$	$
	$	$

─────────────────── **OTHER BEDROOMS** ───────────────────

Item/description	Valuation	Sale price
	$	$
	$	$
	$	$
	$	$
	$	$
	$	$
	$	$
	$	$
	$	$
	$	$
	$	$
	$	$
	$	$
	$	$
	$	$
	$	$

Second Home/Additional Items

	$	$
	$	$
	$	$
	$	$
	$	$

BATHROOMS / CLOSETS

Item/description	Valuation	Sale price
	$	$
	$	$
	$	$
	$	$
	$	$
	$	$
	$	$
	$	$
	$	$
	$	$
	$	$
	$	$
	$	$
	$	$
	$	$
	$	$

Second Home/Additional Items

	$	$
	$	$
	$	$
	$	$
	$	$

R O O M - B Y - R O O M   I N V E N T O R Y

ATTIC/BASEMENT

Item/description	Valuation	Sale price
	$	$
	$	$
	$	$
	$	$
	$	$
	$	$
	$	$
	$	$
	$	$
	$	$
	$	$
	$	$
	$	$
	$	$
	$	$
	$	$

Second Home/Additional Items

	$	$
	$	$
	$	$
	$	$
	$	$

R O O M - B Y - R O O M I N V E N T O R Y

───── GARAGE/STORAGE BUILDINGS ─────

Item/description	Valuation	Sale price
	$	$
	$	$
	$	$
	$	$
	$	$
	$	$
	$	$
	$	$
	$	$
	$	$
	$	$
	$	$
	$	$
	$	$
	$	$
	$	$

Second Home/Additional Items

	$	$
	$	$
	$	$
	$	$
	$	$

PORCH/PATIO/OUTDOOR

Item/description	Valuation	Sale price
	$	$
	$	$
	$	$
	$	$
	$	$
	$	$
	$	$
	$	$
	$	$
	$	$
	$	$
	$	$
	$	$
	$	$
	$	$
	$	$

Second Home/Additional Items

Item/description	Valuation	Sale price
	$	$
	$	$
	$	$
	$	$
	$	$

R O O M - B Y - R O O M   I N V E N T O R Y

——— ELECTRONICS/PHOTO/MISCELLANEOUS ———

Item/description	Valuation	Sale price
	$	$
	$	$
	$	$
	$	$
	$	$
	$	$
	$	$
	$	$
	$	$
	$	$
	$	$
	$	$
	$	$
	$	$
	$	$
	$	$

Second Home/Additional Items

	Valuation	Sale price
	$	$
	$	$
	$	$
	$	$
	$	$

ESTATE INVENTORY

—————————————— CASH/NOTES ——————————————

Bank Accounts

Checking

	Joint acct.?	Account #	Amount	Amount
_____	_____	_____	$_____	$_____
_____	_____	_____	$_____	$_____
_____	_____	_____	$_____	$_____

Savings

_____	_____	_____	$_____	$_____
_____	_____	_____	$_____	$_____
_____	_____	_____	$_____	$_____

Certificates

_____	_____	_____	$_____	$_____
_____	_____	_____	$_____	$_____
_____	_____	_____	$_____	$_____

IRAs

_____	_____	_____	$_____	$_____
_____	_____	_____	$_____	$_____

Cash

_____	_____	_____	$_____	$_____

Safe Deposit Box

Location

_____	_____	_____	$_____	$_____
_____	_____	_____	$_____	$_____

Notes Receivable

Maker_____ $_____ $_____

Address_____

Balance $_____   Security_____

Maker_____ $_____ $_____

Address_____

Balance $_____   Security_____

Total Cash/Notes $_____ $_____

──────────────── **STOCKS/BONDS** ────────────────

Stocks/Mutual Funds

Company	Number of shares	CUSIP number	Dollar value	Dollar value
_____	_____	_____	$_____	$_____
_____	_____	_____	$_____	$_____
_____	_____	_____	$_____	$_____
_____	_____	_____	$_____	$_____
_____	_____	_____	$_____	$_____
_____	_____	_____	$_____	$_____
_____	_____	_____	$_____	$_____
_____	_____	_____	$_____	$_____
_____	_____	_____	$_____	$_____
_____	_____	_____	$_____	$_____
_____	_____	_____	$_____	$_____
_____	_____	_____	$_____	$_____
_____	_____	_____	$_____	$_____

Bonds

Company/Government	Cost	Date	Dollar value	Dollar value
_____	$_____	_____	$_____	$_____
_____	$_____	_____	$_____	$_____
_____	$_____	_____	$_____	$_____
_____	$_____	_____	$_____	$_____
_____	$_____	_____	$_____	$_____
_____	$_____	_____	$_____	$_____
_____	$_____	_____	$_____	$_____
_____	$_____	_____	$_____	$_____
_____	$_____	_____	$_____	$_____
_____	$_____	_____	$_____	$_____
_____	$_____	_____	$_____	$_____
Total Stocks/Bonds			$_____	$_____

ESTATE INVENTORY

———————————————————— LIFE INSURANCE ————————————————————

Company——————————————— Policy #—————— Amount $——————
Agent/Address——————————————————————— Phone——————
Name of
insured——————————————— Beneficiary——————————
Alternate beneficiary—————————————————————————

Company——————————————— Policy #—————— Amount $——————
Agent/Address——————————————————————— Phone——————
Name of
insured——————————————— Beneficiary——————————
Alternate beneficiary—————————————————————————

Company——————————————— Policy #—————— Amount $——————
Agent/Address——————————————————————— Phone——————
Name of
insured——————————————— Beneficiary——————————
Alternate beneficiary—————————————————————————

Company——————————————— Policy #—————— Amount $——————
Agent/Address——————————————————————— Phone——————
Name of
insured——————————————— Beneficiary——————————
Alternate beneficiary—————————————————————————

Company——————————————— Policy #—————— Amount $——————
Agent/Address——————————————————————— Phone——————
Name of
insured——————————————— Beneficiary——————————
Alternate beneficiary—————————————————————————

Company——————————————— Policy #—————— Amount $——————
Agent/Address——————————————————————— Phone——————
Name of
insured——————————————— Beneficiary——————————
Alternate beneficiary—————————————————————————

Total Life Insurance $—————— $——————

──────────────── **PERSONAL PROPERTY** ────────────────

Autos, Boats, R.V.s, etc.

Type_____

Model/ID_____   Value   Value

Serial #_____ $_____ $_____

Description_____

_____

Type_____

Model/ID_____   Value   Value

Serial #_____ $_____ $_____

Description_____

_____

Type_____

Model/ID_____   Value   Value

Serial #_____ $_____ $_____

Description_____

_____

Type_____

Model/ID_____   Value   Value

Serial #_____ $_____ $_____

Description_____

_____

Household Effects and Furniture

Description   Value   Value

_____ $_____ $_____

_____ $_____ $_____

_____ $_____ $_____

_____ $_____ $_____

_____ $_____ $_____

_____ $_____ $_____

_____ $_____ $_____

_____ $_____ $_____

(continued)

111

——————————————— **PERSONAL PROPERTY** (*continued*) ———————————————

Jewelry

Description	Value	Value
_____	$_____	$_____
_____	$_____	$_____
_____	$_____	$_____
_____	$_____	$_____
_____	$_____	$_____
_____	$_____	$_____
_____	$_____	$_____

Tools/Hobby/Sporting Goods

Description	Value	Value
_____	$_____	$_____
_____	$_____	$_____
_____	$_____	$_____

Heirlooms and Collections

Description	Value	Value
_____	$_____	$_____
_____	$_____	$_____
_____	$_____	$_____

Antiques

Description	Value	Value
_____	$_____	$_____
_____	$_____	$_____
_____	$_____	$_____

Miscellaneous

Description	Value	Value
_____	$_____	$_____
_____	$_____	$_____
_____	$_____	$_____

Total Personal Property $_____ $_____

―――――――――――――― **ANNUITIES/PENSIONS** ――――――――――――――

Company_____ #_____

Agent_____ Amount $_____

Owner_____ Beneficiary_____

Company_____ #_____

Agent_____ Amount $_____

Owner_____ Beneficiary_____

Company_____ #_____

Agent_____ Amount $_____

Owner_____ Beneficiary_____

Company_____ #_____

Agent_____ Amount $_____

Owner_____ Beneficiary_____

Company_____ #_____

Agent_____ Amount $_____

Owner_____ Beneficiary_____

Company_____ #_____

Agent_____ Amount $_____

Owner_____ Beneficiary_____

Company_____ #_____

Agent_____ Amount $_____

Owner_____ Beneficiary_____

Company_____ #_____

Agent_____ Amount $_____

Owner_____ Beneficiary_____

Company_____ #_____

Agent_____ Amount $_____

Owner_____ Beneficiary_____

Total Annuities/Pensions $_____ $_____

ESTATE INVENTORY

REAL PROPERTY

Residence

House ☐   Condominium ☐   Co-op ☐   Other ☐

Description_____

_____

Address_____

_____

	Market value	Market value
	$_____	$_____

Deed in name of_____

Jointly owned ☐   Community property ☐   Co-owned ☐

Joint owner/Co-owner_____

Second/Vacation Home

Description_____

_____   Property #_____

_____

Address_____

_____

	Market value	Market value
	$_____	$_____

Deed in name of_____

Jointly owned ☐   Community property ☐   Co-owned ☐

Joint owner/Co-owner_____

Commercial/Rental Property

Description_____

_____   Property #_____

_____

Address_____

_____

	Market value	Market value
	$_____	$_____

Deed in name of_____

Jointly owned ☐   Co-owned ☐   Partnership ☐   Corporation ☐   Other ☐

Joint/Co-owner(s)_____

_____

Total Real Property $_____ $_____

─────────────────── **JOINT REAL PROPERTY** ───────────────────

Residence

House ☐   Condominium ☐   Co-op ☐   Other ☐

Description_____

_____

	Market value	Market value
Address_____		
_____	$_____	$_____

Deed in name of_____

Jointly owned ☐   Community property ☐   Co-owned ☐

Joint owner/Co-owner_____

Second/Vacation Home

Description_____

_____   Property #_____

_____

	Market value	Market value
Address_____		
_____	$_____	$_____

Deed in name of_____

Jointly owned ☐   Community property ☐   Co-owned ☐

Joint owner/Co-owner_____

Commercial/Rental Property

Description_____

_____   Property #_____

_____

	Market value	Market value
Address_____		
_____	$_____	$_____

Deed in name of_____

Jointly owned ☐   Co-owned ☐   Partnership ☐   Corporation ☐   Other ☐

Joint/Co-owner(s)_____

_____

Total Joint Real Property $_____ $_____

_____ **FARM/BUSINESS** _____

Farm

Real estate	$_____	$_____
Market value	$_____	$_____
Farm use value	$_____	$_____
Improvements	$_____	$_____
Equipment	$_____	$_____
Supplies	$_____	$_____
Livestock	$_____	$_____
Crops	$_____	$_____
Totals—Market value	$_____	$_____
Totals—Farm use value	$_____	$_____

Real estate % of Market value   _____%

Real estate % of Farm use value   _____%

Owners_____

_____

Operator(s)_____

Business

Real estate	$_____	$_____
Market value	$_____	$_____
Business use value	$_____	$_____
Improvements	$_____	$_____
Equipment	$_____	$_____
Supplies	$_____	$_____
Other	$_____	$_____
Totals—Market value	$_____	$_____
Totals—Business use value	$_____	$_____

Real estate % of Market value   _____%

Real estate % of Business use value   _____%

Owners_____

_____

Management_____

Buy–sell agreement   Yes___   No___

Business life insurance policy $_____ $_____

                                         $_____ $_____

Total Business Life Insurance $_____ $_____

————————————————————————— **DEBTS** —————————————————————————

Mortgages/Notes

Type——————————————————————— Original balance $——————————

Security———

Mortage/Note holder—————————————————————————————————————

Address——

Location of document————————————————————————————————————

Type——————————————————————— Original balance $——————————

Security———

Mortgage/Note holder————————————————————————————————————

Address——

Location of document————————————————————————————————————

Type——————————————————————— Original balance $——————————

Security———

Mortgage/Note holder————————————————————————————————————

Address——

Location of document————————————————————————————————————

Other Debts

Account	Number	Balance
——————————————	——————————————	$——————————————
——————————————	——————————————	$——————————————
——————————————	——————————————	$——————————————
——————————————	——————————————	$——————————————
——————————————	——————————————	$——————————————
——————————————	——————————————	$——————————————
——————————————	——————————————	$——————————————
——————————————	——————————————	$——————————————
——————————————	——————————————	$——————————————
——————————————	——————————————	$——————————————
——————————————	——————————————	$——————————————

Total Debts $——————————————

E S T A T E   I N V E N T O R Y

─────────────── **DEBTS** ───────────────

Mortgages/Notes

Type_____ Original balance $_____

Security_____

Mortage/Note holder_____

Address_____

Location of document_____

Type_____ Original balance $_____

Security_____

Mortgage/Note holder_____

Address_____

Location of document_____

Type_____ Original balance $_____

Security_____

Mortgage/Note holder_____

Address_____

Location of document_____

Other Debts

Account	Number	Balance
_____	_____	$_____
_____	_____	$_____
_____	_____	$_____
_____	_____	$_____
_____	_____	$_____
_____	_____	$_____
_____	_____	$_____
_____	_____	$_____
_____	_____	$_____
_____	_____	$_____
_____	_____	$_____
		$_____

Total Debts

ESTATE INVENTORY

_____ **ESTATE SUMMARY** _____

Estate Component Totals

Cash/Notes	$_____	$_____
Stocks/Bonds	$_____	$_____
Life Insurance	$_____	$_____
Personal Property	$_____	$_____
Annuities/Pensions	$_____	$_____
Real Property	$_____	$_____
Joint Real Property	$_____	$_____
Farm/Business	$_____	$_____
Inheritance	$_____	$_____
Gross estate totals	$_____	$_____
(less debts)	$(_____)	$(_____)
Balance	$_____	$_____
(less charitable gifts)	$(_____)	$(_____)
Balance	$_____	$_____
(less settlement cost estimate)	$(_____)	$(_____)
Actual estate before taxes	$_____	$_____
(less federal estate tax deduction)	$____(600,000)____	$____(600,000)____
Federal taxable estate	$_____	$_____

NOTE: If there is a federal taxable estate, an IRS 706 Return must be filed. A surviving spouse may use the amount of the marital deduction (Schedule M) to reduce the federal taxable estate to zero. Check with State Department of Taxation regarding other state estate, inheritance, gift and/or generation-skip tax liabilities.

Federal taxable estate (less state credit estate tax deduction)	$____(60,000)____	$____(60,000)____
State credit estate taxable estate	$_____	$_____

CHAPTER 5

Before Distribution

Prior to distribution of the balance of the estate, the Personal Representative must collect all assets and receive, review, and pay any liabilities. Once again, a simple list is the basic tool involved. As mentioned earlier, the Personal Representative must identify all debts, expenses, and claims and the amount of resources available to the estate before making any payments.

Liquidity

Liquidity refers to the ease and speed that assets can be converted to cash without loss of value. Bank accounts such as checking and savings accounts are the most obvious liquid assets. Since payment of debts and claims will require cash, the Personal Representative should review the components of the estate in terms of their liquidity. The amount and liquidity of the assets can affect the timing and order that debts and claims against the estate are settled. If a significant portion of the estate consists of highly liquid assets, needed cash is readily available. If, however, the estate consists of relatively illiquid assets, such as real estate and personal property, the Personal Representative may need to develop a liquidation plan to raise necessary funds.

This plan may mean placing real estate and titled personal property on the market early in the probate process. An estate auction of valuable items or general personal property may also be required.

Estate Auctions

An estate auction may be necessary to obtain cash for payment of debts and taxes, to divide an estate into shares, to fund cash bequests, or to dispose of residual property after specific bequests have been fulfilled. In some cases, it may be more advantageous or convenient to sell personal property, rather than to make arrangements for its storage and transportation.

Recognizing that many factors can affect the amount realized at an auction, particularly the weather and other competing events and sales, it is best to plan carefully. Because of the need for advertisement (Figure 5-1), the auction usually is scheduled about 30 days after the auctioneer's contract is

---

• AUCTION •
THE HATTIE BELLE GOODE ESTATE
Saturday, Sept. 15 -- 10 A.M. -- New Castle
Many of the items being sold were used during the filming of
IN A SHALLOW GRAVE

Partial List Includes: **FURNITURE:** Curved glass china cabinet, walnut pie safe, oak kitchen cabinet, walnut Victorian bedroom set, 10-pc. mahogany dining room suite, 2 brass beds, 7-ft. wardrobe w/beveled glass mirrors, oak dressers, oak chest of drawers, oak dressing tables, oak washstand, mission oak rocker & chair, large cedar blanket chest, electric Hammond organ, upright piano, Victorian love seat, ladies' small oak drop front desk, 5-pc. ornate bedroom set, spool bed, 18-ft. frost-free ref/freezer, 36-in. electric range. **CHINA & GLASSWARE:** several sets of china, 8-place setting of Homer Laughlin, pressed glass, Depression glass, Nippon china, carnival glass, children's tea set, matching bowl, pitcher & shaving mug, tea pots, very old set enameled glasses, lots of stemware, old crocks & jugs. **COLLECTIBLES:** Oil hanging lamp (all original), Victorian hanging lamp, baskets, oil lamps, anniversary clock, blue oriental rug, silverplate flatware, costume jewelry, old clothes, hats, purses, books, very old post cards, sheet music dating to early 1900s. **LINENS:** Quilts, bedspreads, woven coverlet, bed linens (some new). **PICTURES & MIRRORS:** Buffet mirror, old shaving mirror, framed sampler, shadow box frames w/prints, old pictures. **HAND & GARDEN TOOLS, AND OTHER MISC. ITEMS.**

CALL FOR DETAILED LIST: FINCASTLE 473-3939 • COVINGTON 962-1155
Sale conducted for: **Mrs. Harriet G. Reubush, Executrix.**

Food Service by: Rocket Booster Club.   **BRING YOUR CHAIR.**

Sale site: 1/2 mi. South of New Castle on Rt. 311

DON CHARLTON • TOMMY GARTEN • PAT CHARLTON
(703) 864-6655   •   (703) 962-1155   •   (703) 473-3939

Greenway's Auction Co.
VAAF 096
Covington, VA 24426 • Fincastle, VA 24090

Figure 5-1

signed. Discuss the best date and time for the auction with the auctioneer to draw on his or her experience and knowledge of other upcoming sales. As you review the personal property to be sold, there may be items for which you wish to establish a minimum or reserve sale price. Be sure to discuss this with the auctioneer, so that the item is not inadvertently sold for less. Reserve prices should be used sparingly in a public auction and, as the Personal Representative, you should have an alternate sale strategy if the minimum price is not met.

Another approach that may be considered is offering the items for sale to individuals at a set price prior to the auction. This may be done either on a continuing basis or just before the sale. The auctioneer may specify a (reduced) percentage of the proceeds of such sales although a minimum commission total may be required. It is essential that you fully understand the auctioneer's contract and have any questions answered in writing before signing.

Although sometimes the entire estate is sold at auction, often the auction includes only the residual personal property left after other sales methods have been pursued. Be sure to examine personal property carefully before a sale, thumbing through books and opening all boxes and drawers to locate any money, certificates, photographs, or other important papers and small items of value that otherwise may be overlooked. If the estate includes antique furniture, rare books, art, or other unusual artifacts, obtaining the advice of an antique dealer can help determine values. Because many antique dealers and dealers in old jewelry purchase a large portion of their inventory directly from estates, it is always wise to get a second opinion of the value of certain items before accepting an offer.

Costs of an estate auction vary as a result of differences in auctioneers' commission rates and the size of sales, both in terms of quantity of items and dollar sales anticipated. Generally, commission rates range from 10 to 25 percent of the gross amount realized for personal property sales. Higher percentages are often charged when the auctioneer feels that the property offered is of little value. When arranging an estate auction the Personal Representative should have several auctioneers review the property. No auctioneer will be able to offer a contract without viewing the items to be sold because the auctioneer's list of major and significant items becomes a part of the formal contract. The auctioneer decides the commission rate he or she will charge after viewing the personal property to be sold. When selecting an auctioneer, be aware that there often are costs in addition to the basic commission. Usually the costs of advertising the sale are passed on, and often additional charges are made for labor (helpers) on the day of the sale, as well as any rental costs for a tent, tables, and chairs. If the sale is not to be held at the home, some firms charge for transportation of the personal property to the auction hall. Discuss and understand fully how these costs are calculated before you select the auctioneer and sign the consignment contract.

The auctioneer usually tags the property to be sold with numbers to track each item or lot of items in order to record the selling prices properly. Some may simply use a handwritten record, while others may provide a computer printout after the sale. When choosing the auctioneer, the Personal Representative should inquire about the type of sales records that will be provided. Whatever their form, these records should show a brief description of the item, the item number, the bidder number, and the actual sale price. The Personal Representative must have a copy of these records to answer any questions that may arise after the sale. It is a good idea to provide a copy of the sales record to the interested beneficiaries or heirs, along with a copy of the auctioneer's contract and final bill.

All interested parties, including beneficiaries, heirs, and friends of the deceased, should be informed of the date and time of the auction so that they can observe and bid if they wish. Auctions of personal property are absolute sales, and once payment is made there is no way to revoke a sale.

Occasionally, real estate is also sold at an estate auction. If real estate is involved, it is advisable to extend the time and frequency of advertisement before the sale. Auctioneers' commissions on these sales generally vary between 6 and 10 percent, comparable to those of real estate agents. If the same auctioneer is selling both real estate and personal property, a lower commission rate can usually be negotiated. Most real estate is sold subject to confirmation by the owner, allowing the Personal Representative, acting on behalf of the estate, to refuse unreasonable offers. Discuss the sale of real estate thoroughly with the auctioneer before committing yourself. You should also verify that there are no liens against the property and confirm with the local probate court your authority to sell.

Debts and Claims

Meeting the living expenses of a surviving spouse, minor children, or other dependents during the period of administration should be considered prior to paying any debts owed by the estate. Life insurance proceeds, survivor's pension or annuity benefits, and Social Security benefits can be used to meet living expenses. Jointly titled bank accounts with the right of survivorship or a surviving spouse's automatic share may also be available. If funds are insufficient, the Personal Representative should request clarification from the probate court of the options available to meet living expenses.

If the estate is solvent, timing of payment of debts is generally at the discretion of the Personal Representative. If there is sufficient liquidity, payment decisions can be made on the basis of a comparison of the interest earned by assets versus the interest being charged on debts. Less liquid estates may have to defer most debts. In either case, certain expenses will have to be paid soon after appointment as the Personal Representative. Any court and filing fees, the cost of certified copies, and the cost of any required notices must be paid in order for the administrative process to advance. The

Personal Representative should pay all expenses of the estate with the estate checking account and obtain receipts as well.

Debts related to real property may include mortgages, home equity credit lines, utility bills for the last month, local real estate taxes, and hazard insurance payments. Property that is transferred outside of probate through joint titling will be liable only for the portion of these expenses incurred up to the date of transfer. If the real estate is part of the probate estate, utility accounts should be changed to the name of the estate and paid when due. The same is true regarding hazard insurance and mortgage payments. Local taxes usually can be deferred, although the taxes and any late payment penalties must be paid before the property can be sold or distributed. If the estate is being settled under supervised administration, the Personal Representative must obtain court approval before paying any of these debts.

Titled personal property that is part of the probate estate may also involve installment financing or outstanding local personal property taxes. The Personal Representative should pay installment payments when due and any outstanding personal property taxes prior to sale or distribution of such property. Secured debts such as mortgages and automobile loans must be paid when due, to retain the estate's equity position in these assets.

Unsecured debts, such as credit cards, store accounts, and other bills due to be paid by the deceased, allow some flexibility in the timing of payment. Similarly, funeral expenses and medical costs can usually be deferred for a time without risk. Most of these bills arrive in the mail, and for this reason the Personal Representative should arrange to receive all mail addressed to the decedent. As these bills are received, it is advisable to respond with a brief letter to inform the creditors that the estate is in the process of being settled and that any future correspondence should be addressed to the Personal Representative. This step is not necessary if there are sufficient funds available and the Personal Representative is authorized to pay liabilities when received. Any bills should be reviewed to determine whether any credit life insurance was in effect. In these cases, the outstanding balance will be paid in full by the insurance provider. Note that the outstanding amount will be listed as a debt of the deceased and the amount paid by the credit insurance policy will be listed as an asset of the estate. This same procedure applies to mortgage insurance on real property and insurance that may be carried on installment notes for titled personal property.

The Personal Representative is responsible for reviewing all debts and claims to determine that they are, in fact, valid claims. Carefully review the decedent's bills for accuracy and verify the account totals. Medical and hospital bills should receive special scrutiny, to be sure they are correct and that there are no duplicate charges. An examination of any health insurance payments made on behalf of the decedent should be reviewed for accuracy. Billing errors should be resolved before final payment is made. When the deadline for filing creditor claims has passed, any remaining questions regarding debts should be referred to the probate court for guidance and determination.

Taxes

The Personal Representative of an estate is responsible for filing and signing all applicable local, state, and federal tax returns. Further, the Personal Representative is personally liable for payment of these taxes, to the full extent of the estate's assets. Consequently, the Personal Representative should determine the amount of tax liability before making any distribution of the estate's assets, to ensure that all taxes due can be paid in full. All tax returns must be filed by their respective deadlines and in most cases payment must accompany the returns. Failure to file in a timely manner usually results in penalties and interest, in addition to the tax owed. If more time will be required, file a formal request for extension of time to file and pay the estimated amount of tax due, to minimize interest costs.

Reports

The Personal Representative is usually required to file an estate inventory and may also be required to file periodic estate status reports with the local probate court. The forms for these reports are available from the court and generally are quite simple. When completed, the forms must be signed by the Personal Representative, usually before a notary or an authorized member of the court's staff, attesting to the accuracy of information therein. Copies of any appraisals required should also be submitted with the inventory. If arithmetic errors need to be corrected or valuations need adjustment, this can be accomplished by filing a supplemental report. The following Estate Summary Worksheets can assist the Personal Representative in organizing the information about the estate that will have to be reported on the court's forms. The Estate Summary Worksheets separate estate principal and liabilities from estate income and expenses related to that income for ease of calculating taxes. Three sets of the Estate Summary Worksheets are provided that can be used for background for the initial inventory, a status report, and the final statement. One follows and two are included in the perforated section of detachable forms at the back of the book.

E S T A T E S U M M A R Y W O R K S H E E T

ESTATE

Court _____ File Number _____

Estate of _____

Resident at _____

Date of death _____ Will: Yes _____ No _____

Personal Representative _____

Address _____

Date of appointment _____

Date(s) of notice to beneficiaries/heirs _____

Date(s) of notice to creditors _____

Date of this summary account _____

PRINCIPAL

Assets	Value
Real estate	$_____
Joint real estate	$_____
Stocks/bonds	$_____
Cash/notes	$_____
Life insurance to estate	$_____
Titled personal property	$_____
Other personal property	$_____
Farm/business interest	$_____
Other assets	$_____
Total Assets	$_____
Adjustments to asset values	$_____
Principal receipts	
Income tax refund(s)	$_____
Other	$_____
Adjusted Principal Balance	$_____

Disbursements	Amount
Court fees	$_____
Advertisements	$_____
Postage	$_____
Certified copies	$_____

Disbursements

Disbursements	Amount
Personal property taxes	$_____
Real estate taxes	$_____
Income taxes	$_____
Other taxes	$_____
Hazard insurance	$_____
Utility bills	$_____
Title transfer fees	$_____
Recordation fees	$_____
Appraisal fees	$_____
Auction/agent commissions	$_____
Stock/bond broker commission(s)	$_____
Funeral expenses	$_____
Monument costs	$_____
Last illness costs	$_____
Other professional fees	$_____
Notary fees	$_____
State estate/inheritance taxes	$_____
Federal estate taxes	$_____
Living expenses/allowances	$_____
Personal Representative commission	$_____
Other expenses (list)	$_____
Debts	$_____
Total Disbursements	$_____
Principal Balance Before Distribution	$_____

Distribution to Beneficiaries/Heirs

Name	Date	Amount
_____	_____	$_____
_____	_____	_____
_____	_____	_____
_____	_____	_____
_____	_____	_____
_____	_____	_____
_____	_____	_____
_____	_____	_____
_____	_____	_____
_____	_____	_____

Total Distribution to Beneficiaries/Heirs $_____

Investments

Investment	Date	Amount
_____	_____	$_____
_____	_____	_____
_____	_____	_____
_____	_____	_____

Capital Changes

Type	Date	Amount
_____	_____	$_____
_____	_____	_____
_____	_____	_____

Principal Balance Remaining

$_____

_____ **INCOME** _____

Period from _____ to _____

Receipts

Type	Amount
Rent	$_____
Stock dividends	$_____
Bond interest	$_____
Cash account interest	$_____
Private note interest	$_____
Royalty payments	$_____
Other income (list)	$_____
	$_____
	$_____

Total Income

$_____

Disbursements

Type	Amount
Management fees	$_____
Bank fees	$_____
Other expenses to produce income (list)	$_____
	$_____
	$_____

Disbursements   Amount

Federal fiduciary income tax $_____

State fiduciary income tax $_____

Other taxes on estate income $_____

Personal Representative income commission $_____

Total Disbursements $_____

Income Balance Before Distribution $_____

Income Distribution to Beneficiaries/Heirs

Name	Date	Amount
_____	_____	$_____
_____	_____	_____
_____	_____	_____
_____	_____	_____
_____	_____	___ _____
_____	_____	_____
_____	_____	_____
_____	_____	_____
_____	_____	_____
_____	_____	_____

Total Income Distribution to Beneficiaries/Heirs $_____

Income Balance Remaining $_____

Total Principal and Income Balance Remaining $_____

CHAPTER 6

Taxes

There are two basic categories of taxes that may have to be paid. The first group consists of the regular taxes the decedent was liable for while still living. Taxes of this nature can include local real estate and personal property taxes, income taxes, taxes on a business or farm operation, and special state taxes, such as Florida's intangible personal property tax. The second group of taxes are taxes that are triggered by the creation of the estate and can include estate income taxes, inheritance taxes, gift taxes, estate taxes, and generation-skipping transfer taxes.

Taxes that the Personal Representative will have to deal with vary, depending on the decedent's location of residence, the type and amount of income, and the type and amount of property included in the estate. The list on page 132 shows taxes that may be encountered in the probate period.

Regular Taxes

The Personal Representative will need to locate copies of regular tax returns of the deceased for guidance in preparing and filing the last year tax returns. If copies of the previous three years' tax returns cannot be found, a review of the decedent's checking accounts should show taxes paid or, possibly, refunds received. If there is such evidence of taxes being paid, copies of

Potential Tax Checklist

REGULAR TAXES

_____   Local personal property taxes

_____   Local real estate taxes

_____   State income tax—last year

_____   Federal income tax—last year

_____   Local income tax—last year

_____   Business taxes—state
                                    federal
                                    local

_____   Special state taxes (intangible personal property, etc.)

ESTATE-RELATED TAXES

_____   State estate income tax

_____   Federal estate income tax

_____   State inheritance (and gift) taxes

_____   State estate (and gift) taxes

ESTATES OVER $600,000

_____   State credit estate tax

_____   Federal estate tax

ESTATES OVER $1,000,000

_____   Generation-skipping transfer taxes

returns should be requested from the appropriate taxation departments, which will supply the copies for a nominal fee. If no evidence of tax payments can be found, a thorough review of the deceased's financial records should be made to ensure that there are no unpaid taxes due from prior years. Occasionally, because of illness or forgetfulness, prior taxes may not have been paid. It is vital for the Personal Representative to be aware of such liabilities.

Often local real estate and personal property taxes will be the first regular taxes due, since they commonly are collected on a semiannual basis. It is particularly important to pay local taxes when due, so that the property will be free of tax liens should it need to be sold quickly. In many jurisdictions, real estate taxes for qualified elderly homeowners may be either frozen or deferred. Inquire at the locality to determine whether deferred taxes will be assessed upon sale of the real estate.

When preparing final income tax returns, copies of state and federal returns for prior years are an important source of information. Unless review of prior returns indicates otherwise, income tax returns are filed on a calendar year basis. The final income tax returns should be filed on the previous filing schedule. A surviving spouse may use joint filing status for the last year income tax returns, if he or she does not remarry during that tax year. Qualified widows and widowers (those who provide over half of the living expenses of a dependent child and do not remarry) may elect to use joint filing status for two years. The Personal Representative should also be alert to the possibility of an income tax refund being available and also should check to see if the Credit for the Elderly and Disabled can be claimed by using schedule R.

Members of the U.S. Armed Forces who die while on active duty in a combat zone are eligible to have any income tax liability abated (forgiven) for all tax years since beginning service in the combat zone. If income tax has been paid, a refund can be claimed on behalf of the estate. This income tax abatement also applies to death resultant from wounds, disease, or injury incurred in a combat zone (after June 24, 1950). Estates of members of the U.S. Armed Forces officially listed as missing in action (MIA) are entitled to the same income tax abatement. Both military and civilian employees of the United States who die as a result of a terrorist or military action outside the United States (after November 17, 1978) are also eligible for income tax abatement from the time the fatal wound or injury was incurred. Special forms available from the Department of Defense or the Department of State must accompany the estate's request for income tax abatement.

In a number of states, income tax must be paid even when there is no federal income tax due. All states impose a state income tax except for Alaska, Florida, Nevada, South Dakota, Texas, Washington, and Wyoming. State income tax is due only on dividends, interest, and capital gains in Connecticut and only on dividends and interest in New Hampshire and Tennessee. Interest on federally tax-exempt state and local government bonds issued in a state other than that of residency is subject to income tax in all states that impose income tax, except Indiana, New Mexico, and Utah. Local income taxes in those jurisdictions that impose them are due at the same time the state income taxes are due.

When there is an ongoing business or farming operation, the Personal Representative needs to make sure that any state registration and/or franchise taxes, as well as any local business license taxes required, are paid when due. Payment should be made from the business or farm operating account, and the Personal Representative should discuss payment with the probate court before taking action. Any quarterly estimated tax payments and employee withholding payments due should be dealt with in a similar manner.

Estate-Related Taxes

The estate becomes a separate entity for taxation purposes when its creator dies. The Personal Representative should apply for a federal employer identification number for the estate soon after its creation, since this number is needed when filing estate income tax returns. Income generated by the assets of the estate, such as rents received, interest, and dividends, is subject to income tax in those states that impose income tax. If the income exceeds $600, it is subject to federal income tax as well. Estate income tax is due on a calendar year basis, for each year the estate remains open.

Estate and gift taxes are taxes levied on the transfer of property, whereas inheritance taxes are taxes imposed on the receipt of property. Estate taxes are based on the total taxable estate after adjustment for taxable gifts and exemptions, where applicable, and are paid from the estate's assets prior to distribution. Inheritance taxes are based on the amount received and the relationship of the beneficiary or heir to the deceased and are paid or deducted from the share involved. Presently, 19 states impose an inheritance tax and seven states impose estate tax affecting estates of less than $600,000. Refer to the following State Taxes Summary for information on these taxes in your state.

State Taxes—Summary

| State | Income | Gift | Inheritance | Estate | Estates over $600,000 | |
					Federal Credit Estate	Generation-Skipping Transfer
Alabama	Yes	No	No	No	Yes	Yes
Alaska	No	No	No	No	Yes	No
Arizona	Yes	No	No	No	Yes	Yes
Arkansas	Yes	No	No	No	Yes	No
California	Yes	No	No	No	Yes	Yes
Colorado	Yes	No	No	No	Yes	No

State Taxes—Summary (continued)

State	Income	Gift	Inheritance	Estate	Estates over $600,000 Federal Credit Estate	Estates over $600,000 Generation-Skipping Transfer
Connecticut	(1)*	No	Yes	No	Yes	No
Delaware	Yes	Yes	Yes	No	Yes	No
District of Columbia	Yes	No	No	No	Yes	No
Florida	No	No	No	No	Yes	Yes
Georgia	Yes	No	No	No	Yes	No
Hawaii	Yes	No	No	No	Yes	Yes
Idaho	Yes	No	No	No	Yes	Yes
Illinois	Yes	No	No	No	Yes	Yes
Indiana	Yes	No	Yes	No	Yes	No
Iowa	Yes	No	Yes	No	Yes	Yes
Kansas	Yes	No	Yes	No	Yes	Yes
Kentucky	Yes	No	Yes	No	Yes	No
Louisiana	Yes	Yes	Yes	No	Yes	No
Maine	Yes	No	No	No	Yes	No
Maryland	Yes	No	Yes	No	Yes	Yes
Massachusetts	Yes	No	No	Yes	Yes	Yes
Michigan	Yes	No	Yes	No	Yes	No
Minnesota	Yes	No	No	No	Yes	No
Mississippi	Yes	No	No	(2)*	Yes	Yes
Missouri	Yes	No	No	No	Yes	No
Montana	Yes	No	Yes	No	Yes	No
Nebraska	Yes	No	Yes	No	Yes	No
Nevada	No	No	No	No	Yes	Yes
New Hampshire	(3)*	No	Yes	No	Yes	No
New Jersey	Yes	No	Yes	No	Yes	No
New Mexico	Yes	No	No	No	Yes	No
New York	Yes	Yes	No	Yes	Yes	Yes
North Carolina	Yes	Yes	Yes	No	Yes	Yes
North Dakota	Yes	No	No	No	Yes	No
Ohio	Yes	No	No	Yes	Yes	Yes
Oklahoma	Yes	No	No	Yes	Yes	No
Oregon	Yes	No	No	No	Yes	No
Pennsylvania	Yes	No	Yes	No	Yes	No
Rhode Island	Yes	No	No	(4)*	Yes	No
South Carolina	Yes	Yes	No	Yes	Yes	Yes
South Dakota	No	No	Yes	No	Yes	No
Tennessee	(3)*	Yes	Yes	No	Yes	Yes

State Taxes—Summary (continued)

State	Income	Gift	Inheritance	Estate	Estates over $600,000	
					Federal Credit Estate	Generation- Skipping Transfer
Texas	No	No	Yes	No	Yes	Yes
Utah	Yes	No	No	No	Yes	No
Vermont	Yes	No	No	No	Yes	No
Virginia	Yes	No	No	No	Yes	Yes
Washington	No	No	No	No	Yes	Yes
West Virginia	Yes	No	No	No	Yes	Yes
Wisconsin	Yes	(5)*	(5)*	No	Yes	No
Wyoming	No	No	No	No	Yes	No

*(1) On interest, dividends, and capital gains only. (2) Phased out as of October 1, 1990. (3) On interest and dividends only. (4) Phased out as of January 1, 1991. (5) Phased out as of January 1, 1992.

If an estate exceeds $600,000, a federal estate tax return (IRS Form 706) must be filed. The federal estate tax return provides a credit against federal estate tax due for state death taxes paid, and all 50 states and the District of Columbia collect this federal credit estate tax. In the 26 states that impose separate estate or inheritance taxes, any amount of the federal credit in excess of the taxes paid is "picked-up" and collected by the state as well. Currently, fewer than 2% of the estates in the United States exceed the $600,000 filing threshold. In a small percentage of these cases, property that is transferred to descendants at least two generations removed from the decedent (to grandchildren, great grandchildren) is subject to a generation-skipping transfer tax. With a $1,000,000 generation-skipping transfer maximum exemption this additional tax applies only to very large estates. Twenty-two states have followed the federal model and impose a generation-skipping transfer tax. Note that when estate-related taxes are due, payment must be made; otherwise both penalties and interest will be charged.

State Tax Information and Forms

Information, tax forms, and instructions regarding estate-related state taxes discussed in the preceding section can be obtained directly from the state departments listed below. Even if the estate will not be subject to taxation, an information return may be required. If real estate is involved, state taxes due must be paid or a certificate of no tax due obtained prior to recording the transfer of the property. Since state forms, rates, and requirements are subject to frequent change, it is important for the Personal Representative to obtain the current information and forms early in the probate process. Current filing due dates for tax forms are also shown below. Generally, tax payment is due at the same time as the tax return(s). Timely filing is important, as most states impose both late filing penalties and interest charges on tax due after the filing date. If an extension of time to file federal estate tax has been granted, a copy of the extension should be forwarded to the state as soon as it is received. In hardship situations, many states can provide special payment terms. It is advisable to contact the department well before the filing due dates to discuss special concerns and to get the correct forms needed for the size and type of estate being settled.

State Tax Information and Forms Summary

State	Address	Filing Due
Alabama	Alabama Department of Revenue Income Tax Division Montgomery, AL 36132-7410	Tax within 9 months of date of death
Alaska	Alaska Department of Revenue Estate Tax Section P.O. Box SA Juneau, AK 99811-0400	*Report within 2 months* of date of death/Tax within 15 months of date of death
Arizona	Arizona Department of Revenue Estate Tax Unit 1600 West Monroe Phoenix, AZ 85007	Tax within 9 months of date of death
Arkansas	Arkansas Department of Finance and Administration Estate Tax P.O. Box 3628 Little Rock, AR 72203-3628	Tax within 9 months of date of death
California	Controller Division of Tax Administration P.O. Box 942004 Sacramento, CA 94250-2004	Tax within 9 months of date of death
Colorado	Colorado Department of Revenue Estate Tax Section 1375 Sherman Street Denver, CO 80261	Tax within 9 months of date of death
Connecticut	Commissioner of Revenue Services Inheritance Tax Division 92 Farmington Avenue Hartford, CT 06105	Tax within 9 months of date of death
Delaware	Delaware Division of Revenue Carvel State Building 820 North French Street Wilmington, DE 19801	Tax within 9 months of date of death

State Tax Information and Forms Summary (*continued*)

State	Address	Filing Due
District of Columbia	Department of Finance and Revenue 300 Indiana Avenue, N.W. Washington, DC 20001	Tax within 10 months of date of death
Florida	Florida Department of Revenue Carlton Building Tallahassee, FL 32399-0100	*Report within 2 months* of date of death or appointment of Personal Representative/Tax within 9 months of date of death
Georgia	Georgia Department of Revenue Income Tax Division Trust and Estate Section Trinity-Washington Building Atlanta, GA 30334	Tax within 9 months of date of death
Hawaii	Hawaii Department of Taxation Estate and Tax Transfer Section P.O. Box 259 Honolulu, HI 96809-0259	Tax within 9 months of date of death
Idaho	Idaho State Tax Commission Estate Tax Audit P.O. Box 36 Boise, ID 83722	Tax within 9 months of date of death
Illinois	*Cook, Dupage, Lake and McHenry Counties:* Attorney General, 13th Floor State of Illinois Center 100 West Randolph Street Chicago, IL 60601 *All other counties:* Attorney General 500 South Second Street Springfield, IL 62706	Tax within 9 months of date of death
Indiana	Indiana Department of Revenue Inheritance Tax and Fiduciary Tax State Office Building, Room 205 100 North Senate Avenue Indianapolis, IN 46204-2253	Tax within 12 months of date of death
Iowa	Iowa Department of Revenue Hoover State Office Building Des Moines, IA 50319	Tax within 9 months of date of death
Kansas	Kansas Department of Revenue Division of Taxation Income and Inheritance Tax Bureau State Office Building Topeka, KS 66625-0001	Tax within 9 months of date of death
Kentucky	Kentucky Revenue Cabinet Frankfort, KY 40620	Tax within 18 months of date of death *Note:* 5% discount if paid within *9 months* of date of death

State Tax Information and Forms Summary (*continued*)

State	Address	Filing Due
Louisiana	Louisiana Department of Revenue and Taxation P.O. Box 201 Baton Rouge, LA 70821-0201	Tax within 9 months of date of death
Maine	Maine Bureau of Taxation Estate Tax Section State Office Building Augusta, ME 04333	Tax within 9 months of date of death
Maryland	Comptroller of the Treasury Office of the Comptroller P.O. Box 466 Annapolis, MD 21404-0466	Tax within 9 months of date of death
Massachusetts	Commonwealth of Massachusetts Department of Revenue Estate Tax Bureau P.O. Box 7023 Boston, MA 02204	Tax within 9 months of date of death
Michigan	Michigan Department of Treasury Treasury Building Lansing, MI 48922	Tax within 9 months of date of death
Minnesota	Minnesota Department of Revenue Minnesota Estate Tax St. Paul, MN 55146-1315	Tax within 9 months of date of death
Mississippi	Mississippi State Tax Commission 501 North West Street Jackson, MS 39215	*Notice within 2 months* of date of death/Tax within 9 months of date of death
Missouri	Missouri Department of Revenue Income Taxes Bureau Estate Tax Unit P.O. Box 27 Jefferson City, MO 65105	Tax within 9 months of date of death
Montana	Montana Department of Revenue Income & Miscellaneous Tax Division Inheritance Tax Mitchell Building Helena, MT 59620	Tax within 9 months of date of death
Nebraska	Nebraska Department of Revenue P.O. Box 94818 Lincoln, NE 68509-4818	Tax within 12 months of date of death
Nevada	Nevada Department of Taxation Revenue Division Capitol Complex 1340 South Curry Street Carson City, NV 89710	Tax within 9 months of date of death
New Hampshire	New Hampshire Department of Revenue Administration P.O. Box 457 Concord, NH 03302-0457	Tax within 12 months of date of death

State Tax Information and Forms Summary (*continued*)

State	Address	Filing Due
New Jersey	New Jersey Department of the Treasury Division of Taxation Transfer, Inheritance and Estate Tax Branch 50 Barrack Street, CN-249 Trenton, NJ 08646-0249	Tax within *8 months* of date of death
New Mexico	New Mexico Taxation and Revenue Department P.O. Box 630 Santa Fe, NM 87509-0630	Tax within 9 months of date of death
New York	New York Department of Taxation and Finance Central Estate Tax Audit W. A. Harriman State Campus Albany, NY 12227	Tax within 9 months of date of death *Note:* Interest on tax charged from *6 months* after date of death
North Carolina	North Carolina Department of Revenue Inheritance and Gift Tax Division P.O. Box 25000 Raleigh, NC 27640	Tax within 9 months of date of death
North Dakota	North Dakota State Tax Department State Capitol 600 E. Boulevard Avenue Bismark, ND 58505-0599	Tax within 9 months of date of death
Ohio	Ohio Department of Taxation Estate Tax Division State Office Tower P.O. Box 530 Columbus, OH 43266-0030	Tax within 9 months of date of death
Oregon	Oregon Department of Revenue Revenue Building 955 Center Street, N.E. Salem, OR 97310	Tax within 9 months of date of death
Oklahoma	Oklahoma Tax Commission McConnors Building 2501 Lincoln Boulevard Oklahoma City, OK 73194	Tax within 9 months of date of death
Pennsylvania	Pennsylvania Department of Revenue Bureau of Individual Taxes Department 280601 Harrisburg, PA 17128-0601	Tax within 9 months of date of death *Note:* 5% discount if paid within *3 months* of date of death
Rhode Island	Rhode Island Department of Administration Division of Taxation One Capitol Hill Providence, RI 02908-5800	Tax within 10 months of date of death

State Tax Information and Forms Summary (*continued*)

State	Address	Filing Due
South Carolina	South Carolina Tax Commission P.O. Box 125 Columbia, SC 29214	Tax within 9 months of date of death
South Dakota	South Dakota Department of Revenue Division of Special Taxes and Licensing Kneip Building 700 Governors Drive Pierre, SD 57501-2276	Tax within 9 months of date of death
Tennessee	Tennessee Department of Revenue Miscellaneous Tax Division Andrew Jackson State Office Building 500 Deaderick Street Nashville, TN 37242-1099	Tax within 9 months of date of death
Texas	Comptroller of Public Accounts Austin, TX 78774	Tax within 9 months of date of death
Utah	Utah State Tax Commission Auditing Division 160 East 300 South Salt Lake City, UT 84134	Tax within 9 months of date of death
Vermont	Vermont Department of Taxes Pavilion Office Building Montpelier, VT 05602	Tax within 9 months of date of death
Virginia	Virginia Department of Taxation Processing Services Division P.O. Box 6-L Richmond, VA 23282	Tax within 9 months of date of death
Washington	Washington Department of Revenue Miscellaneous Tax Division P.O. Box 448 Olympia, WA 98507-0090	Tax within 9 months of date of death
West Virginia	West Virginia Department of Tax and Revenue Estate Tax P.O. Drawer 2389 Charleston, WV 25328	Tax within 9 months of date of death
Wisconsin	Wisconsin Department of Revenue 125 South Webster Madison, WI 53702	Tax within 12 months of date of death
Wyoming	Wyoming Department of Revenue and Taxation Inheritance/Estate Tax Administrator P.O. Box 448 Cheyenne, WY 82003	Tax within 9 months of date of death

How to Get IRS Forms and Publications

You can order tax forms and publications from the IRS Forms Distribution Center for your state at the address below. Or, if you prefer, you can photocopy tax forms from reproducible copies kept at many participating public libraries. In addition, many of these libraries have reference sets of IRS publications which you can read or copy.

If you are located in:

Send to "Forms Distribution Center" for your state

Alaska, Arizona, California, Colorado, Hawaii, Idaho, Montana, Nevada, New Mexico, Oregon, Utah, Washington, Wyoming — Rancho Cordova, Ca. 95743-0001

Alabama, Arkansas, Illinois, Indiana, Iowa, Kansas, Kentucky, Louisiana, Michigan, Minnesota, Mississippi, Missouri, Nebraska, North Dakota, Ohio, Oklahoma, South Dakota, Tennessee, Texas, Wisconsin — P.O. Box 9903, Bloomington, IL 61799

Connecticut, Delaware, District of Columbia, Florida, Georgia, Maine, Maryland, Massachusetts, New Hampshire, New Jersey, New York, North Carolina, Pennsylvania, Rhode Island, South Carolina, Vermont, Virginia, West Virginia — P.O. Box 25866, Richmond, VA 23289

Foreign Addresses—Taxpayers with mailing addresses in foreign countries should send their requests for forms and publications to: Forms Distribution Center, P.O. Box 25866, Richmond, VA 23289, or Forms Distribution Center, Rancho Cordova, Ca. 95743-0001, whichever is closer.

Puerto Rico—Forms Distribution Center, P.O. Box 25866, Richmond, VA 23289

Virgin Islands—V.I. Bureau of Internal Revenue, P.O. Box 3186, St. Thomas, VI 00801

Special Note: Not all items, particularly publications, are available on January 1. All available items will be shipped immediately and remaining items will be shipped as they become available. Please DO NOT reorder.

Detach At This Line
Circle Desired Forms, Instructions and Publications   Pub 2

Order blank—We will send you 2 copies of each form and 1 copy of each set of instructions or publication you circle. Please cut the order blank on the dotted line above and **be sure to print or type your name accurately on both labels.** These labels will be used to return material to you. Enclose this order blank in your own envelope and address your envelope to the IRS address shown above for your state. To help reduce waste, please order only the forms, instructions, and publications you think you will need to prepare your return. Use the blank spaces to order items not listed. If you need more space attach a separate sheet of paper listing the additional forms and publications you may need. Be sure to allow 2 weeks to receive your order.

1040	Schedule C (1040)	2119 & Instructions	Pub. 463	Pub. 524		
Instructions for 1040 & Schedules	Schedule D (1040)	2210 & Instructions	Pub. 502	Pub. 525		
1040A	Schedule D-1 (1040)	2441 & Instructions	Pub. 504	Pub. 527		
Schedule 2 (1040A)	Schedule E (1040)	3903 & Instructions	Pub. 505	Pub. 529		
1040EZ	Schedule R (1040) & Instructions	4868	Pub. 508	Pub. 545		
1040A & 1040EZ Instructions	1040-ES (1990)	8283 & Instructions	Pub. 521	Pub. 917		
Schedules A&B (1040)	2106 & Instructions	8606	Pub. 523	Pub. 929		

Internal Revenue Service

2

Name
Number and street
City or town, State, and ZIP code

Internal Revenue Service

2

Name
Number and street
City or town, State, and ZIP code

☆U.S. GOVERNMENT PRINTING OFFICE:

Figure 6-1

Federal Tax Information and Forms

The Personal Representative must obtain tax forms and instructions for filing any federal tax returns required in the settlement of the estate. Because federal tax forms are revised frequently it is important to obtain the correct forms and instructions for the reporting period covered by the tax return(s) to be filed. The Personal Representative should request information and tax forms early in the probate process, so that the extent of federal tax liability can be established soon enough to allow timely distribution of the balance of the estate. Forms, instructions, and publications can be ordered by mail from the Internal Revenue Service as set out in Figure 6-1 or by telephone by calling (800) 424-3676. Allow two to four weeks for delivery. When ordering forms it is advisable to order at least two copies of each. Request the instructions also, as they often are separate from the forms. In the case of income tax forms, request any additional schedules that may be required. Review of the prior year's forms filed by the deceased will help you determine what is needed. The following table lists specific publications and forms you may need.

Federal Tax Publications and Forms

Most Estates

Publication 559	Tax Information for Survivors, Executors, and Administrators
Form SS-4	Application for Employer Identification Number
Form 1040	U.S. Individual Income Tax Return Instructions for Form 1040 *Note:* Schedule R—Credit for the Elderly or the Disabled may be appropriate
	or
Form 1040A	U.S. Individual Tax Return
Form 1040EZ	U.S. Individual Tax Return Instructions for Forms 1040A, 1040EZ
Form 1310	Statement of Person Claiming Refund Due a Deceased Tax Payer
Form 4810	Request for Prompt Assessment Under Internal Revenue Code Section 6501(d)
Form 56	Notice Concerning Fiduciary Relationship

Estates with Income over $600

Form 1041	U.S. Fiduciary Income Tax Return Instructions for Form 1041 and Schedules A, B, D, G, J, and K-1

Estates over $600,000

Publication 448	Federal Estate and Gift Taxes

Federal Tax Publications and Forms (*continued*)

Estates over $600,000

Form 706	United States Estate (and Generation-Skipping Transfer) Tax Return
	Instructions for Form 706
Form 4768	Application for Extension of Time to File U.S. Estate (and Generation-Skipping Transfer) Tax Return and/or Pay Estate (and Generation-Skipping Transfer) Taxes

The Personal Representative of a small estate may need only publication 559 and form 1040EZ and instructions, while a large estate may require a 1040 form and all the others as well. Sample federal tax returns for an estate with assets in excess of $600,000 and annual income in excess of $600 are included in Chapter 8.

CHAPTER 7

Distribution and Closing

When all the assets of the estate have been collected, all debts reviewed and paid, and taxes due determined and funds reserved for payment, the remaining balance can be distributed to the heirs or beneficiaries. Clearly, the size and complexity of the estate will affect the amount of time required to determine the estate's balance available for distribution. However, for many estates this can be accomplished soon after the period for filing creditor claims has expired.

Distribution with a Will

If there is a will, the distribution of all estate assets is specified and the Personal Representative simply follows the directions contained therein. Gifts made by a will are called bequests. Bequests identify the beneficiary and specify the property involved. In some cases a specific amount of time is set out in the will that must elapse before bequests can be distributed. Instructions contained in a valid will must be followed by the Personal Representative. Some wills specify the estate property to be distributed and contain a residual bequest naming the recipient of any balance remaining after the specific bequests have been made. Obviously, residual bequests are distributed last.

Bequests may consist of individual items of property, monetary amounts, or shares. If the beneficiaries agree, monetary amounts or shares may be distributed *in kind*. For example, a beneficiary may choose to receive a number of shares of stocks equal to a monetary amount specified in the will, rather than having the stock sold to fund the cash bequest. In cases of in-kind distribution, the asset's value at the date of death is used.

In a similar fashion those who have shares in an estate under a will may elect to receive real or personal property as all or a portion of their share rather than having everything sold and the proceeds divided. The Personal Representative should discuss this type of distribution with the beneficiaries and clear plans for in-kind distribution with the probate court before transferring assets.

Bequests received under a will are not taxable as income to those who receive them. Any taxes required are either paid by the estate or deducted from the share to be received (in the case of inheritance taxes) before distribution. If there are any questions regarding interpretation of the distribution instructions contained in the will, the probate court will rule as to how to fulfill those bequests. Whenever making a distribution from the estate, the Personal Representative should obtain a receipt from the beneficiary.

Distribution without a Will

Every state has its own laws of succession that govern the distribution of estates of its residents who die without a valid will (intestate). If the decedent left a will that is successfully challenged, then there is no valid will, and the estate is to be distributed in accord with the state's laws of intestate succession. Since the laws of intestate succession cover every possible combination of heirs that might survive the decedent, they are necessarily rather complex. However, all states grant a surviving spouse a portion of the intestate estate, with the amount affected by the number and relationship of other surviving relatives. To simplify the presentation that follows, the distributive shares when there is a surviving spouse are addressed separately from the distributive shares available when there is no surviving spouse. In all cases where there is no valid will, the distribution of the estate must be in accord with the state law. The following summary material regarding distribution of an intestate estate is given to provide general guidance and understanding; always contact the local probate court for the exact distribution that is required.

SURVIVING SPOUSE—INTESTATE SHARE SUMMARY

The three intestate succession summary tables that follow show the share that a surviving spouse would receive in community-property states, in states that grant life estate interests, and in the remaining states. In all cases this share varies depending on the existence and number of other living potential heirs. These potential heirs are classified under five headings:

1. Children of the marriage (per stirpes).
2. Other children of the deceased spouse (per stirpes), which includes children from previous marriage(s) and illegitimate children.
3. No children but living parents of the deceased spouse.
4. No children and no living parents but brother(s) and/or sister(s) (per stirpes) of the deceased spouse.
5. No children, no living parents, and no brother(s) and/or sister(s).

In most states, in the last category (no children, no parents, and no brother(s) and/or sister(s) of the deceased spouse), the surviving spouse inherits the entire estate. However, in Arkansas, Maine, Massachusetts, Oklahoma, Rhode Island, South Carolina, Texas, Vermont, and the District of Columbia, the surviving spouse receives the entire estate only if there are also no living grandparents and no living descendants of the deceased spouse's grandparents as well.

Other special cases occur in Georgia, Mississippi, and Oklahoma, which provide for the spouse and the children to receive equal shares, meaning that the more children there are, the smaller the surviving spouse's share becomes. Arkansas requires the spouse to have been married for three years to obtain the full intestate succession share; otherwise, the share is diminished proportionally. Although not a community-property state, Oklahoma treats property gained during the marriage separately from other property. Louisiana, a community-property state, grants the surviving spouse a life estate interest in real property as long as the surviving spouse does not remarry. Tennessee grants homestead and a one-year living allowance to the surviving spouse, not to be less than one-third of the estate.

COMMUNITY-PROPERTY STATES. There are two types of property in community-property states: *community property* and *separate property*. Community property is property owned by the couple during their marriage, and each has a one-half interest in it. Separate property is property owned solely by one spouse, such as an inheritance or assets identified in a valid prenuptial agreement. These two types of property are treated differently under intestate succession in all community-property states except Wisconsin.

LIFE ESTATE. A *life estate* is an interest in, and right to use, real property for the lifetime of the estate holder. It is not ownership, but a terminable

Surviving Spouse Share in Community-Property States

State	If Deceased Had Children		If Deceased Had No Children, and There Are		
	Children of Marriage Only	Other Children of Deceased	Living Parents of Deceased	No Living Parents but Living Siblings of Deceased	No Living Parents or Siblings of Deceased
			Then the Surviving Spouse Receives		
Arizona					
Community	½	None	All	All	All
Separate	All	½	All	All	All
California					
Community	All	All	All	All	All
Separate			½	½	All
1 Child	½	½			
2 or more	⅓	⅓			
Idaho					
Community	All	All	All	All	All
Separate	$50,000 + ½	½	$50,000 + ½	All	All
Louisiana					
Community	Life estate if no remarriage		All	All	All
Separate	None	None	None	None	All
Nevada					
Community	All	All	All	All	All
Separate			½	½	All
1 Child	½	½			
2 or more	⅓	⅓			
New Mexico					
Community	All	All	All	All	All
Separate	¼	¼	All	All	All
Texas					
Community	½	½	All	All	All
Separate	⅓	⅓	½	½	All*
Washington					
Community	All	All	All	All	All
Separate	½	⅓	¾	¾	All
Wisconsin					
Community	All	½	All	All	All
Separate	All	½	All	All	All

*If no living grandparents and no living descendants of deceased spouse's grandparents; otherwise, same as previous category.

interest that ends with the death of the life estate holder. Six states and the District of Columbia grant a life estate interest in real property to the surviving spouse under intestate succession. Louisiana (listed in the table showing community-property states) also grants life estate interest if the surviving spouse does not marry again.

Surviving Spouse Share in States with Life Estate Interests

State	If Deceased Had Children		If Deceased Had No Children, and There Are		
	Children of Marriage Only	Other Children of Deceased	Living Parents of Deceased	No Living Parents but Living Siblings of Deceased	No Living Parents or Siblings of Deceased
	Then the Surviving Spouse Receives				
Arkansas					
Real property	Life estate + ⅓	Life estate + ⅓	All*	All*	All*
Personal property	⅓	⅓	All*	All*	All*
Delaware					
Real property	Life estate	Life estate	Life estate	Life estate	All
Personal property	$5,000 + ½	½	$50,000 + ½	All	All
District of Columbia					
Real property	Life estate + ⅓	Life estate	Life estate + ⅓	Life estate + ⅓	All
Personal property	⅓	⅓	½	½	All**
Indiana					
Real property	Life estate	Life estate	¾	All	All
Personal property			¾	All	All
1 Child	½	½			
2 or more	⅓	⅓			
Kentucky					
Real property	Life estate + ⅓	Life estate + ⅓	½	½	All
Personal property	½	½	½	½	All
Rhode Island					
Real property	Life estate	Life estate	Life estate + $75,000	Life estate + $75,000	All**
Personal property	½	½	$50,000 + ½	$50,000 + ½	All**
West Virginia					
Real property	⅓	Life estate	All	All	All
Personal property	⅓	⅓	All	All	All

*If married 3 years; otherwise ½.

**If no living grandparents and no living descendants of deceased spouse's grandparents; otherwise, same as previous category.

Surviving Spouse Share in All Other States

	If Deceased Had Children		If Deceased Had No Children, and There Are		
State	**Children of Marriage Only**	**Other Children of Deceased**	**Living Parents of Deceased**	**No Living Parents but Living Siblings of Deceased**	**No Living Parents or Siblings of Deceased**
			Then the Surviving Spouse Receives		
Alabama	$50,000 + ½	½	$100,000 + ½	All	All
Alaska	$50,000 + ½	½	$5,000 + ½	All	All
Colorado	$25,000 + ½	½	All	All	All
Connecticut	$100,000 + ½	½	$100,000 + ¾	All	All
Florida	$20,000 + ½	½	All	All	All
Georgia	Equal shares with children (spouse ¼ minimum)		All	All	All
Hawaii	½	½	½	All	All
Illinois	½	½	All	All	All
Iowa	All	½ (Not less than $50,000)	All	All	All
Kansas	½	½	All	All	All
Maine	$50,000 + ½	½	$50,000 + ½	$50,000 + ½	All*
Maryland	$15,000 + ½	$15,000 + ½	$15,000 + ½	All	All
Minor child	½	½			
Massachusetts	½	½	$200,000 + ½	$200,000 + ½	All
Michigan	$60,000 + ½	½	$60,000 + ½	All	All
Minnesota	$70,000 + ½	½	All	All	All
Mississippi	Equal shares with children		All	All	All
Missouri	$20,000 + ½	½	$20,000 + ½	All	All
Montana			All	All	All
1 Child	All	½			
2 or more	All	⅓			

*If married 3 years; otherwise ½.

**If no living grandparents and no living descendants of deceased spouse's grandparents; otherwise, same as previous category.

(continued)

Surviving Spouse Share in All Other States (continued)

| State | If Deceased Had Children | | If Deceased Had No Children, and There Are | | |
	Children of Marriage Only	Other Children of Deceased	Living Parents of Deceased	No Living Parents but Living Siblings of Deceased	No Living Parents or Siblings of Deceased
	Then the Surviving Spouse Receives				
Nebraska	$50,000 + ½	½	$50,000 + ½	All	All
New Hampshire	$50,000 + ½	⅓	$50,000 + ½	All	All
New Jersey	$50,000 + ½	⅓	$50,000 + ½	All	All
New York			$25,000 + ½	All	All
1 Child	$4,000 + ½	$4,000 + ½			
2 or more	$4,000 + ⅓	$4,000 + ⅓			
North Carolina			$25,000 + ½	All	All
1 Child	$15,000 + ½	$15,000 + ½			
2 or more	$15,000 + ⅓	$15,000 + ⅓			
North Dakota	$50,000 + ½	½	$50,000 + ½	All	All
Ohio			All	All	All
1 Child	$30,000 + ½	$10,000 + ½			
2 or more	$10,000 + ⅓	$10,000 + ⅓			
Oklahoma			All	All	All
Marriage property	½	½			
Balance	½	Equal shares with children			
Oregon	½	½	All	All	All
Pennsylvania	$30,000 + ½	½	$30,000 + ½	All	All
South Carolina	½	½	All	All	All
South Dakota			$100,000 + ½	$100,000 + ½	All
1 Child	½	½			
2 or more	⅓	⅓			
Tennessee	Homestead + 1 year living allowance (⅓ minimum)		All	All	All
Utah	$50,000 + ½	½	$100,000 + ½	All	All

*If no living grandparents and no living descendants of deceased spouse's grandparents; otherwise, same as previous category.

Surviving Spouse Share in All Other States (continued)

State	If Deceased Had Children		If Deceased Had No Children, and There Are		
	Children of Marriage Only	Other Children of Deceased	Living Parents of Deceased	No Living Parents but Living Siblings of Deceased	No Living Parents or Siblings of Deceased
	Then the Surviving Spouse Receives				
Vermont Real property			$25,000 + ½	$25,000 + ½	All*
1 Child	½	½			
2 or more	⅓	⅓			
Personal property	⅓	⅓			
Virginia	All	⅓	All	All	All
Wyoming	½	½	All	All	All

*If no living grandparents and no living descendants of deceased spouse's grandparents; otherwise, same as previous category.

NO SURVIVING SPOUSE—INTESTATE SHARE SUMMARY

When there is no surviving spouse, the distinction between community property and separate property does not apply and a life estate is not available under intestate succession. With no surviving spouse, state laws governing intestate share distribution are considerably more uniform. If the deceased is survived by a child or children but not a spouse, the child or children receive the entire estate, in all 50 states and the District of Columbia. The children who can inherit under intestate succession are the issue or descendants of the deceased and any legally adopted children. Step-brothers and step-sisters have no claim on the estate, unless they were legally adopted. If the deceased had any children who died before he or she did, that child's issue are entitled to an equal division of the share their parent would have received. This descendant's right to a parent's share is known as *per stirpes.*

When the deceased is not survived by a spouse or any children, but one or both parents of the deceased are still living, the entire estate goes to the parents equally or to the surviving parent in all states and the District of Columbia, with the following exceptions:

- In Georgia, Mississippi, Missouri, South Carolina, and Wyoming the estate is divided in equal shares among the deceased's parent(s) and his or her brother(s) and sister(s), per stirpes.

- In Illinois the above division applies, except that if there is only one surviving parent, that parent gets two shares, calculated as if both parents were living.

- In Indiana each surviving parent gets one-fourth of the estate, with the rest being divided equally between the deceased's brother(s) and sister(s), per stirpes. If no brothers or sisters or their issue survive the deceased, the entire estate goes to the parent(s).

- In Louisiana, any surviving brothers or sisters of the deceased share equally, per stirpes. If no brothers or sisters or their issue survive the deceased, the entire estate goes to the parent(s).

- In Texas, if there are two surviving parents, they inherit the entire estate. If there is only one surviving parent, he or she gets one-half of the estate, with the balance equally divided between the deceased's brothers and sisters, per stirpes. If there are no brothers or sisters or their issue, the entire estate goes to the surviving parent.

In all states and the District of Columbia, except for Maine, if there is no surviving spouse, no issue, and no surviving parents, the entire estate is divided in equal shares among the deceased's brothers and sisters, per stirpes. In Maine, one-half of the estate goes to each of the deceased's grandparents or their issue on a per capita basis.

As the foregoing makes obvious, when there is no surviving spouse and no issue, the distribution becomes further removed and more complex. If no spouse, no issue of the deceased, no parents, and no brothers or sisters or their issue survive the deceased, the estate goes to the deceased's grandparents equally or to their issue, per stirpes, everywhere in the United States, with the following exceptions:

- In Maine and New York the shares to the deceased's grandparents' issue are divided on a per capita basis (among the survivors only).

- In Mississippi and Missouri the estate is divided equally among the deceased's grandparents and uncles and aunts, per stirpes.

The final level of intestate distribution covered is the case in which there is no surviving spouse, no issue, no surviving parent, no surviving brother or sister or their issue, and no surviving issue of the deceased's grandparents. In this case the estate is divided into equal shares for the issue of the deceased's great grandparents, per stirpes, in all states except Alabama and Iowa and in the District of Columbia. In Alabama and Iowa the estate would go to the deceased's spouse's next of kin. If, at this final level of intestate succession distribution, there are no known inheritors, the estate will be *escheated,* that is, claimed by the state.

The state laws of intestate succession establish the shares that each heir may receive. The Personal Representative must simply distribute the estate in accord with the distribution schedule supplied by the probate court. If the heirs agree, in-kind distribution may be made, subject to the court's approval, as discussed earlier under Distribution with a Will.

Transferring Assets

After the balance of the estate available for distribution has been identified and its recipients defined by the will or intestate succession, the Personal Representative may distribute the estate. If the estate is being settled under supervised administration, approval must be obtained from the court before actual distribution. If all assets of the estate have been converted to cash that has been placed in the estate checking account, the distribution consists of writing checks for the appropriate shares. If specific property is to be distributed or in-kind distribution has been agreed to by both the recipients and the court, the transfer of ownership is effected by recording new deeds, titles, and account ownership documents or issuing new certificates or bonds. With the exception of mortgages with the lender's approval, all liens and encumbrances on the property must be paid before transfer. If these liabilities have been deferred, they must be paid before the assets can be distributed. In many cases a certificate of no tax due or evidence of payment of taxes will be required before the deed, title, or ownership transfer can be made. In states that require certificates of no tax due, these certificates can be obtained through the department of taxation listed in the previous chapter. A canceled check drawn on the estate checking account may be used as evidence of payment of tax. The Personal Representative should release the assets to be transferred to the beneficiary or heir and record the change in ownership records as if a sale had been made. Deed and title recordation fees are the responsibility of the new owner, unless the will or court directs otherwise. Whenever making a distribution of any of the estate's assets to a beneficiary or heir, be sure to obtain a signed receipt.

Since the Personal Representative is responsible for seeing that all estate-related taxes are paid, it is generally preferable to pay such taxes before making final distribution. This may mean that tax returns are filed before the due date, but such a course can speed the settlement and closing of the estate.

Dividing Personal Property

If the will of the decedent contains a bequest such as "I give my household goods to my three children in equal shares," the Personal Representative is faced with the task of making the equal distribution. One way to do this is to sell the property at fair market value and divide the net proceeds equally among the beneficiaries. Property such as automobiles and other large items is usually disposed of in this manner. This method is simple and may, if the beneficiaries are unable to agree, be the only option available.

If the family is in agreement the *take one* method may be used to divide property. In this situation each beneficiary, usually in the order of age, is allowed to select one item of personal property in rotation. Each beneficiary continues to choose an item in turn until the property is totally divided. If an estate contains one or two extremely valuable items, this method can present problems. The last beneficiary to choose may feel unfairly treated because he or she will be prevented from acquiring an item of significant value. If this situation exists, the beneficiaries may agree to some form of compensation among themselves or may simply withdraw particular items and deal with them individually. The beneficiaries may agree to sell the one or two items that have significant value separately and divide the proceeds. Arrangements of this type must be agreed to by the beneficiaries in advance and should be noted in some formal manner so that no misunderstandings arise later.

Closing the Estate

After distribution to heirs or beneficiaries, the final step is the submission of a final accounting of the estate's transactions to the local probate court. The specific forms or format required will be provided by the probate court. This final account will list all the assets of the estate at either their appraised or actual sale values, any income received by the estate, expenses related to that income, the debts of the estate (with receipts to prove payment), the taxes paid (or certification that no taxes were due), and the distribution of the balance to the beneficiaries or heirs, again with receipts. The final account will be affirmed to present a true and correct accounting by the Personal Representative. One of the detachable Estate Summary Worksheets can be used to organize the information needed for the final report form. The probate court will review the account and upon its verification discharge the Personal Representative from his or her duties. At this point the probate process is completed and the estate is formally closed. The Personal Representative should retain all records regarding administration of the estate for at least three years. If the estate had to pay state estate-related taxes and there is a surviving spouse, the tax records should be kept for 10 years because a partial credit may be available to the estate of that spouse.

CHAPTER 8

Settlement Sample

This chapter illustrates the settlement of the estate of James Robert Kent, whose will and self-proving certificate were shown in Chapter 2. James Robert Kent's will named his eldest son, Robert Lee Kent, as Executor. The steps Robert followed in settling his father's estate are discussed and the Sample Forms section at the end of the chapter shows the forms he used in the process. The settlement shares and methods in this case would have been the same had James Robert Kent died intestate, but one of his sons would have had to petition the probate court for appointment as the Personal Representative.

This fictional example is intended to provide a general "walk through" of the process involved in settling an estate. When you find yourself in a position like that of Robert Lee Kent, remember to select the information pertinent to the estate that you are settling from the various State Summaries presented in earlier chapters and recognize that the local probate court will have the specific information you will need.

The Estate of James Robert Kent

James Robert Kent retired from his production management position at the Martin Marietta plant in Gainesville, Florida, at the end of 1987 and was retained under a consultant contract at the rate of $1,500 per month. His wife, Lillian Lee, had died the previous year. She had left her family silver and jewelry to their sons, Robert Lee Kent and James Byrd Kent, and he had received her share of their real estate and certificates of deposit, as well as her AT&T and Detroit Edison Company stock.

The senior Mr. Kent had arranged for 10 percent withholding on his interest and dividend income, taking the balance of interest income on a monthly basis, and had authorized automatic dividend reinvestment of the balance of his stock dividends. With his Social Security being paid at the top rate and both his residence in Gainesville and the Gulf side retreat at Cedar Key fully paid for, James R. Kent enjoyed a comfortable standard of living in his semi-retirement. He had estimated his potential estate's value when he made his new will after his wife died and felt that it would be below the $600,000 federal estate taxation threshold. He directed that his estate be equally divided between his two sons, and since the younger, James Byrd Kent, lived in Atlanta, Georgia, he named the elder, Robert Lee Kent, who was also a Florida resident, as his Executor.

Their father had seemed to be in excellent health and spirits when Robert and James and their families had visited him after Christmas. The children were fascinated with their grandfather's newly acquired big-screen television, and they all watched the bowl games together. Robert was shocked when he got the call that Monday afternoon in February telling him that his father had had a severe heart attack at the plant. His father was gone less than 10 hours after Robert drove up to the hospital from Tampa. Robert was familiar with his father's affairs and made all the necessary arrangements.

After the funeral Robert and James discussed the general distribution of the estate and decided to wait until January 5, 1990, to transfer ownership of assets, after all expenses had been identified. They took turns selecting small personal items and decided to have the real estate and major personal property appraised to provide a basis for equal distribution.

After getting several copies of his father's death certificate from the hospital and removing his father's self-proved will from their joint safety deposit box, Robert went to the Alachua County Circuit Court to file the will and open the estate. Since the estate contained income-producing property, he filed an Application For Employer Identification Number (IRS Form SS-4) for estate income tax identification purposes, after being confirmed as Executor. That weekend he made an inventory list of all the personal property at both houses and also listed the items he and his brother had removed. Working with the list and his father's financial records, he filled out the Florida Preliminary Notice and Report form (DR-301) he had been given by the court, had it notarized, and mailed it in with the $5 filing fee. These forms are shown in the Sample Forms section at the end of this chapter.

Robert placed a legal notice for creditors of the estate in the Gainesville newspaper, and the ad ran once a week for two consecutive weeks. There was no response from creditors that Robert was not already aware of. His father's only debts were the balance for the television, his hospital bill, funeral expenses, 1988 income tax balance due, and current utility bills. Robert applied for the Veterans Administration plot benefits his father was entitled to and sent a copy of the death certificate to the insurance company and asked that an IRS Form 712 be completed for the policy. He reviewed the final hospital bill and established the portion the estate would have to pay after the health insurance company made its payment.

As soon as he received the Employer Identification Number for the estate, Robert took proof of his appointment as Executor to the bank and opened new accounts for the estate, transferring the current balances at the bank and the listing of stock accounts. Next he chose a firm to appraise the real estate and another to appraise the tangible personal property. He used the personal property tax bill to value the car. He then calculated his father's 1988 federal income tax.

With the debts identified and property values established, Robert prepared the following brief financial statement of the estate's position on April 5, 1989.

Estate of James Robert Kent—Summary, April 5, 1989

		Value on Feb. 21, 1989
Assets		
Gainesville house		$130,000
Cedar Key retreat		60,000
1987 Audi (Distributed JBK)		14,500
Piano		2,500
Personal Items		7,500
Distributed: RLK ($2,000)		
JBK ($2,000)		
Household furnishings		
Gainesville		$ 32,500
Cedar Key		7,500
Stock		
Martin Marietta	5,351 shares	$234,106
AT&T	360 shares	11,250
Florida Progress	799 shares	27,965
Detroit Edison	658 shares	11,679
Cash		
Certificates of deposit		$60,000
Savings account		750
Checking account		11,250
Life insurance (to checking account)		10,000
Total assets		$621,500

Estate of James Robert Kent—Summary, April 5, 1989 (*continued*)

	Value on Feb. 21, 1989
Liabilities	
Funeral expenses	($ 5,305)
Less burial benefits applied for	235
Hospital final bill—after health insurance	(1,348)
1988 Income tax balance due 4-15-89	(3,506)
Credit card balance—TV	(2,296)
Last utility bills	(163) paid
Total liabilities	($12,383)
Subtotal	$609,117
Expenses	
Copies, fees	($108) paid
Legal advertising	(147) paid
Appraisals	(625)
Total expenses	($880)
Income	
Interest/CDs—net after 10% withholding	$415

Estate Checking Account Summary

	Transaction	Balance
Transfer balance	$11,250	$11,250
Deposit—life insurance	10,000	21,250
Payments—copies/fees	(108)	21,142
Payments—legal advertising	(147)	20,995
Payments—utilities	(163)	20,832
Deposit—interest/CDs net	415	21,247
4-5-89 Balance		$21,247

Robert called James and reviewed the estate's value and the checking transactions carried out. They agreed that it was best to file and pay the 1988 federal income taxes without requesting an extension. Robert told James he would file the Florida intangible personal property tax when due as well, and they agreed to let the interest income accumulate without distribution until after the end of the year when the income tax liability for 1989 could be finally determined. James confirmed to Robert his desire for the house at Cedar Key, and they agreed that they would equal out their final distribution shares with proceeds from sale of the stock.

Robert filed his father's 1988 income tax return with payment the next week, as shown in the Sample Forms section. The estate checking account balance was reduced accordingly.

Estate Checking Account

		Balance
Balance—April 5, 1989		$21,247
Payment—April 10, 1989, IRS	($3,506)	$17,741

Next Robert completed and filed an Initial Notice Concerning Fiduciary Relationship (IRS Form 56) with the IRS in Atlanta, to document his position administering his father's estate and to receive all relevant correspondence at his Tampa address. (See Sample Forms section.)

Robert Kent checked the stock market quotes for August 21, 1989, and was relieved to see that all of the estate's stocks had risen in value. He had had to wait to find out their value six months after the date of his father's death to determine whether the estate would use *alternate valuation* when he filed the federal estate tax return (see table). Estates are valued as of the date of death for federal estate tax purposes unless their value is less under alternate valuation. Alternate valuation applies to marketable securities whose market value is less six months after the date of death and to other property that is sold at less than its appraised value. Since the brothers had decided to retain all of the estate property and the total market value of the stocks had not gone down, taxes on their father's estate would be based on its value when he died. While this meant that a United States Estate Tax Return (IRS Form 706) had to be filed, the estate would have had to lose over $8,068 in value (the amount by which the estate exceeded $600,000 after allowable deductions) to have avoided the $2,985 in federal credit estate taxes it owed to the state. Clearly, the brothers were better off paying the tax.

Alternate Valuation Analysis

	Feb. 21, 1989 (Date of Death)		Aug. 21, 1989 (Alternate Valuation Date)	
	Share Price	Total	Share Price	Total
Martin Marietta (5,351 shares)	$43.75	$234,106	$48.875	$261,530
AT&T (360 shares)	31.25	11,250	38.25	13,770
Florida Progress (799 shares)	35.00	27,965	37.25	29,763
Detroit Edison (658 shares)	17.75	11,679	21.75	14,311
Balance of estate assets		336,500		336,500
Total estate assets		$621,500		$655,874

Robert had paid the real estate taxes on both properties when they came due, as well as the appraisal fees and miscellaneous administration costs. He had also paid a friend who was a lawyer to review his estate inventory and distribution plans. He filed his U.S. Estate Tax Return (IRS Form 706) on November 20, 1989 (within nine months of his father's death), and included the Life Insurance Statement (IRS Form 712) he had received, as shown in the Sample Forms section, along with a certified copy of the will. At the same time he filed a copy, accompanied by a check for $2,985, with the Florida Department of Taxation. Further, he filed a Request for Prompt Assessment Under Internal Revenue Code Section 6501(d) (IRS Form 4810), along with a copy of the U.S. Estate Tax Return and a certified copy of his letters testamentary. This form (also shown in the Sample Forms section) shortened the time for final acceptance of the U.S. Estate Tax Return from the usual three years to 18 months.

All of these transactions are reflected in the table showing the changes in the estate checking account balance.

Estate Checking Account

	Transaction	Balance
Balance, April 10, 1989		$17,741
Payment—Florida intangible personal property tax	($ 280)	17,461
Payment—Appraisals	(625)	16,836
Payment—Credit card	(2,296)	14,540
Payment—Credit card interest	(14)	14,526
Payment—Hospital bill	(1,348)	13,178
Deposit—Interest CDs net	1,760	14,938
Payment—Funeral expenses net	(5,070)	9,868
Payment—Legal fee	(120)	9,748
Deposits Interest CDs net	1,380	11,128
Payment—Real estate taxes	(3,420)	7,708
Payment—Administration	(50)	7,658
Payment—Florida federal credit estate tax	(2,985)	4,673
Balance, November 20, 1989		4,673
Deposit Interest/CDs net	545	5,218
Balance, December 31, 1989		$ 5,218

Robert calculated his father's 1989 income tax and found that the estate would be due a $649 refund. He then prepared the U.S. Fiduciary Income Tax Return (IRS Form 1041) for the estate for the period between February 21, 1989, and December 31, 1989, and found that $454 would be the balance due. He reviewed this information with his brother James, and they decided to file both returns early and to sell the stock so that the final distribution of assets could be made. Samples of the U.S. Individual Income Tax Return (IRS Form 1040A) for the last (partial) year of life and the estate income tax form (IRS Form 1041) are included in the Sample Forms section.

Robert Kent called his stock broker and instructed him to sell all of the stock holdings on January 5, 1990. Fortunately, the market had risen and all the stocks, except for the Martin Marietta, sold at a higher level than was shown in the August alternate valuation analysis. The number of shares had also increased, as a result of the dividend re-investment. An outline of the sale follows:

Stock Sale Summary, January 5, 1990

Company	Share Price	Total
Martin Marietta (5,565 shares)	$45.875	$255,294
AT&T (374 shares)	44.625	16,690
Florida Progress (831 shares)	39.75	33,032
Detroit Edison (684 shares)	24.875	17,014
Total		$322,030
Less brokerage fee @ 1.75%		($5,635)
Total net to estate checking		$316,395

After depositing the proceeds of the stock sale in the estate checking account and recording other transactions that had taken place since December 31, 1989, Robert updated the Estate Checking Account Summary to arrive at a balance available for distribution to be used in preparing a new summary of the estate. The following table shows the updated status of the estate checking account.

Estate Checking Account Summary

	Transaction	Balance
Balance on December 31, 1989		$ 5,218
Payment—Estate income tax balance	(454)	4,764
Deposit—Stock sale net	316,395	321,159
Payment—Florida intangible personal property tax	(322)	320,837
Deposit—1989 1040A tax refund	649	321,486
Balance for distribution		321,486

Robert then prepared a new summary of the estate, now that all expenses had been identified and paid and actual values of all assets were available.

The following summary provides the basis for calculating the final equal distribution of estate assets between the brothers.

Estate of James Robert Kent—Summary, January 15, 1990

	Distribution Value
Assets	
Gainesville house	$130,000
Cedar Key retreat	60,000
1987 Audi (Distributed JBK)	14,500
Piano	2,500
Personal items	7,500
Distributed: RLK ($2,000)	
JBK ($2,000)	
Stock—Sold 1-5-90	—
Cash	
Certificates of deposit	$ 60,000
Savings account	784
Checking account	321,486
Cash total	$382,270
Total assets	$636,770
Liabilities	—
Total Estate	$636,770

Estate Asset Distribution

	Robert Lee Kent	James Byrd Kent
1989 Distribution		
Personal items	$2,000	$ 2,000
1987 Audi	—	14,500
1990 Distribution		
Gainesville house	$130,000	—
Gainesville furnishings	32,500	—
Piano	2,500	—
Cedar Key house	—	$60,000
Cedar Key furnishings	—	7,500
Personal items	500	3,000
Subtotal	$167,500	$ 87,000
Cash	$150,885	$231,385
Distribution total	$318,385	$318,385

RLK share	$318,385	
JBK share	318,385	
Total estate	$636,770	

After reviewing the above estate asset distribution summary with his brother and a representative of the County Circuit Court, Robert transferred title to the real estate and closed the estate bank accounts by having two certified bank checks prepared, one in the amount of $231,385 for James Byrd Kent and one in the amount of $150,885 for himself.

After obtaining a signed, notarized acknowledgment of receipt of his portion of the estate distribution from James, Robert filed the final accounting with the court and requested that the estate be closed. When he received the court order discharging him from his Executor duties, he then filed a second Notice Concerning Fiduciary Relationship (IRS Form 56) indicating that these responsibilities were completed in Part IV, box 5a. (Refer to previous IRS Form 56 in the Sample Form section.) Since the estate had not received over $600 in income in 1990, no further estate income tax reporting was required. Robert took satisfaction in the completion of the settlement process and readied the Gainesville house for rent to a college professor and his family, to start in the spring.

Sample Forms

The forms used by Robert Lee Kent in settling his father's estate are listed in the following table and shown on the following pages in the order in which they are discussed in the text of this chapter.

Forms Used in Settling the Estate of James Robert Kent

Form		
SS-4	Application for Employer Identification Number	167
	NOTE: The basic Application for Employer Identification Number (IRS Form SS-4) was revised in August of 1990. The sample shown uses the new form.	
DR-301	Preliminary Notice and Report	168
1040	U.S. Individual Income Tax Return, 1988	169
	Schedule B, Interest and Dividend Income	171
56	Notice Concerning Fiduciary Relationship	172
706	U.S. Estate Tax Return*	173
	Schedule A, Real Estate	176
	Schedule B, Stocks and Bonds	177
	Schedule C, Mortgages, Notes, and Cash	178
	Schedule D, Insurance on the Decedent's Life	179
712	Life Insurance Statement	180

Forms Used in Settling the Estate of James Robert Kent (continued)

Form		
706	Schedule F, Other Miscellaneous Property	181
	Schedule J, Funeral Expenses and Expenses Incurred in Administering Property Subject to Claims	182
	Schedule K, Debts of the Decedent, and Mortgages and Liens	183
4810	Request for Prompt Assessment Under Internal Revenue Code Section 6501(d)	184
1040A	U.S. Individual Income Tax Return, 1989	185
	Schedule 1	187
1041	U.S. Fiduciary Income Tax Return, 1989	188

*IRS Form 706 also has the following schedules that are not included in this sample: Schedule A-1, Section 2032A Valuation; Schedule E, Jointly owned Property; Schedule G, Transfers During Decedent's Life; Schedule H, Powers of Appointment; Schedule I, Annuities; Schedule L, Net Losses During Administration and Expenses Incurred in Administering Property Not Subject to Claims; Schedule M, Bequest, etc., to Surviving Spouse; Schedule N, Qualified ESOP Sales (under Section 2057); Schedule O, Charitable, Public, and Similar Gifts and Bequests; Schedule P, Credit for Foreign Death Taxes; Schedule Q, Credit for Tax on Prior Transfers; Schedule R, Generation-Skipping Transfer Tax.

Application for Employer Identification Number

(For use by employers and others. Please read the attached instructions
before completing this form.) Please type or print clearly.

EIN

OMB No. 1545-0003
Expires 7-31-91

1 Name of applicant (True legal name) (See instructions.)

Estate of James Robert Kent

2 Trade name of business, if different from name in line 1

3 Executor, trustee, "care of name"

Robert L. Kent

4a Mailing address (street address) (room, apt., or suite no.)

115 Gulf View Drive

5a Address of business. (See instructions.)

4b City, state, and ZIP code

Tampa, Florida 33601

5b City, state, and ZIP code

6 County and state where principal business is located

ESTATE: Alachua County, Florida

7 Name of principal officer, grantor, or general partner. (See instructions.) ▶

N/A

8a Type of entity (Check only one box.) (See instructions.)

☐ Individual SSN _____
☐ REMIC   ☐ Personal service corp.
☐ State/local government ☐ National guard
☐ Other nonprofit organization (specify) _____
☐ Other (specify) ▶

☒ Estate
☐ Plan administrator SSN _____
☐ Other corporation (specify) _____
☐ Federal government/military
If nonprofit organization enter GEN (if applicable) _____

☐ Trust
☐ Partnership
☐ Farmers' cooperative
☐ Church or church controlled organization

8b If a corporation, give name of foreign country (if applicable) or state in the U.S. where incorporated ▶

Foreign country

State

9 Reason for applying (Check only one box.)

☐ Started new business
☐ Hired employees
☐ Created a pension plan (specify type) ▶ _____
☐ Banking purpose (specify) ▶

☐ Changed type of organization (specify) ▶ _____
☐ Purchased going business
☐ Created a trust (specify) ▶ _____
☒ Other (specify) ▶   ESTATE

10 Date business started or acquired (Mo., day, year) (See instructions.)

February 21, 1989

11 Enter closing month of accounting year. (See instructions.)

DECEMBER

12 First date wages or annuities were paid or will be paid (Mo., day, year). **Note:** If applicant is a withholding agent, enter date income will first be paid to nonresident alien. (Mo., day, year). . . . . ▶   N/A

13 Enter highest number of employees expected in the next 12 months. **Note:** If the applicant does not expect to have any employees during the period, enter "0." . . . . ▶

Nonagricultural	Agricultural	Household
0	0	0

14 Does the applicant operate more than one place of business? . . . . ☐ Yes ☒ No

If "Yes," enter name of business. ▶

15 Principal activity or service (See instructions.) ▶   N/A

16 Is the principal business activity manufacturing? . . . . ☐ Yes ☒ No

If "Yes," principal product and raw material used ▶

17 To whom are most of the products or services sold? Please check the appropriate box.   ☐ Business (wholesale)

☐ Public (retail)   ☐ Other (specify) ▶   ☒ N/A

18a Has the applicant ever applied for an identification number for this or any other business? . . . . ☐ Yes ☒ No

Note: If "Yes," please complete lines 18b and 18c.

18b If you checked the "Yes" box in line 18a, give applicant's true name and trade name, if different than name shown on prior application.

True name ▶

Trade name ▶

18c Enter approximate date, city, and state where the application was filed and the previous employer identification number if known.

Approximate date when filed (Mo., day, year)

City and state where filed

Previous EIN

Under penalties of perjury, I declare that I have examined this application, and to the best of my knowledge and belief, it is true, correct, and complete.

Telephone number (include area code)

Name and title (Please type or print clearly.) ▶   Robert L. Kent, Executor

(813) 687-2921

Signature ▶   *Robert Lee Kent*

Date ▶ 3-15-89

Note: Do not write below this line.   For official use only.

Please leave blank ▶	Geo.	Ind.	Class	Size	Reason for applying

For Paperwork Reduction Act Notice, see attached instructions.

☆U.S. Government Printing Office 1989-262-257/80163

Form **SS-4** (Rev. 8-89)

PRELIMINARY NOTICE AND REPORT

TO: FLORIDA DEPARTMENT OF REVENUE, TALLAHASSEE, FLORIDA, 32399-0100

IN COMPLIANCE WITH THE PROVISIONS OF THE ESTATE TAX LAW OF THE STATE OF FLORIDA, CHAPTER 198, FLORIDA STATUTES, NOTICE IS HEREBY GIVEN OF THE DEATH OF

Please Print

Decedent's first name and middle initial	Decedent's last name	Decedent's social security number
James R.	Kent	013-62-1458

Residence (domicile) at time of death (County, State)	Florida counties in which decedent owned real estate	Date of death
Alachua County, Florida	Alachua, Levy	2-21-89

Name, Title, and address of personal representative, or person in possession of decedent's property

Robert L. Kent, Executor, 115 Gulf View Drive, Tampa, FL 33601

Name, address, and telephone number of attorney for estate

If estate is being administered, give title and location of court and date of appointment as representative

Alachua County Circuit Court, Gainesville, FL 32601   3-15-89

Send the Non-Taxable Certificate to the following address:

115 Gulf View Drive, Tampa, Florida 33601

Is This Estate subject to Federal Estate Tax Return? _____ Yes

The decedent left an Estate which consisted of (X) only Florida property, ( ) property situated both within and outside the State of Florida. The property is described below. The amount set opposite each being the estimated value thereof.

Real Estate in Florida (Give legal description of all real property in which decedent owned an interest.)

17 Crest Hill Drive, Gainesville, FL 32601
Tax # 408-13-17
175 Shell Lane, Cedar Key, FL 32626
Tax # 105-0045

(Continue on separate schedule if necessary)

	$ 175,000.00
Tangible personal property in Florida	$ 65,000.00
All Other Property Wherever Situate:	
Real Estate not in Florida	-0-
Stock, bonds, Mortgages, notes, and cash	$ 357,000.00
Insurance on decedent's life and Annuities	$ 10,000.00
All other property including, but not limited to, jointly owned property (other than real estate) and Powers of Appointment	-0-
Transfers during decedent's life	-0-
TOTAL	$ 607,000.00

FOR OFFICE USE ONLY

I, _____ Robert Lee Kent _____ hereby acknowledge
(must be signed by person qualifying under F.S. 198.01 (2))
under oath that I have read the foregoing report and that the statements therein contained are true
and that the same correctly disclose all of the assets of the decedent named therein wherever located
to the best of my knowledge and belief.

3-20-89   *Robert Lee Kent*   Executor
(Date)   (Signature of personal representative or person authorized under F.S. 198.01 (2))   (Title)

State of County of

Sworn to and subscribed before me this the _____ 20th _____ day of _____ March _____ 19 89 _____ in
the State and County aforesaid.

Austin L. Healey
Notary Public - XXXXXX

IMPORTANT NOTICE	**WARNING!** FAILURE TO COMPLETE ALL BLANK SPACES IN THE ABOVE FORM WILL RESULT IN DELAYING THE ISSUANCE OF THE PROPER CERTIFICATE. IF NONE SHOW "NONE," FIVE DOLLARS ($5.00) FEE REQUIRED FOR THE ISSUANCE OF A NONTAXABLE CERTIFICATE.

DECEASED

Department of the Treasury—Internal Revenue Service
U.S. Individual Income Tax Return **1988** (O)

For the year Jan.–Dec. 31, 1988, or other tax year beginning _____ , 1988, ending _____ , 19 ___ | OMB No. 1545-0074

Label

Use IRS label.
Otherwise,
please print or
type.

Your first name and initial (if joint return, also give spouse's name and initial) | Last name
James R. Kent   deceased 2-21-89

Your social security number
013 : 62 : 1458

Present home address (number, street, and apt. no. or rural route). (If a P.O. Box, see page 6 of Instructions.)
17 Crest Hill Drive

Spouse's social security number
: :

City, town or post office, state, and ZIP code
Gainesville, Florida 32601

For Privacy Act and Paperwork
Reduction Act Notice, see Instructions.

Presidential Election Campaign ▶
Do you want $1 to go to this fund? .... Yes ☐ X No ☐
If joint return, does your spouse want $1 to go to this fund? .... Yes ☐ No ☐

Note: Checking "Yes" will
not change your tax or
reduce your refund.

Filing Status

Check only
one box.

1 ☒ Single
2 ☐ Married filing joint return (even if only one had income)
3 ☐ Married filing separate return. Enter spouse's social security no. above and full name here. _____
4 ☐ Head of household (with qualifying person). (See page 7 of Instructions.) If the qualifying person is your child but not your dependent, enter child's name here. _____
5 ☐ Qualifying widow(er) with dependent child (year spouse died ▶ 19 ___). (See page 7 of Instructions.)

Exemptions

(See
Instructions
on page 8.)

6a ☒ Yourself If someone (such as your parent) can claim you as a dependent, do not check box 6a.
But be sure to check the box on line 33b on page 2. . . . .
b ☐ Spouse . . . .

No. of boxes
checked on 6a
and 6b | 1

c Dependents:

(1) Name (first, initial, and last name)	(2) Check if under age 5	(3) If age 5 or older, dependent's social security number	(4) Relationship	(5) No. of months lived in your home in 1988
	:			
	:			
	:			
	:			
	:			
	:			

No. of your
children on 6c
who:
● lived with you
● didn't live with
you due to divorce
or separation

No. of other
dependents listed
on 6c

If more than 6
dependents, see
Instructions on
page 8.

d If your child didn't live with you but is claimed as your dependent under a pre-1985 agreement, check here ▶ ☐
e Total number of exemptions claimed . . . .

Add numbers
entered on
lines above ▶ | 1

Income

Please attach
Copy B of your
Forms W-2, W-2G,
and W-2P here.

If you do not have
a W-2, see
page 6 of
Instructions.

7	Wages, salaries, tips, etc. (attach Form(s) W-2)	7	$ 18,000	–
8a	**Taxable** interest income (also attach Schedule B if over $400)	8a	$ 4,800	
b	**Tax-exempt** interest income (see page 11). DON'T include on line 8a **8b**	0			
9	Dividend income (also attach Schedule B if over $400)	9	$ 14,850	–
10	Taxable refunds of state and local income taxes, if any, from worksheet on page 11 of Instructions . .	10	–0–	
11	Alimony received	11	–0–	
12	Business income or (loss) (attach Schedule C)	12	–0–	
13	Capital gain or (loss) (attach Schedule D)	13	–0–	
14	Capital gain distributions not reported on line 13 (see page 11) . . .	14	–0–	
15	Other gains or (losses) (attach Form 4797)	15	–0–	
16a	Total IRA distributions . . **16a**	16b Taxable amount (see page 11)	16b	–0–	
17a	Total pensions and annuities **17a**	17b Taxable amount (see page 12)	17b	–0–	
18	Rents, royalties, partnerships, estates, trusts, etc. (attach Schedule E) . .	18	–0–	
19	Farm income or (loss) (attach Schedule F)	19	–0–	
20	Unemployment compensation (insurance) (see page 13)	20	–0–	
21a	Social security benefits (see page 13) **21a**	$ 9,750	–		
b	Taxable amount, if any, from the worksheet on page 13	21b	$ 4,875	–
22	Other income (list type and amount—see page 13) _____	22	–0–	
23	Add the amounts shown in the far right column for lines 7 through 22. This is your **total income** ▶	23	$ 42,525	–

Please
attach check
or money
order here.

Adjustments to Income

(See
Instructions
on page 13.)

24	Reimbursed employee business expenses from Form 2106, line 13 . .	24	–0–		
25a	Your IRA deduction, from applicable worksheet on page 14 or 15	25a	–0–		
b	Spouse's IRA deduction, from applicable worksheet on page 14 or 15	25b	–0–		
26	Self-employed health insurance deduction, from worksheet on page 15 .	26	–0–		
27	Keogh retirement plan and self-employed SEP deduction . .	27	–0–		
28	Penalty on early withdrawal of savings	28	–0–		
29	Alimony paid (recipient's last name _____ and social security no. : :) .	29	–0–		
30	Add lines 24 through 29. These are your **total adjustments** ▶	30		–0–	

Adjusted Gross Income

31 Subtract line 30 from line 23. This is your **adjusted gross income.** If this line is less than $18,576 and a child lived with you, see "Earned Income Credit" (line 56) on page 19 of the Instructions. If you want IRS to figure your tax, see page 16 of the Instructions ▶ | 31 | $ 42,525 | – |

	32	Amount from line 31 (adjusted gross income)	32	$ 42,525	-

Tax Computation

33a Check if: ☒ **You** were 65 or older ☐ Blind; ☐ **Spouse** was 65 or older ☐ Blind.
Add the number of boxes checked and enter the total here . . . . ▶ │ **33a** │ 1

b If someone (such as your parent) can claim you as a dependent, check here . . ▶ **33b** ☐

c If you are married filing a separate return and your spouse itemizes deductions, or you are a dual-status alien, **see** page 16 and check here . . . . . ▶ **33c** ☐

34 Enter the larger of:
{ ● Your **standard deduction** (from page 17 of the Instructions), **OR**
● Your **itemized deductions** (from Schedule A, line 26).
If you itemize, attach Schedule A and check here ▶ ☐ }

			34	$ 3,750	-
35	Subtract line 34 from line 32. Enter the result here	35	$ 38,775	-
36	Multiply $1,950 by the total number of exemptions claimed on line 6e	36	$ 1,950	-
37	**Taxable income.** Subtract line 36 from line 35. Enter the result (if less than zero, enter zero)	37	$ 36,825	-

Caution: If under age 14 and you have more than $1,000 of investment income, check here ▶ ☐ and see page 17 to see if you have to use Form 8615 to figure your tax.

38	Enter tax. Check if from: ☒ Tax Table, ☐ Tax Rate Schedules, or ☐ Form 8615	38	$ 7,991	-
39	Additional taxes (see page 17). Check if from: ☐ Form 4970 ☐ Form 4972	39	-0-	
40	Add lines 38 and 39. Enter the total . . . . ▶	40	$ 7,991	-

Credits
(See Instructions on page 18.)

41	Credit for child and dependent care expenses (attach Form 2441)	41	-0-
42	Credit for the elderly or the disabled (attach Schedule R) . . .	42	-0-
43	Foreign tax credit (attach Form 1116)	43	-0-
44	General business credit. Check if from: ☐ Form 3800 or ☐ Form (specify) _____	44	-0-
45	Credit for prior year minimum tax (attach Form 8801) . . .	45	-0-

46	Add lines 41 through 45. Enter the total	46		
47	Subtract line 46 from line 40. Enter the result (if less than zero, enter zero) . . . . ▶	47	$ 7,991	-

Other Taxes
(Including Advance EIC Payments)

48	Self-employment tax (attach Schedule SE)	48	-0-
49	Alternative minimum tax (attach Form 6251)	49	-0-
50	Recapture taxes (see page 18). Check if from: ☐ Form 4255 ☐ Form 8611	50	-0-
51	Social security tax on tip income not reported to employer (attach Form 4137)	51	-0-
52	Tax on an IRA or a qualified retirement plan (attach Form 5329) . . .	52	-0-

53	Add lines 47 through 52. This is your **total tax** . . . . ▶	53	$ 7,991	-

Payments
Attach Forms W-2, W-2G, and W-2P to front.

54	Federal income tax withheld (If any is from Form(s) 1099, check ▶ ☐)	54	$ 4,485	-
55	1988 estimated tax payments and amount applied from 1987 return	55	-0-	
56	Earned income credit (see page 19)	56	-0-	
57	Amount paid with Form 4868 (extension request)	57	-0-	
58	Excess social security tax and RRTA tax withheld (see page 20)	58	-0-	
59	Credit for Federal tax on fuels (attach Form 4136)	59	-0-	
60	Regulated investment company credit (attach Form 2439) . .	60	-0-	

61	Add lines 54 through 60. These are your **total payments** . . . . ▶	61	$ 4,485	-

Refund or Amount You Owe

62	If line 61 is larger than line 53, enter amount **OVERPAID** . . . . . ▶	62	-0-
63	Amount of line 62 to be **REFUNDED TO YOU** . . . . ▶	63	-0-
64	Amount of line 62 to be applied to your 1989 estimated tax . . ▶ │ 64 │ -0- │		
65	If line 53 is larger than line 61, enter **AMOUNT YOU OWE.** Attach check or money order for full amount payable to "Internal Revenue Service." Write your social security number, daytime phone number, and "1988 Form 1040" on it	65	$ 3,506	-

Check ▶ ☐ if Form 2210 (2210F) is attached. See page 21. **Penalty: $**

Please Sign Here

Under penalties of perjury, I declare that I have examined this return and accompanying schedules and statements, and to the best of my knowledge and belief, they are true, correct, and complete. Declaration of preparer (other than taxpayer) is based on all information of which preparer has any knowledge.

▶ Your signature *Robert Lee Hart* │ Date 4-10-89 │ Your occupation Consultant

Spouse's signature (If a joint return, BOTH must sign) │ Date │ Spouse's occupation
EXECUTOR

Paid Preparer's Use Only

Preparer's signature ▶	Date	Check if self-employed ☐	Preparer's social security no.
Firm's name (or yours if self-employed) and address ▶		E.I. No.	
		ZIP code	

☆U.S. Government Printing Office: 1988-205-104 23-0916700

Name(s) as shown on Form 1040. (Do not enter name and social security number if shown on other side.)	Your social security number
James R. Kent deceased 2-21-89	013 :62 :1458

Schedule B—Interest and Dividend Income

Attachment Sequence No. **08**

Part I
Interest Income

(See Instructions on pages 10 and 26.)

If you received more than $400 in taxable interest income, you must complete Part I and Part III and list ALL interest received. You must report all interest on Form 1040, even if you are not required to complete Part I and Part III. If you received, as a nominee, interest that actually belongs to another person, or you received or paid accrued interest on securities transferred between interest payment dates, see page 27.

Interest Income		Amount	
1 Interest income from seller-financed mortgages. (See Instructions and list name of payer.) ▶	**1**	-0-	
2 Other interest income (list name of payer) ▶			
.... Gainesville National Bank, Gainesville FL		$ 4,800	-
....			
....			
....			
....	**2**		
....			
....			
....			
....			
....			
....			
3 Add the amounts on lines 1 and 2. Enter the total here and on Form 1040, line 8a. ▶	**3**	$ 4,800	-

Note: If you received a Form 1099–INT or Form 1099–OID from a brokerage firm, list the firm's name as the payer and enter the total interest shown on that form.

Part II
Dividend Income

(See Instructions on pages 11 and 27.)

If you received more than $400 in gross dividends and/or other distributions on stock, complete Part II and Part III. You must report all taxable dividends on Form 1040, even if you are not required to complete Part II and Part III. If you received, as a nominee, dividends that actually belong to another person, see page 27.

Dividend Income		Amount	
4 Dividend income (list name of payer—include on this line capital gain distributions, nontaxable distributions, etc.) ▶			
.... Martin Marietta Corporation		$12,193	-
.... AT&T		$ 579	-
.... Florida Progress Corporation		$ 1,455	-
.... Detroit Edison Company		$ 623	-
....			
....			
....	**4**		
....			
....			
....			
....			
....			

Note: If you received a Form 1099-DIV from a brokerage firm, list the firm's name as the payer and enter the total dividends shown on that form.

5 Add the amounts on line 4. Enter the total here	**5**	$14,850	-	
6 Capital gain distributions. Enter here and on line 13, Schedule D.*	**6**	-0-		
7 Nontaxable distributions. (See Schedule D Instructions for adjustment to basis.)	**7**	-0-		
8 Add the amounts on lines 6 and 7. Enter the total here	**8**	-0-		
9 Subtract line 8 from line 5. Enter the result here and on Form 1040, line 9 . . . ▶	**9**	$14,850	-	

If you received capital gain distributions but do not need Schedule D to report any other gains or losses, enter your capital gain distributions on Form 1040, line 14.

Part III
Foreign Accounts and Foreign Trusts

(See Instructions on page 27.)

If you received more than $400 of interest or dividends, OR if you had a foreign account or were a grantor of, or a transferor to, a foreign trust, you must answer both questions in Part III.

	Yes	No
10 At any time during the tax year, did you have an interest in or a signature or other authority over a financial account in a foreign country (such as a bank account, securities account, or other financial account)? (See page 27 of the Instructions for exceptions and filing requirements for Form TD F 90-22.1.)		X
If "Yes," enter the name of the foreign country ▶		
11 Were you the grantor of, or transferor to, a foreign trust which existed during the current tax year, whether or not you have any beneficial interest in it? If "Yes," you may have to file Form 3520, 3520-A, or 926 . . .		X

For Paperwork Reduction Act Notice, see Form 1040 Instructions.   ☆ U.S.G.P.O. 1988 - 205-109   **Schedule B (Form 1040) 1988**

Form **56**
(Rev. February 1989)
Department of the Treasury
Internal Revenue Service

Notice Concerning Fiduciary Relationship

(Internal Revenue Code sections 6036 and 6903)

OMB No. 1545-0013
Expires 1-31-92

Part I   Identification

Name of person for whom you are acting (as shown on the tax return)

James Robert Kent, Estate of

Identifying number

54-1048375

Address of person for whom you are acting (number and street, including apartment number)

17 Crest Hill Drive   (SS# 013-62-1458)

City, town, or post office, state, and ZIP code

Gainesville, Florida 32601

Fiduciary's name

Robert L. Kent

Fiduciary's address (number and street, including apartment number, or P.O. Box)

115 Gulf View Drive

City, town, or post office, state, and ZIP code

Tampa, Florida 33601

Telephone number (optional)

(813) 687-2921

Part II   Authority

1 Evidence of fiduciary authority (check applicable boxes):

a [X] Certified copy of will and codicils attached . . . . Date of death   2-21-89

b [ ] Certified copy of court order appointing the fiduciary attached . . . Date (see instructions) ....

c [ ] Copy of valid trust instrument and amendments attached

d [ ] Other evidence of creation of fiduciary relationship (describe) ▶ ....

Part III   Tax Notices

Send all notices and other written communications addressed to the fiduciary(ies) (listed in Part I) involving the following tax matters :

2 Type of tax (estate, gift, generation-skipping transfer, income, excise, etc.)   income, estate ....

3 Federal tax form number (706, 1040, 1041, 1120, etc.)   1040, 1040-A, 1041, 706 ....

4 Year(s) or period(s) (If estate tax, date of death)   1988/ 1989 / 2-21-89

Part IV   Revocation or Termination of Notice

Section A.—Total Revocation or Termination

5 Check this box if you are revoking or terminating all prior notices concerning fiduciary relationships on file with the Internal Revenue Service for the same tax matters and years or periods covered by this notice concerning fiduciary relationship . . . . ▶ [ ]

Evidence of termination of fiduciary authority (check applicable boxes):

a [ ] Certified copy of court order revoking fiduciary authority attached

b [ ] Copy of certificate of dissolution or termination of a business entity attached

c [ ] Other evidence of termination of fiduciary relationship (describe) ▶

Section B.—Partial Revocation

6a Check this box if you are revoking earlier notices concerning fiduciary relationships on file with the Internal Revenue Service for the same tax matters and years or periods covered by this notice concerning fiduciary relationship . . . . ▶ [ ]

b Specify to whom granted, date, and address, including ZIP code, or refer to attached copies of earlier notices and authorizations.
....

Section C.—Substitute Fiduciary

7 Check this box if a new fiduciary or fiduciaries have been or will be substituted for the revoking or terminating fiduciary(ies) and specify the name(s) and address(es), including ZIP code(s), of the new fiduciary(ies) . . . . ▶ [ ]

Part V   Court and Administrative Proceedings

Name of court (if other than a court proceeding, identify the type of proceeding and name of agency)

Date proceeding initiated

Address of court or other proceeding

Docket number of proceeding

City, town, or post office, state and ZIP code	Date	Time	a.m. p.m.	Place of other proceedings

I certify that I have the authority to execute this notice concerning fiduciary relationship on behalf of the taxpayer.

Please Sign Here

▶ _Robert Lee Kent_   Executor   4-20-89
Fiduciary's signature   (Title, if applicable)   Date

▶ _____   _____   _____
Fiduciary's signature   (Title, if applicable)   Date

For Paperwork Reduction Act and Privacy Act Notices, see back page.

Form **56** (Rev 2-89)

Form 706
(Rev. October 1988)
Department of the Treasury
Internal Revenue Service

United States Estate (and Generation-Skipping Transfer) Tax Return

Estate of a citizen or resident of the United States (see separate instructions). To be filed for decedents dying after October 22, 1986, and before January 1, 1990.
For Paperwork Reduction Act Notice, see page 1 of the instructions.

OMB No. 1545-0015
Expires 8-30-91

Part 1.—Decedent and Executor

1a Decedent's first name and middle initial (and maiden name, if any) James R.	**1b** Decedent's last name Kent	**2** Decedent's social security no. 013 : 62 : 1458

3a Domicile at time of death Gainesville, Florida	**3b** Year domicile established 1955	**4** Date of birth 12/10/22	**5** Date of death 2/21/89

6a Name of executor (see instructions) Robert L. Kent	**6b** Executor's address (number and street including apartment number or rural route; city, town, or post office; state; and ZIP code) 115 Gulf View Drive Tampa, Florida 33601
6c Executor's social security number (see instructions) 021 : 52 : 0331	

7a Name and location of court where will was probated or estate administered Alachua County Circuit Court, Gainesville, Florida 32601	**7b** Case number 89-00153

8 If decedent died testate, check here ▶ [X] and attach a certified copy of the will.   **9** If Form 4768 is attached, check here ▶ ☐

10 If Schedule R-1 is attached, check here ▶ ☐   *See page 2 for representative's authorization.*

Part 2.—Tax Computation

1	Total gross estate (from Part 5, Recapitulation, page 3, item 10)	**1**	$621,500 -
2	Total allowable deductions (from Part 5, Recapitulation, page 3, item 25)	**2**	$ 13,433 -
3	Taxable estate (subtract line 2 from line 1)	**3**	$608,067 -
4	Adjusted taxable gifts (total taxable gifts (within the meaning of section 2503) made by the decedent after December 31, 1976, other than gifts that are includible in decedent's gross estate (section 2001(b)))	**4**	-0-
5	Add lines 3 and 4	**5**	$608,067
6	Tentative tax on the amount on line 5 from Table A in the instructions	**6**	$195,785 -

Note: *If decedent died before January 1, 1988, skip lines 7a-c and enter the amount from line 6 on line 8.*

7a If line 5 exceeds $10,000,000, enter the lesser of line 5 or $21,040,000. If line 5 is $10,000,000 or less, skip lines 7a and 7b and enter zero on line 7c	**7a**		
b Subtract $10,000,000 from line 7a	**7b**		
c Enter 5% (.05) of line 7b		**7c**	-0-
8 Total tentative tax (add lines 6 and 7c)		**8**	$195,785 -
9 Total gift tax payable with respect to gifts made by the decedent after December 31, 1976. Include gift taxes paid by the decedent's spouse for split gifts (section 2513) only if the decedent was the donor of these gifts and they are includible in the decedent's gross estate (see instructions)		**9**	-0-
10 Gross estate tax (subtract line 9 from line 8)		**10**	
11 Unified credit against estate tax from Table B in the instructions	**11** $192,800 -		
12 Adjustment to unified credit. (This adjustment may not exceed $6,000. See instructions.)	**12** -0-		
13 Allowable unified credit (subtract line 12 from line 11)		**13**	$192,800 -
14 Subtract line 13 from line 10 (but do not enter less than zero)		**14**	$ 2,985 -
15 Credit for state death taxes. Do not enter more than line 14. Compute credit by using amount on line 3 less $60,000. See Table C in the instructions and **attach credit evidence** (see instructions)		**15**	$ 2,985 -
16 Subtract line 15 from line 14		**16**	-0-
17 Credit for Federal gift taxes on pre-1977 gifts (section 2012)(attach computation)	**17** -0-		
18 Credit for foreign death taxes (from Schedule(s) P). (Attach Form(s) 706CE)	**18** -0-		
19 Credit for tax on prior transfers (from Schedule Q)	**19** -0-		
20 Total (add lines 17, 18, and 19)		**20**	-0-
21 Net estate tax (subtract line 20 from line 16)		**21**	-0-
22 Generation-skipping transfer taxes (from Schedule R, Part 2, line 12)		**22**	-0-
23 Section 4980A increased estate tax (attach Schedule S (Form 706)) (see instructions)		**23**	-0-
24 Total transfer taxes (add lines 21, 22, and 23)		**24**	-0-
25 Prior payments. Explain in an attached statement	**25** -0-		
26 United States Treasury bonds redeemed in payment of estate tax	**26** -0-		
27 Total (add lines 25 and 26)		**27**	-0-
28 Balance due (subtract line 27 from line 24)		**28**	-0-

Under penalties of perjury, I declare that I have examined this return, including accompanying schedules and statements, and to the best of my knowledge and belief, it is true, correct, and complete. Declaration of preparer other than the executor is based on all information of which preparer has any knowledge.

Robert Lee Kent   11-20-89
Signature(s) of executor(s)   Date

_____

_____
Signature of preparer other than executor   Address (and ZIP code)   Date

173

Estate of: James R. Kent

Part 3.—Elections by the Executor

Please check the "Yes" or "No" box for each question.	Yes	No
1 Do you elect alternate valuation?		X
2 Do you elect special use valuation? . . . . If "Yes," you must complete and attach Schedule A–1		X
3 Do you elect to pay the taxes in installments as described in section 6166? . . . . If "Yes," you must attach the additional information described in the instructions.		X
4 Do you elect to postpone the part of the taxes attributable to a reversionary or remainder interest as described in section 6163?	X	
5 Do you elect to have part or all of the estate tax liability assumed by an Employee Stock Ownership Plan (ESOP) as described in section 2210?		X
If "Yes," enter the amount of tax assumed by the ESOP here ▶ $ _____ and attach the supplemental statements described in the instructions.		

Part 4.—General Information Note: *Please attach the necessary supplemental documents.* **You must attach the death certificate.**

Authorization to receive confidential tax information under Regulations section 601.502(c)(3)(ii), to act as the estate's representative before the Internal Revenue Service, and to make written or oral presentations on behalf of the estate if return prepared by an attorney, accountant, or enrolled agent for the executor:

Name of representative (print or type)	State	Address (number and street, city, state, and ZIP code)

I declare that I am the attorney/accountant/enrolled agent (strike out the words that do not apply) for the executor and prepared this return for the executor. I am not under suspension or disbarment from practice before the Internal Revenue Service and am qualified to practice in the state shown above.

Signature	CAF Number	Date	Telephone Number

1 Death certificate number and issuing authority (attach a copy of the death certificate to this return).

0-0089216   Gainesville Community Hospital, Gainesville, Florida 32601

2 Decedent's business or occupation. If retired, check here ▶ ☒ and state decedent's former business or occupation. CONSULTANT

3 Marital status of the decedent at time of death:

☐ Married

☒ Widow or widower—Name, SSN and date of death of deceased spouse ▶ Lillian Lee Byrd Kent,
SSN: 017-03-6091, 11/11/86

☐ Single

☐ Legally separated

☐ Divorced—Date divorce decree became final ▶

4a Surviving spouse's name	4b Social security number	4c Amount received (see instructions)

5 Individuals (other than the surviving spouse), trusts, or other estates who receive benefits from the estate (do not include charitable beneficiaries shown in Schedule O) (see instructions). For Privacy Act Notice (applicable to individual beneficiaries only), see the Instructions for Form 1040.

Name of individual, trust or estate receiving $5,000 or more	Identifying number	Relationship to decedent	Amount (see instructions)
Robert Lee Kent	021-52-0331	Son	$302,541.00
James Byrd Kent	023-42-9720	Son	$302,541.00
All unascertainable beneficiaries and those who receive less than $5,000 . . . . ▶			-0-
Total			$605,082.00

(Continued on next page)

Form 706 (Rev. 10-88)

Part 4.—General Information (continued)   James R. Kent

Please check the "Yes" or "No" box for each question.

		Yes	No
6	Does the gross estate contain any section 2044 property (see instructions)?		X
7a	Have Federal gift tax returns ever been filed?		X
	If "Yes," please attach copies of the returns, if available, and furnish the following information:		

7b Period(s) covered	7c Internal Revenue office(s) where filed		

If you answer "Yes" to any of questions 8–16, you must attach additional information as described in the instructions.

		Yes	No
8a	Was there any insurance on the decedent's life that is not included on the return as part of the gross estate?		X
b	Did the decedent own any insurance on the life of another that is not included in the gross estate?		X
9	Did the decedent at the time of death own any property as a joint tenant with right of survivorship in which (1) one or more of the other joint tenants was someone other than the decedent's spouse, and (2) less than the full value of the property is included on the return as part of the gross estate? If "Yes," you must complete and attach Schedule E.		X
10	Did the decedent, at the time of death, own any interest in a partnership or unincorporated business or any stock in an inactive or closely held corporation?		X
11a	Did the decedent make any transfer described in section 2035, 2036, 2037 or 2038 (see the instructions for Schedule G)? If "Yes," you must complete and attach Schedule G		X
b	If "Yes," was it a valuation freeze subject to section 2036(c)?		
12	Were there in existence at the time of the decedent's death:		
a	Any trusts created by the decedent during his or her lifetime?		X
b	Any trusts not created by the decedent under which the decedent possessed any power, beneficial interest, or trusteeship?		X
13	Did the decedent ever possess, exercise, or release any general power of appointment? If "Yes," you must complete and attach Schedule H.		X
14	Was the marital deduction computed under the transitional rule of Public Law 97-34, section 403(e)(3) (Economic Recovery Tax Act of 1981)?		X
	If "Yes," attach a separate computation of the marital deduction, enter the amount on item 18 of the Recapitulation, and note on item 18 "computation attached."		
15	Was the decedent, immediately before death, receiving an annuity described in the "General" paragraph of the instructions for Schedule I? If "Yes," you must complete and attach Schedule I.		X
16	Did the decedent have a total "excess retirement accumulation" (as defined in section 4980A(d)) in qualified employer plan(s) and individual retirement plan(s)? If "Yes," you must attach Schedule S (Form 706) (see instructions)		X

Part 5.—Recapitulation

Item number	Gross estate	Alternate value	Value at date of death	
1	Schedule A—Real Estate		$ 190,000	–
2	Schedule B—Stocks and Bonds		$ 285,000	–
3	Schedule C—Mortgages, Notes, and Cash		$ 72,000	–
4	Schedule D—Insurance on the Decedent's Life (attach Form(s) 712)		$ 10,000	–
5	Schedule E—Jointly Owned Property (attach Form(s) 712 for life insurance)		-0-	
6	Schedule F—Other Miscellaneous Property (attach Form(s) 712 for life insurance) . .		$ 64,500	–
7	Schedule G—Transfers During Decedent's Life (attach Form(s) 712 for life insurance) .		-0-	
8	Schedule H—Powers of Appointment.		-0-	
9	Schedule I—Annuities		-0-	
10	Total gross estate (add items 1 through 9). Enter here and on line 1 of the Tax Computation.		$ 621,500	–

Item number	Deductions	Amount	
11	Schedule J—Funeral Expenses and Expenses Incurred in Administering Property Subject to Claims	$ 6,120	–
12	Schedule K—Debts of the Decedent	$ 7,313	–
13	Schedule K—Mortgages and Liens	-0-	
14	Total of items 11 through 13	$ 13,433	–
15	Allowable amount of deductions from item 14 (see the instructions for item 15 of the Recapitulation) . . .	$ 13,433	–
16	Schedule L—Net Losses During Administration	-0-	
17	Schedule L—Expenses Incurred in Administering Property Not Subject to Claims	-0-	
18	Schedule M—Bequests, etc., to Surviving Spouse	-0-	
19	Schedule O—Charitable, Public, and Similar Gifts and Bequests	-0-	
20	Total of items 15 through 19—If you did not complete Schedule N, skip lines 21-24 and enter the line 20 amount on line 25 .	$ 13,433	–
21	Intermediate taxable estate (subtract item 20 from item 10)		
22	Maximum ESOP deduction (from Table D in the Instructions)		
23	Enter the amount from Schedule N, line 8.		
24	Allowable ESOP deduction—enter the lesser of item 22 or 23		
25	Total allowable deductions (add items 20 and 24). Enter here and on line 2 of the Tax Computation	$ 13,433	–

Page 3

175

Estate of: James R. Kent

SCHEDULE A—Real Estate

(For jointly owned property that must be disclosed on Schedule E, see the Instructions for Schedule E.)

(Real estate that is part of a sole proprietorship should be shown on Schedule F. Real estate that is included in the gross estate under section 2035, 2036, 2037, or 2038 should be shown on Schedule G. Real estate that is included in the gross estate under section 2041 should be shown on Schedule H.)

(If you elect section 2032A valuation, you must complete Schedule A and Schedule A-1.)

Item number	Description	Alternate valuation date	Alternate value	Value at date of death
1	17 Crest Hill Drive Gainesville, Florida 32601 TAX # 408 - 1317 (Appraisal attached)			$130,000.00
2.	175 Shell Lane Cedar Key, Florida 32626 TAX # 105-0045 (Appraisal attached)			$ 60,000.00
	Total from continuation schedule(s) (or additional sheet(s)) attached to this schedule			-0-
	TOTAL. (Also enter on Part 5, Recapitulation, page 3, at item 1.)			$190,000.00

(If more space is needed, attach the continuation schedule from the end of this package or additional sheets of the same size.)

Schedule A—Page 4

Estate of: James R. Kent

SCHEDULE B—Stocks and Bonds

(For jointly owned property that must be disclosed on Schedule E, see the Instructions for Schedule E.)

Item number	Description including face amount of bonds or number of shares and par value where needed for identification. Give CUSIP number if available.	Unit value	Alternate valuation date	Alternate value	Value at date of death
1	5,351 Shares Martin Marietta Corporation common stock (CUSIP NO: 876543219	$43.75			$234,106.00
2.	360 Shares AT&T Corporation common stock (CUSIP NO: 912345678)	$31.25			$ 11,250.00
3.	799 Shares Florida Progress Corporation common stock (CUSIP NO: 456789123)	$35.00			$ 27,965.00
4.	658 Shares Detroit Edison Company common stock (CUSIP NO: 456342198)	$17.75			$ 11,679.00
	Total from continuation schedule(s) (or additional sheet(s)) attached to this schedule . . .				-0-
	TOTAL. (Also enter on Part 5, Recapitulation, page 3, at item 2.)				$285,000.00

(If more space is needed, attach the continuation schedule from the end of this package or additional sheets of the same size.)

(The instructions to Schedule B are in the **separate instructions**.)

Schedule B—Page 10

Estate of: James R. Kent

SCHEDULE C—Mortgages, Notes, and Cash

(For jointly owned property that must be disclosed on Schedule E, see the Instructions for Schedule E.)

Item number	Description	Alternate valuation date	Alternate value	Value at date of death
1	CHECKING ACCOUNT # 055 728 641 GAINESVILLE NATIONAL BANK 118 High Street, Gainesville, FL 32601			$11,250.00
2.	SAVINGS ACCOUNT # 857-94372 GAINESVILLE NATIONAL BANK 118 High Street, Gainesville, FL 32601			$ 750.00
3.	CERTIFICATES OF DEPOSIT - 6 GAINESVILLE NATIONAL BANK 118 High Street, Gainesville, FL 32601			$60,000.00
	Total from continuation schedule(s) (or additional sheet(s)) attached to this schedule			-0-
	TOTAL. (Also enter on Part 5, Recapitulation, page 3, at item 3.)			$72,000.00

(If more space is needed, attach the continuation schedule from the end of this package or additional sheets of the same size.)

Schedule C—Page 11

Estate of: Janes R. Kent

SCHEDULE D—Insurance on the Decedent's Life
You must attach a Form 712 for each policy.

Item number	Description	Alternate valuation date	Alternate value	Value at date of death
1	Sunshine State Mutual Life Insurance Company - paid up J-306-14827-A-11953			$10,000.00
	Total from continuation schedule(s) (or additional sheet(s)) attached to this schedule . . .			-0-
	TOTAL. (Also enter on Part 5, Recapitulation, page 3, at item 4.)			$10,000.00

(If more space is needed, attach the continuation schedule from the end of this package or additional sheets of the same size.)

Schedule D—Page 13

Form **712**
(Rev. January 1989)
Department of the Treasury
Internal Revenue Service

Life Insurance Statement

OMB No. 1545-0022

Expires 2-28-91

Part I   Decedent—Insured (To Be Filed With United States Estate Tax Return, Form 706)

1 Decedent's first name and middle initial	2 Decedent's last name	3 Decedent's social security number (if known)	4 Date of death
James R.	Kent	013-62-1458	2-21-89

5 Name and address of insurance company   Sunshine State Mutual Life Insurance Company
1218 Front Street, Tallahassee, FL   33323

6 Kind of policy	7 Policy number
Basic Life Insurance	J-306-14827-A-11953

8 Owner's name. If decedent is not owner, please attach copy of application.	9 Date issued	10 Assignor's name. Please attach copy of assignment.	11 Date assigned
James R. Kent	2-15-46	DNA	DNA

12 Value of the policy at the time of assignment	13 Amount of premium (see instructions)	14 Name of beneficiaries
DNA	Paid up in full	Estate of James R. Kent

15 Face amount of policy	$ 10,000.00
16 Indemnity benefits	$ -0-
17 Additional insurance	$ -0-
18 Other benefits	$ -0-
19 Principal of any indebtedness to the company deductible in determining net proceeds	$ -0-
20 Interest on indebtedness (item 19) accrued to date of death	$ -0-
21 Amount of accumulated dividends	$ -0-
22 Amount of post-mortem dividends	$ -0-
23 Amount of returned premium	$ -0-
24 Amount of proceeds if payable in one sum	$ 10,000.00
25 Value of proceeds as of date of death (if not payable in one sum)	$ -0-

26 Policy provisions concerning deferred payments or installments.

   Note: *If other than lump-sum settlement is authorized for a surviving spouse, please attach a copy of the insurance policy.*

   -

   -

27 Amount of installments $ ---

28 Date of birth, sex, and name of any person the duration of whose life may measure the number of payments.

   -

   -

29 Amount applied by the insurance company as a single premium representing the purchase of installment benefits $ ---

30 Basis (mortality table and rate of interest) used by insurer in valuing installment benefits.

- -

31 Was the insured the annuitant or beneficiary of any annuity contract issued by the company?   ☐ Yes   ☒ No

32 Names of companies with which decedent carried other policies and amount of such policies if this information is disclosed by your records.

                              UNKNOWN

- -

- -

The undersigned officer of the above-named insurance company hereby certifies that this statement sets forth true and correct information.

Signature ▶ *Ralph H. Snodgrass*   Title ▶ Vice-President   Date of Certification ▶ 8-15-89

Instructions

Paperwork Reduction Act Notice.—We ask for this information to carry out the Internal Revenue laws of the United States. We need it to ensure that you are complying with these laws and to allow us to figure and collect the right amount of tax. You are required to give us this information.

The time needed to complete and file this form will vary depending on individual circumstances. The estimated average time is:

Form	Recordkeeping	Preparing the form
712	18 hrs., 25 min.	18 min.

If you have comments concerning the accuracy of this time estimate or suggestions for making this form more simple, we would be happy to hear

from you. You can write to IRS or the Office of Management and Budget at the addresses listed in the instructions of the tax return with which this form is filed.

Statement of Insurer.—This statement must be made, on behalf of the insurance company which issued the policy, by an officer of the company having access to the records of the company. For purposes of this statement, a facsimile signature may be used in lieu of a manual signature and if used, shall be binding as a manual signature.

Separate Statements.—A separate statement must be filed for each policy.

Line 13.—The premium to be reported on line 13 should be the annual premium, not the cumulative premium to date of death. If death occurred after the end of the premium period, the last annual premium should be reported.

Form **712** (Rev. 1-89)

Estate of: James R. Kent

SCHEDULE F—Other Miscellaneous Property Not Reportable Under Any Other Schedule
(For jointly owned property that must be disclosed on Schedule E, see the Instructions for Schedule E.)
(If you elect section 2032A valuation, you must complete Schedule F and Schedule A-1.)

		Yes	No
1	Did the decedent at the time of death own any articles of artistic or collectible value in excess of $3,000 or any collections whose artistic or collectible value combined at date of death exceeded $10,000?		X
	If "Yes," full details must be submitted on this schedule.		
2	Has the decedent's estate, spouse, or any other person, received (or will receive) any bonus or award as a result of the decedent's employment or death?		X
	If "Yes," full details must be submitted on this schedule.		
3	Did the decedent at the time of death have, or have access to, a safe deposit box?	X	

If "Yes," state location, and if held in joint names of decedent and another, state name and relationship of joint depositor.

Gainesville National Bank, 118 High Street, Gainesville,
FL 32601
Robert L. Kent, Son

If any of the contents of the safe deposit box are omitted from the schedules in this return, explain fully why omitted.

Does Not Apply

Item number	Description For securities, give CUSIP number, if available.	Alternate valuation date	Alternate value	Value at date of death
1	Household Furnishing			$40,000.00
	Piano			$ 2,500.00
	Personal Items			$ 7,500.00
	1987 AUDI 5000 S			$14,500.00
	Total from continuation schedule(s) (or additional sheet(s)) attached to this schedule . . .			-0-
	TOTAL. (Also enter on Part 5, Recapitulation, page 3, at item 6.)			$64,500.00

(If more space is needed, attach the continuation schedule from the end of this package or additional sheets of the same size.)

Schedule F—Page 17

Estate of: James R. Kent

SCHEDULE J—Funeral Expenses and Expenses Incurred in Administering Property Subject to Claims

Note: *Do not list on this schedule expenses of administering property not subject to claims. For those expenses, see the Instructions for Schedule L.*

If executors' commissions, attorney fees, etc., are claimed and allowed as a deduction for estate tax purposes, they are not allowable as a deduction in computing the taxable income of the estate for Federal income tax purposes. They are allowable as an income tax deduction on Form 1041 if a waiver is filed to waive the deduction on Form 706 (see the Form 1041 instructions).

Item number	Description	Expense amount	Total Amount
	A. Funeral expenses:		
1	Gainesville Funeral Home - FUNERAL SERVICES, CASKET	$3,505.00	
	Gainesville Funeral Home - GRANITE MONUMENT	$1,800.00	
	LESS BURIAL BENEFITS (VA)	$ (235.00)	
	Total funeral expenses		$5,070.00
	B. Administration expenses:		
1	Executors' commissions—amount estimated/agreed upon/paid. (Strike out the words that do not apply.)		-0-
2	Attorney fees—amount estimated/agreed upon/paid. (Strike out the words that do not apply.)		$ 120.00
3	Accountant fees—amount estimated/agreed upon/paid. (Strike out the words that do not apply.)		-0-
4	Miscellaneous expenses:	**Expense amount**	
	Alachua County Circuit Court - Letters, Testamentary, Certified copies, Fees	$108.00	
	Gainesville Sun - Legal advertising	$147.00	
	Sunshine State Appraisal Co. - Real Estate Appraisals	$400.00	
	Williams & Sons, Inc. - Appraisals of Personal Property	$225.00	
	Additional Administration Expenses - registered mail, copies, etc.	$ 50.00	
	Total miscellaneous expenses from continuation schedule(s) (or additional sheet(s)) attached to this schedule		
	Total miscellaneous expenses		$ 930.00
	TOTAL. (Also enter on Part 5, Recapitulation, page 3, at item 11.)		$6,120.00

(If more space is needed, attach the continuation schedule from the end of this package or additional sheets of the same size.)

Schedule J—Page 21

Estate of: James R. Kent

SCHEDULE K—Debts of the Decedent, and Mortgages and Liens

Item number	Debts of the Decedent—Creditor and nature of claim, and allowable death taxes	Amount unpaid to date	Amount in contest	Amount claimed as a deduction
1	Gainesville Community Hospital Gainesville, Florida - Final Bill (Net after health insurance settlement)			$ 1,348.12
2.	Florida Power Company-electric bill			$ 126.73
3.	Central Florida Telephone Company telephone bill			$ 36.18
4.	Southeast Bank - credit card balance			$ 2,295.65
5.	IRS - Balance 1988 Income tax due (4-15-89)			$ 3,506.00
	Total from continuation schedule(s) (or additional sheet(s)) attached to this schedule			-0-
	TOTAL. (Also enter on Part 5, Recapitulation, page 3, at item 12.)			$ 7,312.68

Item number	Mortgages and Liens—Description	Amount
1	NONE	
	Total from continuation schedule(s) (or additional sheet(s)) attached to this schedule	-0-
	TOTAL. (Also enter on Part 5, Recapitulation, page 3, at item 13.)	-0-

(If more space is needed, attach the continuation schedule from the end of this package or additional sheets of the same size.)

(The instructions to Schedule K are in the separate instructions.)   **Schedule K —Page 23**

Department of the Treasury — Internal Revenue Service

Request for Prompt Assessment
Under Internal Revenue Code Section 6501(d)

(Please see instructions on reverse)

OMB Clearance Number
1545-0430
Expires 4-30-91

To

Director, Internal Revenue Service

Kind of tax

Estate Tax

Tax returns for which prompt assessment of any additional tax is requested

Form Number	Tax Period Ended	Social Security or Employer Identification Number	Name and Address Shown on Return	Internal Revenue Service Office Where Filed	Date Filed
706	11-21-89	013-62-1458 FEIN 54-1048375	James R. Kent 17 Crest Hill Drive Gainesville, FL 33326	Atlanta, GA 31101	11-20-89

Remarks

	Spouse's name *(surviving or deceased)*	Spouse's social security number
If applicable, please provide the following information ▶		

If the forms listed above are corporation income tax returns, please check one of the boxes below

☐ Dissolution has been completed.

☐ Dissolution has begun and will be completed either before or after the 18-month period of limitation.

☐ Dissolution has not begun but is expected by the expiration of the 18-month period of limitation; dissolution will begin before the period expires and will be completed either before or after that period expires.

I have attached the following item(s) to help expedite action on my request:

☒ Letters testamentary, or

☐ Letters of administration

☐ Copies of returns listed above *(See "What to File" on the back)*

☐ Other:

I request a prompt assessment of any additional tax for the kind of tax and periods shown above, as provided by section 6501(d) of the Internal Revenue Code.

Requester's name and address

Robert L. Kent
115 Gulf View Drive
Tampa, FL 33336

Requester's signature

Robert Lee Kent

Date
11-20-89

Title

Executor

Form
1040A

Department of the Treasury – Internal Revenue Service
U.S. Individual
Income Tax Return (o)   1989

DECEASED

OMB No. 1545-0085

Step 1
Label

Use IRS label. Otherwise, please print or type.

LABEL HERE

Your first name and initial	Last name		Your social security no.
James R.	Kent deceased 2-21-89		013 : 62 : 1458

If a joint return, spouse's first name and initial   Last name

Spouse's social security no.
: :

Home address (number and street). (If you have a P.O. box, see page 15 of the instructions.)   Apt. no.

17 Crest Hill Drive

City, town or post office, state and ZIP code. (If you have a foreign address, see page 15.)

Gainesville, Florida   32601

For Privacy Act and Paperwork Reduction Act Notice, see page 3.

Presidential Election Campaign Fund

Do you want $1 to go to this fund?. . . . . ☐ Yes ☒ No
If joint return, does your spouse want $1 to go to this fund? ☐ Yes ☐ No

Note: Checking "Yes" will not change your tax or reduce your refund.

Step 2
Check your filing status

(Check only one.)

1 ☒ Single (See if you can use Form 1040EZ.)
2 ☐ Married filing joint return (even if only one had income)
3 ☐ Married filing **separate** return. Enter spouse's social security number above and spouse's full name here. _____
4 ☐ Head of household (with qualifying person). (See page 16.) If the qualifying person is your child but not your **dependent**, enter this child's name here. _____
5 ☐ Qualifying widow(er) with dependent child (year spouse died ▶ 19 ___). (See page 17.)

Step 3
Figure your exemptions

(See page 17 of instructions.)

If more than 7 dependents, see page 20.

Attach Copy B of Form(s) W-2 here.

6a ☒ **Yourself** If someone (such as your parent) can claim you as a dependent on his or her tax return, do not check box 6a. But be sure to check the box on line 15b on page 2.
6b ☐ **Spouse**

c **Dependents:** 1. Name (first, initial, and last name)	2. Check if under age 2	3. If age 2 or older, dependent's social security number	4. Relationship	5. No. of months lived in your home in 1989

d If your child didn't live with you but is claimed as your dependent under a pre-1985 agreement, check here . . . . ▶ ☐
e Total number of exemptions claimed.

No. of boxes checked on 6a and 6b   **1**

No. of your children on 6c who:
● lived with you ___
● didn't live with you due to divorce or separation (see page 20) ___

No. of **other** dependents listed on 6c ___

Add numbers entered on lines above   **1**

Step 4
Figure your total income

Attach check or money order here.

7	Wages, salaries, tips, etc. This should be shown in Box 10 of your W-2 form(s). (Attach Form(s) W-2.)	7	$ 2,625 –
8a	**Taxable** interest income (see page 24). (If over $400, also complete and attach Schedule 1, Part II.)	8a	$ 700 –
b	**Tax-exempt** interest income (see page 24). (DO NOT include on line 8a.) 8b		
9	Dividends. (If over $400, also complete and attach Schedule 1, Part III.)	9	$ 2,140 –
10	Unemployment compensation (insurance) from Form(s) 1099-G.	10	-0-
11	Add lines 7, 8a, 9, and 10. Enter the total. This is your **total income**. ▶	11	$ 5,465 –

Step 5
Figure your adjusted gross income

12a	Your IRA deduction from applicable worksheet. Rules for IRAs begin on page 25. 12a		
b	Spouse's IRA deduction from applicable worksheet. Rules for IRAs begin on page 25. 12b		
c	Add lines 12a and 12b. Enter the total. These are your **total adjustments.**	12c	-0-
13	Subtract line 12c from line 11. Enter the result. This is your **adjusted gross income.** (If this line is less than $19,340 and a child lived with you, see "Earned Income Credit" (line 25b) on page 37 of instructions.) ▶	13	$ 5,465 –

Step 6

14 Enter the amount from line 13.   14 $ 5,465 -

15a Check   [X] **You were** 65 or older   [ ] Blind   **Enter number of**
if: [ ] **Spouse was** 65 or older   [ ] Blind   **boxes checked** ▶ 15a | 1 |

Figure your standard deduction,

   b If someone (such as your parent) can claim you as a dependent, check here . . . . ▶15b [ ]

   c If you are married filing separately and your spouse files Form 1040 and itemizes deductions, see page 29 and check here . . . ▶15c [ ]

16 **Enter your standard deduction. See page 30 for the chart (or worksheet) that applies to you. Be sure to enter your standard deduction here.**   16 $ 3,850 -

exemption amount, and

17 Subtract line 16 from line 14. Enter the result. (If line 16 is more than line 14, enter -0-.)   17 $ 1,615 -

18 Multiply $2,000 by the total number of exemptions claimed on line 6e.   18 $ 2,000 -

taxable income

19 Subtract line 18 from line 17. Enter the result. (If line 18 is more than line 17, enter -0-.) This is your **taxable income.** ▶ 19   -0-

If You Want IRS To Figure Your Tax, See Page 31 of the Instructions.

Step 7

Figure your tax, credits, supplemental Medicare premium, and payments (including advance EIC payments)

Caution: If you are under age 14 and have more than $1,000 of investment income, check here . . . . ▶ [ ]
   Also see page 31 to see if you have to use Form 8615 to figure your tax.

20 Find the tax on the amount on line 19. Check if from:
[X] Tax Table (pages 41–46) or   [ ] Form 8615   20   -0-

21 Credit for child and dependent care expenses. Complete and attach Schedule 1, Part I.   21   -0-

22 Subtract line 21 from line 20. Enter the result. (If line 21 is more than line 20, enter -0-.)   22   -0-

23 **Supplemental Medicare premium.** See page 35. Complete and attach Schedule 2 (Form 1040A).   23   N/A

24 Add lines 22 and 23. **Enter the total.** This is your **total tax** and any supplemental Medicare premium. ▶ 24   -0-

25a Total Federal income tax withheld—from Box 9 of your W-2 form(s). (If any is from Form(s) 1099, check here ▶ [X] .)   25a $ 649 -

   b **Earned income credit,** from the worksheet on page 38 of the instructions. Also see page 37.   25b

26 Add lines 25a and 25b. Enter the total. These are your **total payments.** ▶ 26 $ 649 -

Step 8

Figure your refund or amount you owe

27 If line 26 is more than line 24, subtract line 24 from line 26. Enter the result. This is your **refund.**   27 $ 649 -

28 If line 24 is more than line 26, subtract line 26 from line 24. Enter the result. This is the **amount you owe.** Attach check or money order for full amount payable to "Internal Revenue Service." Write your social security number, daytime phone number, and "1989 Form 1040A" on it.   28

Step 9

Sign your return

(Keep a copy of this return for your records.)

Under penalties of perjury, I declare that I have examined this return and accompanying schedules and statements, and to the best of my knowledge and belief, they are true, correct, and complete. Declaration of preparer (other than the taxpayer) is based on all information of which the preparer has any knowledge.

Your signature   Date   Your occupation

X _Robert Lee West_   EXECUTOR   1-10-90   Consultant

Spouse's signature (if joint return, both must sign)   Date   Spouse's occupation

X

Paid preparer's use only

Preparer's signature   Date   Preparer's social security no.

X

Firm's name (or yours if self-employed)   Employer identification no.

Address and ZIP code   Check if self-employed [ ]

1989 **Schedule 1 (Form 1040A)**

OMB No. 1545-0085

Name(s) shown on Form 1040A. (Do not complete if shown on other side.)

James R. Kent

Your social security number

013 : 62 : 1458

Part I
(continued)

Complete lines 13 through 20 only if you received employer-provided dependent care benefits. Be sure to also complete lines 1 and 2 of Part I.

13 Enter the total amount of employer-provided dependent care benefits you received for 1989. (This amount should be separately shown on your W-2 form(s) and labeled as "DCB.") DO NOT include amounts that were reported to you as **wages** in Box 10 of Form(s) W-2. **13**

14 Enter the total amount of **qualified** expenses incurred in 1989 for the care of a qualifying person. (See page 34 of the instructions.) **14**

15 Compare the amounts on lines 13 and 14. Enter the **smaller** of the two amounts here. **15**

16 You **must** enter your **earned income.** (See page 34 of the instructions for the definition of earned income.) **16**

17 If you were married at the end of 1989, you **must** enter your spouse's earned income. (If your spouse was a full-time student or disabled, see page 34 of the instructions for the amount to enter.) **17**

18 ● If you were married at the end of 1989, compare the amounts on lines 16 and 17 and enter the **smaller** of the two amounts here.
● If you were unmarried, enter the amount from line 16 here. **18**

Note: *If you are also claiming the child and dependent care credit, first fill in Form 1040A through line 20. Then complete lines 3–12 of Part I.*

19 **Excluded benefits.** Enter here the **smallest** of the following:
● The amount from line 15, or
● The amount from line 18, or
● $5,000 ($2,500 if married filing a separate return). **19**

20 **Taxable benefits.** Subtract line 19 from line 13. Enter the result. (If zero or less, enter -0-.) Include this amount in the total on Form 1040A, line 7. In the space to the left of line 7, write "DCB." **20**

Part II

Interest income (see page 24 of the instructions)

Complete this part and attach Schedule 1 to Form 1040A if you received over $400 in taxable interest.

Note: *If you received a Form 1099-INT or Form 1099-OID from a brokerage firm, enter the firm's name and the total interest shown on that form.*

1 List name of payer	Amount
Gainesville National Bank, Gainesville, FL 1	$ 700 -
2 Add amounts on line 1. Enter the total here and on Form 1040A, line 8a. 2	$ 700 -

Part III

Dividend income (see page 24 of the instructions)

Complete this part and attach Schedule 1 to Form 1040A if you received over $400 in dividends.

Note: *If you received a Form 1099-DIV from a brokerage firm, enter the firm's name and the total dividends shown on that form.*

1 List name of payer	Amount
Martin Marietta Corporation 1	$1,757 -
AT&T	$ 83 -
Florida Progress Corporation	$ 210 -
Detroit Edison Company	$ 90 -
2 Add amounts on line 1. Enter the total here and on Form 1040A, line 9. 2	$2,140 -

Department of the Treasury—Internal Revenue Service

U.S. Fiduciary Income Tax Return | 1989 | IRS Use Only

For the calendar year 1989 or fiscal year beginning , 1989, and ending , 19 | OMB No. 1545-0092

Check applicable boxes:

[X] Decedent's estate	Name of estate or trust (grantor type trust, see instructions)	Employer identification number
[ ] Simple trust	Estate of James Robert Kent	54-1048375
[ ] Complex trust	Name and title of fiduciary	Date entity created
[ ] Grantor type trust	Robert Lee Kent, Executor	2-21-89
[ ] Bankruptcy estate	Address of fiduciary (number and street or P.O. Box)	Nonexempt charitable and split-interest trusts, check applicable boxes (see instructions):
[ ] Family estate trust	115 Gulf View Drive	
[ ] Pooled income fund	City, state, and ZIP code	
[X] Initial return	Tampa, Florida 33601	[ ] Described in section 4947(a)(1)
[ ] Amended return		[ ] Not a private foundation
[ ] Final return	Number of Schedules K-1 attached (see instructions) . . . ▶ 0	[ ] Described in section 4947(a)(2)

Income

1	Dividends	1	$ 13,535 -
2	Interest income	2	$ 4,100 -
3	Income (or losses) from partnerships, other estates, or other trusts (see instructions)	3	-0-
4	Net rental and royalty income (or loss) (attach Schedule E (Form 1040))	4	-0-
5	Net business and farm income (or loss) (attach Schedules C and F (Form 1040))	5	-0-
6	Capital gain (or loss) (attach Schedule D (Form 1041))	6	-0-
7	Ordinary gain (or loss) (attach Form 4797)	7	-0-
8	Other income (state nature of income) _____	8	-0-
9	**Total** income (add lines 1 through 8) . . . ▶	9	$ 17,635 -

Deductions

10	Interest . . .	10	$ 14 -	
11	Taxes	11	$ 3,700 -	
12	Fiduciary fees .	12	-0-	
13	Charitable deduction (from Schedule A, line 6)	13	-0-	
14	Attorney, accountant, and return preparer fees	14	-0-	
15a	Other deductions NOT subject to the 2% floor (attach schedule).	15a	-0-	
b	Allowable miscellaneous itemized deductions subject to the 2% floor	15b	-0-	
c	Add lines 15a and 15b	15c	-0-	
16	**Total** (add lines 10 through 15c) . . .	16	$ 3,714 -	
17	Adjusted total income (or loss) (subtract line 16 from line 9). Enter here and on Schedule B, line 1 . ▶	17	$ 13,921 -	
18	Income distribution deduction (from Schedule B, line 17) (see instructions) (attach Schedules K-1 (Form 1041))	18	-0-	
19	Estate tax deduction (including certain generation-skipping transfer taxes) (attach computation)	19	$ 2,985 -	
20	Exemption . . .	20	$ 600 -	
21	**Total** deductions (add lines 18 through 20) . . . ▶	21	$ 3,585 -	

Tax and Payments

22	Taxable income of fiduciary (subtract line 21 from line 17) . . .	22	$ 10,336 -
23	**Total** tax (from Schedule G, line 7) . . . ▶	23	$ 2,218 -
24a	Payments: 1989 estimated tax payments and amount applied from 1988 return . . .	24a	-0-
b	Treated as credited to beneficiaries . . .	24b	-0-
c	Subtract line 24b from line 24a . . .	24c	-0-
d	Tax paid with extension of time to file: [ ] Form 2758 [ ] Form 8736 [ ] Form 8800 . .	24d	-0-
e	Federal income tax withheld . . .	24e	$ 1,764 -
	Credits: **f** Form 2439 _____ ; **g** Form 4136 _____ ; **h** Other _____ ; Total ▶	24i	-0-
25	**Total** payments (add lines 24c through 24e, and 24i) . . . ▶	25	$ 1,764 -
26	If line 23 is larger than line 25, enter **TAX DUE** . . .	26	$ 454 -
27	If line 25 is larger than line 23, enter **OVERPAYMENT** . . .	27	-0-
28	Amount of line 27 to be: **a** Credited to 1990 estimated tax ▶ _____ ; **b** Refunded ▶	28	-0-
29	**Penalty** for underpayment of estimated tax (see instructions) . . .	29	-0-

Please Sign Here

Under penalties of perjury, I declare that I have examined this return, including accompanying schedules and statements, and to the best of my knowledge and belief, it is true, correct, and complete. Declaration of preparer (other than fiduciary) is based on all information of which preparer has any knowledge.

▶ *Robert Lee Kent* | 1-10-90 | ▶
Signature of fiduciary or officer representing fiduciary | Date | EIN of fiduciary (see instructions)

Paid Preparer's Use Only

Preparer's signature ▶	Date	Check if self-employed ▶ [ ]	Preparer's social security no.
Firm's name (or yours if self-employed) and address ▶		E.I. No. ▶
		ZIP code ▶

For Paperwork Reduction Act Notice, see page 1 of the separate instructions.

Form **1041** (1989)

Schedule A	Charitable Deduction—Do not complete for a simple trust or a pooled income fund.		
	(Write the name and address of each charitable organization to whom your contributions total $3,000 or more on an attached sheet.)		
1	Amounts paid or permanently set aside for charitable purposes from current year's gross income . . .	1	-0-
2	Tax-exempt interest allocable to charitable distribution (see instructions)	2	-0-
3	Subtract line 2 from line 1	3	-0-
4	Enter the net short-term capital gain and the net long-term capital gain of the current tax year allocable to corpus paid or permanently set aside for charitable purposes (see instructions)	4	-0-
5	Amounts paid or permanently set aside for charitable purposes from gross income of a prior year (see instructions)	5	-0-
6	Total (add lines 3 through 5). Enter here and on page 1, line 13	6	-0-

Schedule B	Income Distribution Deduction (see instructions)		
1	Adjusted total income (from page 1, line 17) (see instructions)	1	$ 13,921 -
2	Adjusted tax-exempt interest (see instructions)	2	-0-
3	Net gain shown on Schedule D (Form 1041), line 17, column (a). (If net loss, enter zero.) . .	3	-0-
4	Enter amount from Schedule A, line 4	4	-0-
5	Long-term capital gain included on Schedule A, line 1	5	-0-
6	Short-term capital gain included on Schedule A, line 1	6	-0-
7	If the amount on page 1, line 6, is a capital loss, enter here as a positive figure . . .	7	-0-
8	If the amount on page 1, line 6, is a capital gain, enter here as a negative figure . . .	8	-0-
9	Distributable net income (combine lines 1 through 8)	9	$ 13,921 -
10	Amount of income for the tax year determined under the governing instrument (accounting income) **10**		
11	Amount of income required to be distributed currently (see instructions)	11	-0-
12	Other amounts paid, credited, or otherwise required to be distributed (see instructions) . . .	12	-0-
13	Total distributions (add lines 11 and 12). (If greater than line 10, see instructions.) . . .	13	-0-
14	Enter the total amount of tax-exempt income included on line 13	14	-0-
15	Tentative income distribution deduction (subtract line 14 from line 13)	15	-0-
16	Tentative income distribution deduction (subtract line 2 from line 9)	16	-0-
17	Income distribution deduction. Enter the smaller of line 15 or line 16 here and on page 1, line 18 . .	17	-0-

Schedule G	Tax Computation (see instructions)			
1	Tax: **a** Tax rate schedule _2,218_ ; **b** Other taxes _0_ ; . . . . Total ▶	1c	$ 2,218 -	
2a	Foreign tax credit (attach Form 1116)	2a	-0-	
b	Credit for fuel produced from a nonconventional source.	2b	-0-	
c	General business credit. Check if from:			
	☐ Form 3800 or ☐ Form (specify) ▶	2c	-0-	
d	Credit for prior year minimum tax (attach Form 8801)	2d	-0-	
3	**Total** credits (add lines 2a through 2d) . . . . ▶	3	-0-	
4	Subtract line 3 from line 1c.	4	$ 2,218 -	
5	Recapture taxes. Check if from: ☐ Form 4255 ☐ Form 8611	5	-0-	
6	Alternative minimum tax (attach Form 8656)	6	-0-	
7	**Total** tax (add lines 4 through 6). Enter here and on page 1, line 23 . . ▶	7	$ 2,218 -	

Other Information (see instructions)		Yes	No
1	If the fiduciary's name or address has changed, enter the old information ▶		
2	Did the estate or trust receive tax-exempt income? (If "Yes," attach a computation of the allocation of expenses.) . .		X
	Enter the amount of tax-exempt interest income and exempt-interest dividends ▶ $		
3	Did the estate or trust have any passive activity losses? (If "Yes," enter these losses on **Form 8582**, Passive Activity Loss Limitations, to figure the allowable loss.)		X
4	Did the estate or trust receive all or any part of the earnings (salary, wages, and other compensation) of any individual by reason of a contract assignment or similar arrangement?		X
5	At any time during the tax year, did the estate or trust have an interest in or a signature or other authority over a financial account in a foreign country (such as a bank account, securities account, or other financial account)? (See the instructions for exceptions and filing requirements for Form TD F 90-22.1.)		X
	If "Yes," enter the name of the foreign country ▶		
6	Was the estate or trust the grantor of, or transferor to, a foreign trust which existed during the current tax year, whether or not the estate or trust has any beneficial interest in it? (If "Yes," you may have to file Form 3520, 3520-A, or 926.) . .		X
7	Check this box if this entity has filed or is required to file **Form 8264**, Application for Registration of a Tax Shelter . ▶ ☐		
8	Check this box if this entity is a complex trust making the section 663(b) election . . . . ▶ ☐		
9	Check this box to make a section 643(e)(3) election (attach Schedule D (Form 1041)) . . . . . . ▶ ☐		
10	Check this box if the decedent's estate has been open for more than 2 years . . . . ▶ ☐		
11	Check this box if the trust is a participant in a **Common Trust Fund** that was required to adopt a calendar year . . ▶ ☐		

CHAPTER 9

Probate Planning

While the process of settling an estate is not difficult, the foregoing chapters have made clear the importance of preparation. The ready availability of funeral arrangement plans and specific estate and personal information can simplify the job survivors must face immediately, and often unexpectedly. Locating key documents and papers, such as a will, insurance policies, military service records, tax returns, and financial records can be one of the most difficult tasks facing the Personal Representative. Many Personal Representatives wish too late that they had discussed these matters with the deceased.

The Importance of a Will

As review of the state laws of intestate succession shows, the presence of a current valid will can simplify estate distribution and prevent unintended consequences. The Personal Representative should assess his or her own will in light of the probate process, to be sure that it meets current needs. If you do not have a valid will, settling an estate for another should remove any hesitancy you might feel about preparing one, since you will have gained first-hand knowledge of the effect your failure to do so will have on those close to you. Beneficiaries or heirs of the deceased who receive shares of a solvent estate should be encouraged to prepare or update a will reflecting the changes in their own estate. The information about a simple will found in Chapter 2 and information about the witness requirements found in Chapter 3 will help you use the will forms included at the back of this book. A will should be either typed or written in ink, and all signatures must be in ink.

If you need to make only a minor change in an existing will, such as changing the named Executor or adding a bequest, you may use a *codicil.* A codicil is an amendment to an existing will that must include reference to the date of the will being modified. Witness requirements for a codicil are the same as those for a will. You will also find codicil forms at the back of this book. If extensive changes to a will are needed, it is usually easier to prepare and properly execute a new will. If further information is needed to ensure that your will addresses your needs, refer to our earlier book, *The Complete Will Kit,* published by John Wiley & Sons, Inc., in 1990.

Self-Proving

A properly executed and notarized self-proving certificate simplifies establishing the validity of a will. As any Personal Representative who has had to search for witnesses knows, self-proving a will saves time and inconvenience. A self-proving certificate may be completed by the Testator and witnesses at any time after the execution of the referenced will, by appearing before a notary and having the certificate signed, dated, sealed, and attached to the original will. If you or other family members have a will that has not been self-proved, this procedure is strongly recommended.

Whenever a person prepares a new will or a codicil to an existing will, self-proving the document is advised. The procedure is the same for both. A self-proved codicil also self-proves the will it modifies. Self-proving certificates for a will or for a codicil are also included at the back of the book.

Executor Data

Having a valid will allows you to choose the person who will act as your Personal Representative. He or she will need certain information to settle your estate. Executor Data sheets for listing this key information are provided in the perforated section of detachable forms at the back of the book. It is advisable to discuss this material with your chosen Executor to be sure that there are no questions. Once again, just a few moments spent in advance can save hours and much frustration later.

Joint Title

As explained earlier, not all assets pass through probate administration. Assets owned jointly with a spouse or another person with the right of survivorship or as joint tenants by the entirety transfer to the survivor without being subject to probate. One of these ownership options, available in most non–community-property states, can be used for real property, titled personal property, bank accounts, and ownership of stocks and bonds. Although this approach does not affect the tax liability of an estate, it can simplify probate administration and speed settlement of the estate. Bear in mind that a decision to sell or exchange valuable personal property that is jointly titled will require the co-owner's consent. If an asset is jointly titled, any liens would become the responsibility of the co-title holder upon the death of the other owner.

Gifts

Bequests in a will are gifts made after death that must first pass through the probate process. Depending on the circumstances, making some of these gifts while still alive should be carefully considered, particularly for items of tangible personal property. In this way heirlooms and other items of particular family significance definitely will be received by those whom you wish to have them, and you can provide background about the property yourself. You will be able to share the benefits of your thoughtfulness together. Gifts made while living are not part of your estate, since you did not own them at death. Gifts may be made from one individual to another up to a value of $10,000 per year without being subject to federal gift taxes, which are paid by the giver on gifts exceeding $10,000.

Since the gift and estate tax rates have recently been unified, there is no tax advantage to gifts beyond the first $10,000 exclusion per year. However, if your assets are substantial, making gifts of up to $10,000 can help you transfer these gifts to those you wish while reducing your future taxable estate. The benefits of such an approach can be substantial. For example, a husband and wife could give up to $20,000 a year to each of their three children, which would transfer $180,000 from the estate in a period of three years. The use of gifts can also help reduce the future estate of a surviving spouse below the $600,000 threshold for federal estate tax filing and thus generate significant tax savings later. As review of the tax information shows, there is a substantial difference in the paperwork and taxation due on an estate of the surviving spouse of $595,000 compared to one of $605,000.

Real Estate Options

Although *life estate* interests are often created by intestacy, a life estate can also be created while living. Creation of a life estate involves modifying the property deed to grant the right of property use to a particular individual for the remainder of his or her life, while actual ownership is held by someone else. Creation of a life estate by a surviving spouse for himself or herself with ownership of the property transferred to a child or to children jointly will remove that property from probate jurisdiction.

Another option that may be considered in certain circumstances is the sale-leaseback arrangement. A sale-leaseback generally involves a family member buying the property (usually with conventional financing) and paying the full purchase price to the seller. The seller then pays rent equaling the mortgage payments to the purchaser and continues to live in the house. This method removes the property from the probate process, retains family ownership, and can generate needed cash for the parent by tapping the equity in the property built up over the years. If circumstances are right, the parent(s) can then use the nontaxable gift exclusion discussed above to distribute a portion of the principal received as well.

Life Insurance

Life insurance paid to a beneficiary other than the estate is not subject to probate, although if payable to your Executor it is included in the taxable estate. The use of fully paid up and/or single-premium life insurance policies can thus remove substantial sums from probate administration. Persons with substantial assets may wish to consider using single-premium life insurance policies, payable to their chosen beneficiaries, as an estate planning tool.

Trusts

A *trust* is simply defined as giving assets or property to one party (a trustee) to hold, use, or manage for another party (the trust beneficiary). A trust is legally established by the witnessed and notarized execution of a declaration of trust by the creator of the trust (also called the *settlor, grantor, trustor,* or *donor*). The trust agreement empowers the trustee to administer the trust and sets out its terms and conditions.

The establishment of a trust creates a separate legal entity, which has ownership and/or title of property transferred to it. Functionally, a trust is very similar to a private investment corporation. As a separate legal entity, it must be given an Employer Identification Number, and separate state and federal income tax returns must be filed if the trust's income exceeds $600 annually. Generally, the trust holds title to all its assets, is managed by a trustee, and is owned by the beneficiary(ies). The trustee should keep accurate accounts and report on the trust's status to the beneficiaries (owners) on a regular basis.

Trusts can be established either on a revocable or an irrevocable basis. An irrevocable trust cannot be changed, whereas a revocable trust can be terminated at the trustee's discretion. At present, there are no federal income or estate tax advantages to a revocable trust.

Trusts can be organized either as *living* trusts (*inter vivos* trusts) or as *testamentary* trusts (established upon death). If you set up a living trust, you can also be the trustee. Generally, a revocable trust is preferable if you plan to act as the trustee or wish to assess the performance of a third-party trustee. Living trusts are funded with wholly owned assets such as cash, stock, bonds, and real estate while testamentary trusts can be funded with wholly owned assets or life insurance policy proceeds.

The initial funding of a trust is its principal. Funds earned from the trust principal, such as interest, dividends, and rents, are considered trust income. Many trusts are designed to preserve the principal until termination, with the trust income being distributed to the trust beneficiaries in a timely manner for their benefit. In other cases, the trust may be structured to reinvest all income, thereby creating a larger principal balance to be paid out when the trust is terminated.

Since assets placed in a trust are then owned by another, these assets are not subject to probate administration. However, they are subject to estate taxation. While careful use of properly structured A–B–C living trusts can be useful for tax planning of very large estates, the range of complexity involved is beyond the scope of this book and the needs of its intended audience. Currently fewer than 2 percent of the estates in the United States exceed the $600,000 threshold for required filing of a federal estate tax return and only half of those have to pay federal estate tax. The other probate planning techniques discussed in this chapter offer a more practical approach to asset distribution than creation of a living trust. Also be aware that if assets are not formally transferred to a living trust before death, they must pass through probate and then be placed in the trust. Further, even with an established trust, any assets not owned by the trust are subject to the probate process.

Living Wills

Another consideration in preprobate planning is the possible costs and effects of irreversible illness, which can exhaust all the assets that might make up an estate. For many reasons including recognition that large medical bills can rapidly erode an estate, some people choose to record their wishes regarding extended life-support measures. A living will is a signed, dated, and properly witnessed document in which you state *in advance* your wishes regarding the use of life-support procedures in cases of terminal illness, serious incapacitation, or prolonged coma. In recent years more and more states have begun to accept living wills, and they are now recognized in the District of Columbia and all states except Illinois, Kentucky, Massachusetts, New Jersey, New York, Ohio, Pennsylvania, Rhode Island, and South Dakota. However, witness procedures and notarization requirements vary from state to state. It is especially important to notarize living wills in those states that have no legislation relating to them. You may obtain current information about living wills in your state by contacting your doctor or the Concern for Dying Foundation, 250 West 57th Street, New York, NY 10107.

A *durable power of attorney* is another document that may be of value in the later stages of estate planning. A power of attorney is a signed, witnessed, and notarized statement appointing someone as your *attorney in fact,* with specified powers to act on your behalf. A durable power of attorney continues in effect in the event of the disability or incompetence of the maker. You must have complete trust in the person who holds a durable power of attorney, as he or she is legally authorized to act on your behalf. For this reason, consider this step carefully and only when needed.

Index

Administration, types of, 6, 42, 49, 64–83

Administrator, 1, 5, 27, 51

Affidavit, 6, 30–31

Ancillary administration, 28, 52

Appointment, 3, 27

Appraisals, 64–83, D-2

Auctions, 122–124

Automatic share, 52–57

Benefits, death and burial, 14, 20

Bequests, 61, 145

Bond, surety, 30, D-2

Burial arrangements, 7

Business interests, 63

Capacity, 31

Claims, 58, 124–125

Closing the estate, 89, 155, 163–165

Codicil, 192, D-2

Community property, 43, 148

Compensation, 50–51

Contest, 6, 31

Courts, probate, jurisdiction, 28, 34–43

Creditors, 58–60, 64–83

Curtesy rights, 43

Death benefits, 14, 20

Death certificates, 29, 86, 158

Debts, 58–60, 124–125

Dependents, 8

Distribution, 145

Distributive share, 147–153

Divorce, 20, 22

Domicile, 5, 28

Dower rights, 43

Durable power of attorney, 196

Elective share, 6, 42–47

Employer Identification Number, 62, 167

Estate, 5, 62, 91

Estate inventory, 108–119

Estate summary worksheets, 127–130, R-1

Estate taxes, 62, 134–136, 173–183, 188–189

Executor, 1, 3, 5, 27, 51

Executor data sheets, R-1

Fair market value, 94

Fees, 50–51

F.I.C.A. benefits, 20

Filing accounts, 64–84, 86–89, 126

Funeral expenses, 61

Generation skipping transfer, 2, 134–136
Gift taxes, 134–136, 193
Guardian(s), 8

Heirs, 6, 9, 28, 147–153

Income taxes, 62, 131–136, 169–171, 185–187
Inheritance taxes, 134–136
Insolvent estates, 5, 61
Insurance trust, 194–195
Intangible personal property, 93
Inter vivos (living) trust, 195
Intestate, 1, 6, 31, 147–153
Inventory, 62, 96–107, 108–119
Irrevocable trust, 195
IRS forms
    samples, 168–189
    ordering, 144

Joint income tax return, 133
Joint ownership, 10, 92
Jurisdiction, 28, 34–43

Laws of succession, 6, 146–153
Letters of administration, 6, 30, 49
Letters testamentary, 5, 29, 49, 162
Liens, 10, 124–125, 154
Life estate, 93, 149, 194
Life insurance, 9, 94, 194
Liquidity, 121
Living expenses, 9, 52–57
Living trust, 195
Living will, 196
Lump sum death benefit, 20

Marital deduction, 95
Minors, 6, 8
Mortgages, 10, 92–93

Nonresident personal representative, 51, 64–83
Notices, 27, 34–43, 58–59, 64–83
Notification of creditors, 59, 64–83

Outside appraisals, 64–83, D-2

Personal property, 93–94, 154
Personal representative, 1, 3, 5, 7, 27, 49, 51, 121, 131
Personal representative checklist, 86–89
Per stirpes, 6, 152
Power of attorney, 196
Probate, 1, 2, 5, 27, 31
Probate administration—state summary, 64–83
Probate courts, 34–43
Probate timetable, 84
Property taxes, 10, 93

Real property, 92, 194
Residence, 5, 28
Resident agent, 52
Residue, 61, 146
Revision of will, 29, 192, D-2
Revocable trust, 195
Room-by-room inventory, 96–107

Safe deposit boxes, 29, 88
Samples
    accounts, 159–164
    benefit forms, 11, 15, 18–19, 21, 23–25
    tax forms, 168–189
    will, 32
    will self-proving certificate, 33
Self-proving a will, 6, 31, 33–43, 192, D-2
Settlement of estate, 89, 155, 163–165
Small estates, 31, 42, 50, 64–83
Social security benefits (FICA), 20
State requirements, 34–43, 64–83, 137–141
State taxes—summary, 134–136
State tax information and forms summary, 137–141
Spouse's automatic share—state summary, 53–57
Spouse's elective share—summary, 44–47
Supervised administration, 6, 50, 64–83
Surviving spouse, 6, 8, 10, 14, 20, 42–43, 52, 93–95, 133, 146–152
Survivor benefits, 20–22
Survivorship, right of, 92

Tangible personal property, 93
Taxable gifts, 134–136, 193
Tax checklist, 132
Tax returns, filing, 137–141
Testamentary trust, 195
Transfer of assets, 92, 154, 159
Trust agreement, 195
Trustee, 195
Trusts, 194–195

Unlimited marital deduction, 95
Unsupervised administration, 6, 9, 50, 64–83

Valuation, 95, 161
Veterans benefits, 10–20

Waiver,
    executor bond, 30, D-2
    outside appraisal, D-2
Will, 30, 32, 173, 191, D-2
Will contests, 6, 31
Will probate state summary, 34–43
Witnesses, 30, 34–43
Work-related benefits, 10, 49

Record Set

Using the Detachable Forms

This section contains Estate Summary worksheets and Executor data sheets. The Estate Summary worksheets are for use when you are Personal Representative of an estate. The Executor data sheets can assist you in assembling information that is needed by the Executor you name in your will. These forms are perforated so that you can detach them for ease of use.

ESTATE SUMMARY WORKSHEETS

The two Estate Summary worksheets can assist you in organizing financial and other information about the estate that you will need as Personal Representative to complete tax and other forms required by the court. One worksheet can be used for a status report and the other for a final report.

EXECUTOR DATA SHEETS

Following the Estate Summary worksheets, there are two sets of Executor data sheets that provide space for you to list the key information about yourself and your estate that your Executor will eventually need. Information regarding organ donation; funeral arrangements; people to contact immediately; biographical background for obituary notices; location of keys, documents, and accounts; and beneficiaries and dependent/guardian concerns should be listed. You will probably want to detach these sheets and give them to your Executor for use when they are needed.

E S T A T E   S U M M A R Y   W O R K S H E E T

————————————— **ESTATE** —————————————

Court _____ File Number _____

Estate of _____

Resident at _____

Date of death _____ Will: Yes _____ No _____

Personal Representative _____

Address _____

Date of appointment _____

Date(s) of notice to beneficiaries/heirs _____

Date(s) of notice to creditors _____

Date of this summary account _____

————————————— **PRINCIPAL** —————————————

Assets	Value
Real estate	$_____
Joint real estate	$_____
Stocks/bonds	$_____
Cash/notes	$_____
Life insurance to estate	$_____
Titled personal property	$_____
Other personal property	$_____
Farm/business interest	$_____
Other assets	$_____
Total Assets	$_____
Adjustments to asset values	$_____
Principal receipts	
Income tax refund(s)	$_____
Other	$_____
Adjusted Principal Balance	$_____

Disbursements	Amount
Court fees	$_____
Advertisements	$_____

From *The Complete Probate Kit* by Jens C. Appel, III and F. Bruce Gentry
© 1991 by John Wiley & Sons, Inc.

Disbursements   Amount

Postage $_____
Certified copies $_____
Personal property taxes $_____
Real estate taxes $_____
Income taxes $_____
Other taxes $_____
Hazard insurance $_____
Utility bills $_____
Title transfer fees $_____
Recordation fees $_____
Appraisal fees $_____
Auction/agent commissions $_____
Stock/bond broker commission(s) $_____
Funeral expenses $_____
Monument costs $_____
Last illness costs $_____
Other professional fees $_____
Notary fees $_____
State estate/inheritance taxes $_____
Federal estate taxes $_____
Living expenses/allowances $_____
Personal Representative commission $_____
Other expenses (list) $_____
Debts $_____

Total Disbursements $_____

Principal Balance Before Distribution $_____

Distribution to Beneficiaries/Heirs

Name	Date	Amount
_____	_____	$_____
_____	_____	_____
_____	_____	_____
_____	_____	_____
_____	_____	_____
_____	_____	_____
_____	_____	_____

Distribution to Beneficiaries/Heirs

Name	Date	Amount
_____	_____	_____
_____	_____	_____

Total Distribution to Beneficiaries/Heirs $_____

Investments

Investment	Date	Amount
_____	_____	$_____
_____	_____	_____
_____	_____	_____
_____	_____	_____

Capital Changes

Type	Date	Amount
_____	_____	$_____
_____	_____	_____
_____	_____	_____

Principal Balance Remaining $_____

_____ **INCOME** _____

Period from _____ to _____

Receipts

Type	Amount
Rent	$_____
Stock dividends	$_____
Bond interest	$_____
Cash account interest	$_____
Private note interest	$_____
Royalty payments	$_____
Other income (list)	$_____
	$_____
	$_____

Total Income $_____

Disbursements

Management fees $_____

Bank fees $_____

Other expenses to produce income (list) $_____

                                                   $_____

                                                   $_____

Federal fiduciary income tax $_____

State fiduciary income tax $_____

Other taxes on estate income $_____

Personal Representative income commission $_____

Total Disbursements $_____

Income Balance Before Distribution $_____

Income Distribution to Beneficiaries/Heirs

Name	Date	Amount
_____	_____	$_____
_____	_____	_____
_____	_____	_____
_____	_____	_____
_____	_____	_____
_____	_____	_____
_____	_____	_____
_____	_____	_____
_____	_____	_____
_____	_____	_____

Total Income Distribution to Beneficiaries/Heirs $_____

Income Balance Remaining $_____

Total Principal and Income Balance Remaining $_____

ESTATE SUMMARY WORKSHEET

———— ESTATE ————

Court _____ File Number _____

Estate of _____

Resident at _____

Date of death _____ Will: Yes _____ No _____

Personal Representative _____

Address _____

Date of appointment _____

Date(s) of notice to beneficiaries/heirs _____

Date(s) of notice to creditors _____

Date of this summary account _____

———— PRINCIPAL ————

Assets	Value
Real estate	$_____
Joint real estate	$_____
Stocks/bonds	$_____
Cash/notes	$_____
Life insurance to estate	$_____
Titled personal property	$_____
Other personal property	$_____
Farm/business interest	$_____
Other assets	$_____
Total Assets	$_____
Adjustments to asset values	$_____
Principal receipts	
Income tax refund(s)	$_____
Other	$_____
Adjusted Principal Balance	$_____

Disbursements	Amount
Court fees	$_____
Advertisements	$_____

From *The Complete Probate Kit* by Jens C. Appel, III and F. Bruce Gentry
© 1991 by John Wiley & Sons, Inc.

Disbursements

	Amount
Postage	$_____
Certified copies	$_____
Personal property taxes	$_____
Real estate taxes	$_____
Income taxes	$_____
Other taxes	$_____
Hazard insurance	$_____
Utility bills	$_____
Title transfer fees	$_____
Recordation fees	$_____
Appraisal fees	$_____
Auction/agent commissions	$_____
Stock/bond broker commission(s)	$_____
Funeral expenses	$_____
Monument costs	$_____
Last illness costs	$_____
Other professional fees	$_____
Notary fees	$_____
State estate/inheritance taxes	$_____
Federal estate taxes	$_____
Living expenses/allowances	$_____
Personal Representative commission	$_____
Other expenses (list)	$_____
Debts	$_____
Total Disbursements	$_____
Principal Balance Before Distribution	$_____

Distribution to Beneficiaries/Heirs

Name	Date	Amount
_____	_____	$_____
_____	_____	_____
_____	_____	_____
_____	_____	_____
_____	_____	_____
_____	_____	_____
_____	_____	_____

Distribution to Beneficiaries/Heirs

Name	Date	Amount
_____	_____	_____
_____	_____	_____

Total Distribution to Beneficiaries/Heirs $_____

Investments

Investment	Date	Amount
_____	_____	$_____
_____	_____	_____
_____	_____	_____
_____	_____	_____

Capital Changes

Type	Date	Amount
_____	_____	$_____
_____	_____	_____
_____	_____	_____

Principal Balance Remaining $_____

———————————————— **INCOME** ————————————————

Period from _____ to _____

Receipts

Type	Amount
Rent	$_____
Stock dividends	$_____
Bond interest	$_____
Cash account interest	$_____
Private note interest	$_____
Royalty payments	$_____
Other income (list)	$_____
	$_____
	$_____

Total Income $_____

Disbursements

Management fees $_____

Bank fees $_____

Other expenses to produce income (list) $_____

                                                         $_____

                                                         $_____

Federal fiduciary income tax $_____

State fiduciary income tax $_____

Other taxes on estate income $_____

Personal Representative income commission $_____

Total Disbursements $_____

Income Balance Before Distribution $_____

Income Distribution to Beneficiaries/Heirs

Name	Date	Amount
_____	_____	$_____
_____	_____	_____
_____	_____	_____
_____	_____	_____
_____	_____	_____
_____	_____	_____
_____	_____	_____
_____	_____	_____
_____	_____	_____

Total Income Distribution to Beneficiaries/Heirs $_____

Income Balance Remaining $_____

Total Principal and Income Balance Remaining $_____

E X E C U T O R   D A T A

———————————————— IMMEDIATE ————————————————

Location of Documents/Keys

Location of will_____

Date executed_____ # of Pages _____

Other documents_____

_____

_____

_____

Keys/Safety deposit box_____

_____

_____

_____

Burial/Funeral

Responsible person/Organization

Name_____

Address_____

Phone_____

Interment ☐   Cremation ☐   Crypt ☐   Other ☐

Service Type: Religious ☐   Fraternal ☐   Other ☐

Cemetery/Columbarium_____

_____

Body/Eye/Organ Donations

Organization/Group_____

Contact_____

Phone_____

Address_____

Donation_____

Organization/Group_____

Contact_____

Address_____

Phone_____

Donation_____

From *The Complete Probate Kit* by Jens C. Appel, III and F. Bruce Gentry
© 1991 by John Wiley & Sons, Inc.

EXECUTOR DATA

CONTACTS

Accountant_____ Phone_____

Address_____

Attorney_____ Phone_____

Address_____

Banker_____ Phone_____

Address_____

Clergyman_____ Phone_____

Address_____

Doctor_____ Phone_____

Address_____

Executor_____ Phone_____

Address_____

Alternate Executor_____ Phone_____

Address_____

Insurance agent_____ Phone_____

Address_____

Insurance agent_____ Phone_____

Address_____

Trustee_____ Phone_____

Address_____

Relatives/Friends

Name_____ Phone_____

Address_____

Name_____ Phone_____

Address_____

Name_____ Phone_____

Address_____

Name_____ Phone_____

Address_____

From *The Complete Probate Kit* by Jens C. Appel, III and F. Bruce Gentry
© 1991 by John Wiley & Sons, Inc.

EXECUTOR DATA

───────────── **PERSONAL** ─────────────

Full name_____ Birth date_____

Address_____

_____

Birthplace_____

Social security #_____ Medicare #_____

Military service #_____ Discharge date_____

Father's name_____ Birth date_____

Date deceased_____ Birthplace_____

Mother's maiden name_____ Birth date_____

Date deceased_____ Birthplace_____

Married □   Divorced □   Separated □   Widowed □   Single □   Remarried □

Spouse (name)_____ Marriage date_____

Social security #_____ Medicare #_____

Membership (Religious/Fraternal/Social, Other)_____

_____

_____

Children

Name_____ Birth date_____

Address_____

Name_____ Birth date_____

Address_____

Name_____ Birth date_____

Address_____

Name_____ Birth date_____

Address_____

Name_____ Birth date_____

Address_____

From *The Complete Probate Kit* by Jens C. Appel, III and F. Bruce Gentry
© 1991 by John Wiley & Sons, Inc.

_____ **FINAL ARRANGEMENTS** _____

Person responsible_____ Phone_____

Address_____

Alternate person_____ Phone_____

Funeral home (name)_____ Phone_____

Address_____

Location of service_____ Viewing: Yes ☐   No ☐

Address_____

Service type: Religious ☐   Military ☐   Fraternal ☐   Memorial ☐

Person officiating_____ Phone_____

Cemetery_____

Location_____

Section_____ Plot #_____

Interment_____ Entombment_____ Cremation_____

Location of deed_____

Music/Reading selections_____

_____

_____

_____

Flowers/Memorials_____

_____

Pallbearers   (Honorary)

_____   _____

_____   _____

_____   _____

_____   _____

_____   _____

_____   _____

EXECUTOR DATA

BENEFICIARIES

Name_____ Relationship_____

Address_____ Phone_____

Bequest(s)_____

_____

Name_____ Relationship_____

Address_____ Phone_____

Bequest(s)_____

_____

Name_____ Relationship_____

Address_____ Phone_____

Bequest(s)_____

_____

Name_____ Relationship_____

Address_____ Phone_____

Bequest(s)_____

_____

Name_____ Relationship_____

Address_____ Phone_____

Bequest(s)_____

_____

Name_____ Relationship_____

Address_____ Phone_____

Bequest(s)_____

_____

Name_____ Relationship_____

Address_____ Phone_____

Bequest(s)_____

_____

Name_____ Relationship_____

Address_____ Phone_____

Bequest(s)_____

_____

From *The Complete Probate Kit* by Jens C. Appel, III and F. Bruce Gentry
© 1991 by John Wiley & Sons, Inc.

E X E C U T O R   D A T A

―――――――――― DEPENDENTS/GUARDIANS ――――――――――

Guardian(s)

Name_____ Relationship_____

Address_____

Name_____ Relationship_____

Address_____

Dependent Name

		Birth date	S.S. #
1.	_____	_____	_____
2.	_____	_____	_____
3.	_____	_____	_____
4.	_____	_____	_____

Medical Information

		Blood type	Doctor
1.	_____	_____	_____
2.	_____	_____	_____
3.	_____	_____	_____
4.	_____	_____	_____

Health Insurance (Company/Policy #) _____

Special Instructions (Education, Religion, Guardianship agreement)

_____

_____

_____

_____

Assets (Accounts, Stocks, Bonds, Other) Manager: Guardian ☐ Executor ☐ Trustee ☐ Bank ☐ Other ☐

_____

_____

_____

Insurance

Company/Agent_____ Amt./Type_____

Policy #_____ Address/Phone_____

Company/Agent_____ Amt./Type_____

Policy #_____ Address/Phone_____

From *The Complete Probate Kit* by Jens C. Appel, III and F. Bruce Gentry
© 1991 by John Wiley & Sons, Inc.

EXECUTOR DATA

———————————— IMMEDIATE ————————————

Location of Documents/Keys

Location of will_____

Date executed_____ # of Pages _____

Other documents_____

_____

_____

_____

Keys/Safety deposit box_____

_____

_____

_____

Burial/Funeral

Responsible person/Organization

Name_____

Address_____

Phone_____

Interment ☐   Cremation ☐   Crypt ☐   Other ☐

Service Type: Religious ☐   Fraternal ☐   Other ☐

Cemetery/Columbarium_____

_____

Body/Eye/Organ Donations

Organization/Group_____

Contact_____

Phone_____

Address_____

Donation_____

Organization/Group_____

Contact_____

Address_____

Phone_____

Donation_____

EXECUTOR DATA

CONTACTS

Accountant_____ Phone_____
Address_____

Attorney_____ Phone_____
Address_____

Banker_____ Phone_____
Address_____

Clergyman_____ Phone_____
Address_____

Doctor_____ Phone_____
Address_____

Executor_____ Phone_____
Address_____

Alternate Executor_____ Phone_____
Address_____

Insurance agent_____ Phone_____
Address_____

Insurance agent_____ Phone_____
Address_____

Trustee_____ Phone_____
Address_____

Relatives/Friends

Name_____ Phone_____
Address_____

Name_____ Phone_____
Address_____

Name_____ Phone_____
Address_____

Name_____ Phone_____
Address_____

From *The Complete Probate Kit* by Jens C. Appel, III and F. Bruce Gentry
© 1991 by John Wiley & Sons, Inc.

EXECUTOR DATA

——————————— PERSONAL ———————————

Full name_____ Birth date_____

Address_____

_____

Birthplace_____

Social security #_____ Medicare #_____

Military service #_____ Discharge date_____

Father's name_____ Birth date_____

Date deceased_____ Birthplace_____

Mother's maiden name_____ Birth date_____

Date deceased_____ Birthplace_____

Married ☐ Divorced ☐ Separated ☐ Widowed ☐ Single ☐ Remarried ☐

Spouse (name)_____ Marriage date_____

Social security #_____ Medicare #_____

Membership (Religious/Fraternal/Social, Other)_____

_____

_____

Children

Name_____ Birth date_____

Address_____

Name_____ Birth date_____

Address_____

Name_____ Birth date_____

Address_____

Name_____ Birth date_____

Address_____

Name_____ Birth date_____

Address_____

From *The Complete Probate Kit* by Jens C. Appel, III and F. Bruce Gentry
© 1991 by John Wiley & Sons, Inc.

E X E C U T O R D A T A

——— FINAL ARRANGEMENTS ———

Person responsible_____ Phone_____

Address_____

Alternate person_____ Phone_____

Funeral home (name)_____ Phone_____

Address_____

Location of service_____ Viewing: Yes ☐ No ☐

Address_____

Service type: Religious ☐ Military ☐ Fraternal ☐ Memorial ☐

Person officiating_____ Phone_____

Cemetery_____

Location_____

Section_____ Plot #_____

Interment_____ Entombment_____ Cremation_____

Location of deed_____

Music/Reading selections_____

_____

_____

_____

Flowers/Memorials_____

_____

Pallbearers   (Honorary)

_____   _____

_____   _____

_____   _____

_____   _____

_____   _____

From *The Complete Probate Kit* by Jens C. Appel, III and F. Bruce Gentry
© 1991 by John Wiley & Sons, Inc.

EXECUTOR DATA

BENEFICIARIES

Name_____ Relationship_____

Address_____ Phone_____

Bequest(s)_____

_____

Name_____ Relationship_____

Address_____ Phone_____

Bequest(s)_____

_____

Name_____ Relationship_____

Address_____ Phone_____

Bequest(s)_____

_____

Name_____ Relationship_____

Address_____ Phone_____

Bequest(s)_____

_____

Name_____ Relationship_____

Address_____ Phone_____

Bequest(s)_____

_____

Name_____ Relationship_____

Address_____ Phone_____

Bequest(s)_____

_____

Name_____ Relationship_____

Address_____ Phone_____

Bequest(s)_____

_____

Name_____ Relationship_____

Address_____ Phone_____

Bequest(s)_____

_____

From *The Complete Probate Kit* by Jens C. Appel, III and F. Bruce Gentry
© 1991 by John Wiley & Sons, Inc.

EXECUTOR DATA

DEPENDENTS/GUARDIANS

Guardian(s)

Name_____ Relationship_____

Address_____

Name_____ Relationship_____

Address_____

Dependent Name

	Birth date	S.S. #
1. _____	_____	_____
2. _____	_____	_____
3. _____	_____	_____
4. _____	_____	_____

Medical Information

	Blood type	Doctor
1. _____	_____	_____
2. _____	_____	_____
3. _____	_____	_____
4. _____	_____	_____

Health Insurance (Company/Policy #) _____

Special Instructions (Education, Religion, Guardianship agreement)

_____

_____

_____

_____

Assets (Accounts, Stocks, Bonds, Other) Manager: Guardian ☐ Executor ☐ Trustee ☐ Bank ☐ Other ☐

_____

_____

_____

Insurance

Company/Agent_____ Amt./Type_____

Policy #_____ Address/Phone_____

Company/Agent_____ Amt./Type_____

Policy #_____ Address/Phone_____

From *The Complete Probate Kit* by Jens C. Appel, III and F. Bruce Gentry
© 1991 by John Wiley & Sons, Inc.

Document Set

Using the Detachable Forms

There are two will forms in this section which are perforated for easy removal and use. These forms, completed in ink or on a typewriter, may be used as original documents. The forms may also be used as a guide if you prefer typed originals or need additional documents. Forms should be completed carefully with no crossed out words or erasures. All signatures should be written in ink. If you desire copies of your will and other documents, make them *before* you sign the originals. Never sign anything but the original document(s). *Do not* sign copies. Preparing a draft outline of your will can help avoid mistakes when you prepare the final document.

Be sure that your Executor, alternate Executor, guardian, and/or other persons involved with your estate plan are fully informed and consent to act on your behalf on mutually agreed-on terms. It is recommended that your chosen agents be given specific information as listed in the Executor Data sheets in the preceding record set. Detailed information allows your Executor to act effectively and efficiently in settling your estate.

Forms Provided

Last Will and Testament (two-page form)—2 copies

Codicil—2 copies

Will Self-Proving Certificate—2 copies

Codicil Self-Proving Certificate—2 copies

LAST WILL AND TESTAMENT

The will forms offer space to set out your plans, from a single bequest to extensive gifts or instructions. They also contain printed provisions that save expense to the estate. The following additional provisions are usually appropriate for all estates that name a beneficiary or other trusted person as Executor.

- The EXECUTOR named shall not be required to post surety bond.
- I direct that no outside appraisal be made of my estate unless required for estate tax purposes.

Space is provided under the Executor heading on the forms to add these provisions if desired.

If you use multiple pages, be sure to indicate the page number and page total at the bottom of each page. You and your witnesses should also initial each page in the space provided at the bottom when you execute your will. All multiple-page wills should be fastened together before execution. Remember, you can't add pages after you've executed your will.

If you live in or have property in the states of Louisiana or Vermont, you must have three witnesses; everywhere else two witnesses are sufficient. Sign and date documents in front of all witnesses together at the same time and have them sign, date, and list their addresses on the document. You may keep the specific contents of wills and codicils confidential—your witnesses are attesting to your intent to make a will, not to the content of it. Remember, witnesses should *not* be relatives or others with an interest in your estate. Proper witness procedure should always be followed when executing your will or other documents.

CODICIL

Two codicil forms are included for use if minor amendments to your will are needed. Have your original will before you when you prepare your codicil to verify its date of execution. Witness procedure for a codicil is the same as for a will.

WILL SELF-PROVING CERTIFICATE

Self-proving is an optional step that does not affect the validity of your will. A self-proving certificate, properly completed and notarized, eliminates the need for witnesses to be contacted when the will is presented for probate. The two self-proving certificates included may be completed by a notary public and attached to your will. To self-prove your will, you must appear before the notary with your witnesses and your original will. The notary can complete the self-proving certificate; after all have signed, the notary notarizes and seals the document before attaching it to your will. Be sure the expiration date of the notary commission is listed and that the notary seal is affixed. All states except Vermont and Wisconsin recognize properly notarized self-proving certificates.

CODICIL SELF-PROVING CERTIFICATE

A codicil may be self-proved in the same manner as a will in those states that recognize self-proving certificates. A self-proved codicil self-proves the will it amends. Note that the date of the original will must be filled in on the codicil self-proving certificate.

LAST WILL AND TESTAMENT

I, _____ , resident
of the _____ of _____ in the State of _____ ,
being of sound mind, do make and declare the following to be my LAST WILL AND TESTAMENT
and expressly revoke all my prior wills and codicils and certify that I am not acting under undue
influence, duress or menace.

I. EXECUTOR

I appoint _____ EXECUTOR
of this, my LAST WILL AND TESTAMENT. If this EXECUTOR is unable to serve for any reason,

then I appoint _____ EXECUTOR.
The EXECUTOR is empowered to carry out all provisions of this WILL.
The EXECUTOR shall have all statutory powers available under State law.

II. BEQUESTS

From *The Complete Probate Kit* by Jens C. Appel, III and F. Bruce Gentry
© 1991 by John Wiley & Sons, Inc.

IN WITNESS WHEREOF, I have hereunto set my hand this_____ day

of _____ , 19 _____ .

_____
(Testator signature)

III. WITNESSED

This LAST WILL AND TESTAMENT of _____
was signed and declared to be his/her LAST WILL AND TESTAMENT in our presence at his/her request
and in his/her presence and the presence of each other as witnesses this _____

day of _____ , 19 _____ .

_____   _____
(Witness signature)   (Address)

_____   _____
(Witness signature)   (Address)

_____   _____
(Witness signature)   (Address)

LAST WILL AND TESTAMENT

I, _____ , resident
of the _____ of _____ in the State of _____ ,
being of sound mind, do make and declare the following to be my LAST WILL AND TESTAMENT
and expressly revoke all my prior wills and codicils and certify that I am not acting under undue
influence, duress or menace.

I. EXECUTOR

I appoint _____ EXECUTOR
of this, my LAST WILL AND TESTAMENT. If this EXECUTOR is unable to serve for any reason,

then I appoint _____ EXECUTOR.
The EXECUTOR is empowered to carry out all provisions of this WILL.
The EXECUTOR shall have all statutory powers available under State law.

II. BEQUESTS

IN WITNESS WHEREOF, I have hereunto set my hand this_____ day

of _____ , 19 _____ .

_____
(Testator signature)

III. WITNESSED

This LAST WILL AND TESTAMENT of _____
was signed and declared to be his/her LAST WILL AND TESTAMENT in our presence at his/her request
and in his/her presence and the presence of each other as witnesses this _____

day of _____ , 19 _____ .

_____   _____
(Witness signature)   _(Address)_

_____   _____
(Witness signature)   _(Address)_

_____   _____
(Witness signature)   _(Address)_

CODICIL

I, _____ , resident

of the _____ of _____ in the State of

_____ , being of sound mind, do make and declare this codicil to

be my LAST WILL AND TESTAMENT dated_____ , 19 _____ and

certify that I am not acting under undue influence, duress or menace.

In all other respects I ratify and confirm my Will and in witness whereof, I have hereunto set

my hand this _____ day of _____ , 19 _____ .

_____
(Testator signature)

This codicil to the LAST WILL AND TESTAMENT of_____

was signed and declared to be his/her codicil to his/her LAST WILL AND TESTAMENT in our presence

at his/her request and in his/her presence and the presence of each other as witnesses on this_____

_____ day of _____ , 19 _____ .

_____   _____
(Witness signature)   (Address)

_____   _____
(Witness signature)   (Address)

_____   _____
(Witness signature)   (Address)

From *The Complete Probate Kit* by Jens C. Appel, III and F. Bruce Gentry
© 1991 by John Wiley & Sons, Inc.

CODICIL

I, _____ , resident

of the _____ of _____ in the State of

_____ , being of sound mind, do make and declare this codicil to

be my LAST WILL AND TESTAMENT dated_____ , 19 _____ and

certify that I am not acting under undue influence, duress or menace.

In all other respects I ratify and confirm my Will and in witness whereof, I have hereunto set

my hand this _____ day of _____ , 19 _____ .

_____
(Testator signature)

This codicil to the LAST WILL AND TESTAMENT of_____

was signed and declared to be his/her codicil to his/her LAST WILL AND TESTAMENT in our presence

at his/her request and in his/her presence and the presence of each other as witnesses on this_____

_____ day of _____ , 19 _____ .

_____
(Witness signature)   *(Address)*

_____
(Witness signature)   *(Address)*

_____
(Witness signature)   *(Address)*

From *The Complete Probate Kit* by Jens C. Appel, III and F. Bruce Gentry
© 1991 by John Wiley & Sons, Inc.

WILL
SELF-PROVING CERTIFICATE

State of _____

County/City of _____

Before me, the undersigned authority, on this day personally appeared

_____
Testator

_____
Witness

_____
Witness

_____
Witness

known to me to be the Testator and Witnesses, respectively, whose names are signed to the attached or foregoing instrument and, all of these persons being by me first duly sworn, _____ _____ , the testator, declared to me and to the witnesses in my presence that said instrument is his/her LAST WILL AND TESTAMENT and that he/she had willingly signed or directed another to sign the same for him/her, and executed it in the presence of said witnesses as his/her free and voluntary act for the purposes therein expressed; that said witnesses stated before me that the foregoing will was executed and acknowledged by the testator as his/her LAST WILL AND TESTAMENT in the presence of said witnesses who, in his/her presence and at his/her request, and in the presence of each other, did subscribe their names thereto as attesting witnesses on the day of the date of said will, and that the testator, at the time of the execution of said will was over the age of eighteen years and of sound and disposing mind and memory.

_____
(Witness signature)

_____   _____
(Testator signature)   *(Witness signature)*

_____
(Witness signature)

Subscribed, sworn and acknowledged before me by _____ , the Testator,

and subscribed and sworn before me by_____

_____ , Witnesses,

this _____ day of _____ , 19 _____ A.D.

Signed: _____
Notary Public
My Commission Expires: _____

(Seal)

From *The Complete Probate Kit* by Jens C. Appel, III and F. Bruce Gentry
© 1991 by John Wiley & Sons, Inc.

WILL
SELF-PROVING CERTIFICATE

State of _____

County/City of _____

               Before me, the undersigned authority, on this day personally appeared

_____
Testator

_____
Witness

_____
Witness

_____
Witness

known to me to be the Testator and Witnesses, respectively, whose names are signed to the attached or foregoing instrument and, all of these persons being by me first duly sworn, _____

_____ , the testator, declared to me and to the witnesses in my presence that said instrument is his/her LAST WILL AND TESTAMENT and that he/she had willingly signed or directed another to sign the same for him/her, and executed it in the presence of said witnesses as his/her free and voluntary act for the purposes therein expressed; that said witnesses stated before me that the foregoing will was executed and acknowledged by the testator as his/her LAST WILL AND TESTAMENT in the presence of said witnesses who, in his/her presence and at his/her request, and in the presence of each other, did subscribe their names thereto as attesting witnesses on the day of the date of said will, and that the testator, at the time of the execution of said will was over the age of eighteen years and of sound and disposing mind and memory.

_____
(Witness signature)

_____
(Testator signature)

_____
(Witness signature)

_____
(Witness signature)

         Subscribed, sworn and acknowledged before me by

_____ , the Testator,

and subscribed and sworn before me by_____

_____

_____ , Witnesses,

this _____ day of _____ , 19 _____ A.D.

         Signed: _____
                 Notary Public
             My Commission Expires: _____

(Seal)

From *The Complete Probate Kit* by Jens C. Appel, III and F. Bruce Gentry
© 1991 by John Wiley & Sons, Inc.

CODICIL
SELF-PROVING CERTIFICATE

State of _____

County/City of _____

Before me, the undersigned authority, on this day personally appeared

_____
Testator

_____
Witness

_____
Witness

_____
Witness

known to me to be the Testator and Witnesses, respectively, whose names are signed to the attached or foregoing instrument and, all of these persons being by me first duly sworn, _____

_____ , the testator, declared to me and to the witnesses in my presence that said instrument is a codicil to his/her LAST WILL AND TESTAMENT dated

_____ , 19 _____ , and that he/she had willingly signed or directed another to sign the codicil for him/her, and executed it in the presence of said witnesses as his/her free and voluntary act for the purposes therein expressed; that said witnesses stated before me that the foregoing codicil was executed and acknowledged by the testator as a codicil to his/her LAST WILL AND TESTAMENT in the presence of said witnesses who, in his/her presence and at his/her request, and in the presence of each other, did subscribe their names thereto as attesting witnesses on the day of the date of said codicil, and that the testator, at the time of the execution of said codicil was of sound and disposing mind and memory.

_____
(Witness signature)

_____
(Testator signature)

_____
(Witness signature)

_____
(Witness signature)

Subscribed, sworn and acknowledged before me by

_____ , the Testator,

and subscribed and sworn before me by _____

_____

_____ , Witnesses,

this _____ day of _____ , 19 _____ A.D.

Signed: _____
Notary Public
My Commission Expires: _____

(Seal)

From *The Complete Probate Kit* by Jens C. Appel, III and F. Bruce Gentry
© 1991 by John Wiley & Sons, Inc.

CODICIL
SELF-PROVING CERTIFICATE

State of _____

County/City of _____

Before me, the undersigned authority, on this day personally appeared

_____
Testator

_____
Witness

_____
Witness

_____
Witness

known to me to be the Testator and Witnesses, respectively, whose names are signed to the attached or foregoing instrument and, all of these persons being by me first duly sworn, _____ _____ , the testator, declared to me and to the witnesses in my presence that said instrument is a codicil to his/her LAST WILL AND TESTAMENT dated _____ , 19 _____ , and that he/she had willingly signed or directed another to sign the codicil for him/her, and executed it in the presence of said witnesses as his/her free and voluntary act for the purposes therein expressed; that said witnesses stated before me that the foregoing codicil was executed and acknowledged by the testator as a codicil to his/her LAST WILL AND TESTAMENT in the presence of said witnesses who, in his/her presence and at his/her request, and in the presence of each other, did subscribe their names thereto as attesting witnesses on the day of the date of said codicil, and that the testator, at the time of the execution of said codicil was of sound and disposing mind and memory.

_____
(Witness signature)

_____
(Testator signature)

_____
(Witness signature)

_____
(Witness signature)

Subscribed, sworn and acknowledged before me by _____ , the Testator,

and subscribed and sworn before me by_____

_____

_____ , Witnesses,

this _____ day of _____ , 19 _____ A.D.

Signed: _____
Notary Public
My Commission Expires: _____

(Seal)

From *The Complete Probate Kit* by Jens C. Appel, III and F. Bruce Gentry
© 1991 by John Wiley & Sons, Inc.